Junior High Catalog   8083

DATE			
MAR 23 1984			
MAR 25 1986			
DEC 27 1988			
FEB 01 1995			
FEB 15 1995			
OCT 08 2016			

THE EGYPTIANS

HISTORICAL BOOKS BY

ISAAC ASIMOV

THE GREEKS

THE ROMAN REPUBLIC

THE ROMAN EMPIRE

THE EGYPTIANS

THE
EGYPTIANS

BY ISAAC ASIMOV

HOUGHTON MIFFLIN COMPANY BOSTON

To Walter Lorraine,
firmly!

CONTENTS

THE EGYPTIANS

1

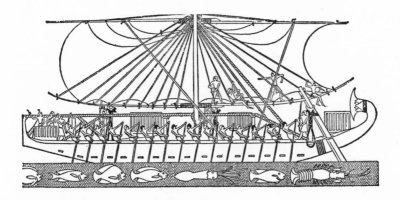

PREHISTORIC EGYPT

THE NILE

In northeastern Africa, there flows a most unusual river. It is 4157 miles long — the longest river in the world — and is called the Nile River, from the Greek name Neilos. Where the Greeks got that name is unknown, for to the people who lived on its banks, it was simply "The River."

Along the northernmost section of the Nile there grew up one of the world's two most ancient civilizations, and for some six thousand years a complex society has lined its shores with villages.

Through most of that time, the question of where the Nile arose was a mystery. Its waters came flowing upward from the far south, but no man from the ancient Mediterranean world ever succeeded in penetrating southward far enough to find its beginning. To the ancients, the problem of the "sources of the

Nile" was as intriguing and puzzling as the problem of the "back of the moon" was to us until satellites finally took photographs of that other side.

It was not until the second half of the nineteenth century that European and American explorers traced the Nile all the way to its sources. In 1857 the Englishman John Hanning Speke reached a great lake which he named Lake Victoria, for the British queen who then reigned. It was just on the equator, and out of it issued the Nile. Other rivers flowed into the lake from the mountains of Kenya near the central East African coast.

As the Nile flows northward to the sea, it passes through a number of regions where the valley grows narrow and steep. The water tumbles wildly over rocks and down inclines to form cataracts. Ships cannot pass these regions of rough water, and the cataracts therefore serve to divide the river into sections.

The cataracts are numbered from the north downward. The First Cataract is located about six hundred miles up the river from its mouth. At present this cataract is just south of a city named Aswan, but in ancient times the city at the site was known to the Greeks as Syene (sigh-ee'nee).

The northernmost stretch of the Nile, from the First Cataract to the mouth, is the chief scene of the events to be described in this book. It was along this stretch of river, all of which could be safely navigated north and south by even the simplest ships, that a remarkable civilization grew up.

The Nile flows through the eastern edge of the Sahara Desert. The Sahara (the very word is Arabic for "desert") covers almost all of northern Africa and is as large in area as the United States. It is, in fact, the largest desert in the world. Through all that region, there is virtually no rain. What water there is can only be found at great depths, except for occasional oases, where the groundwater level rises near the surface.

But the Sahara was not always a desert region. Twenty thousand years ago, glaciers covered much of Europe and cool winds brought moisture to northern Africa. What is now desert was then a pleasant land with rivers and lakes, forests and grassland. Primitive men roamed the area and left behind their crude stone tools.

Gradually, however, the glaciers retreated and the climate grew hotter and drier. Droughts came and slowly grew worse. Plants died, and animals retreated to regions that were still wet enough to support them.

Men retreated also, some south toward the tropics and others north toward the seacoast. Many crowded nearer and nearer to the Nile River, which in that long-distant time was a wider river, snaking lazily through broad areas of marsh and swamp. Indeed, the valley of the Nile was not at all an inviting place for human occupancy until after it had dried out somewhat.

Once that happened, the Nile was a godsend. No matter how dry the weather became, the Nile could be counted upon to provide water for the land and the people, making life along its shores not only possible but comfortable as well.

All winter long, the snows accumulate on the mountaintops of east Central Africa. In the spring, the rains come and the snow melts. Water in tremendous quantities goes tumbling down the mountain slopes and into the streams and great lakes of the region. This water pours out into the Nile, and slowly the flood works its way northward.

The Nile River, filled to overflowing with this water, starts rising in July and reaches its maximum height about the beginning of September. It does not settle back into its usual place until well into October. In the months during which it is spread outward, it brings water to the thirsty land and deposits a layer of fresh silt that it has brought down from the mountains far to the south. In this way, the soil along its banks is constantly renewed and kept fertile.

When men first penetrated the Nile Valley, the floods were vast, and the huge marshes on each side abounded with hippopotamuses, antelopes, cranes, and all sorts of game that could be hunted by men. Slowly, the increasing dryness limited the flood. Eventually, it was confined to the immediate banks, and for many thousands of years now, the section of land benefiting from it, along most of its length, has been only some twelve miles wide at most.

What's more, the fertile land that can be cultivated stops sharply at the limits of the flood, so sharply that nowadays there are many places where a man can stand with one foot on soil and the other on desert.

THE NEOLITHIC

As game continued to decrease in supply and as the population crowded in ever greater numbers closer to the Nile, something had to be done. The food supply had to be increased somehow. Fortunately, a new way of life had originated about 8000 B.C. — when the glaciers to the north were starting their last retreat — in certain communities in southwestern Asia. In well-watered uplands in what are now the nations of Iraq and Iran, about a thousand miles east of the Nile, men had learned to plant seeds and then to gather the grain that grew from them.

This is one of the marks of the beginning of the "Neolithic Age" or "New Stone Age." The Neolithic people still lacked metal and therefore had to use stone tools. These stone tools, however, were carefully polished and were far more sophisticated than the comparatively crude chipped and flaked tools of the earlier Old Stone Age and Middle Stone Age.

Other characteristics of the Neolithic were the development of pottery, the taming and herding of animals and, as I said, the sowing and harvesting of plants. We still don't know exactly how this invention of agriculture ("cultivation of fields") came about, but its advantages were obvious, for it made the food supply more secure.

Before the Neolithic way of life reached any particular area, men lived by hunting game and by picking fruits and berries. But there was only so much game, fruits and berries in any given region, and in a bad year men might have to wander far indeed to find enough. The number of people a particular area would support was rather low.

Once men learned how to herd animals and grow plants, they could produce each in considerably greater quantities than they were ever likely to find them in nature. By confining such animals and plants to a certain definite area, the herdsmen and farmers could make sure that wild animals or other tribes of men did not appropriate them. The supply of food became both greater and more dependable, and this was particularly true in the case of farming, since plants proved easier to grow and tend (once the art had been learned) than animals were. Because an acre of farmland could support more men than an acre of forest, there was what amounted to a "population explosion" wherever the Neolithic culture penetrated.

Furthermore, whereas men who hunted game (and, to a certain extent, those who herded animals) were always on the move, people who farmed land had to settle down. They had to remain where the growing grain was. They had to live together as mutual protection against raiding hunters or herdsmen (who didn't grow grain but had no objection to taking grain that others grew) and build villages — the first primitive cities.

As men were forced to learn how to get along with each other in villages, the free independence of the hunting-band days was gone. The village-dwellers developed, instead, methods of cooperation in building structures, in organizing defense, in cultivating land. In short, they developed *civilization* (a term that comes from the Latin word for "city").

The practice of agriculture spread outward from its source in the Iranian highlands during the millennia that followed its invention. Agriculture was taken up by other tribes and led to new and startling advances in two areas in particular. One was the valley of the twin rivers, the Tigris (tigh'gris) and the Euphrates (yoo-fray'teez), just to the south. The other was the valley of the Nile, a thousand miles to the west. The Tigris-Euphrates region was closer, began the practice earlier, and developed civilization sooner — but the Nile Valley was not far behind.

The Neolithic way of life had arrived in full force in Egypt by 5000 B.C. The Nile Valley proper was still, at this time, somewhat too wet and too wild for a comfortable agriculture, but west of the Nile and about 130 miles south of the Mediterranean was a lake that was ideally suited for it.

In later times, this body of water came to be called Lake Moeris (mee'ris) because the Greek traveler and historian Herodotus (heh-rod'oh-tus), who visited it about 450 B.C., thought it was an artificial lake that had been built by a legendary King Moeris.

But it was not artificial at all and "Moeris" is only from an Egyptian word meaning "lake." It existed naturally as a reminder of a northern Africa that had once been much better watered than it was in the time of Herodotus. There were hippopotamuses in Lake Moeris and other, smaller game, and for the five centuries from 4500 to 4000 B.C., flourishing Neolithic villages lined its edges.

The lake suffered, however, from the continued drying out of the land. As its level fell, and the animal life it supported grew sparser, the villages along its shores withered. At the same time, though, civilization grew more elaborate on the nearby Nile, which grew more manageable, and whose water came from the far southern mountains.

By 3000 B.C., Lake Moeris could only exist in decent size if it were somehow connected with the Nile, and the dwellers along the river had to exert considerable effort (which increased with the centuries) to keep that connection.

The battle to do so was lost a thousand years ago and more, and the lake is now almost gone. In its place is a depression, mostly dry, at the bottom of which is a shallow lake about thirty miles long and five miles wide. This body of water, called Birket Qarun by the Arabic-speaking people of the land, is all that is left of ancient Lake Moeris. On the shores of this bit of water stands the modern city of El Fayum (fay-yoom'), and it gives its name to the entire depression.

The Neolithic settlements that gradually grew up on the banks of the Nile (somewhat later than along Lake Moeris) have been excavated. The remains of each succeeding village lie above those of its predecessor, and to each level (or age), archaeologists have given a name derived from the name of the modern village where the excavations proved particularly rewarding.

Thus, one speaks of the Tasian, the Badarian, the Amratian cultures, and so on. The Tasian people were already practicing agriculture. The Badarians were good potters. The Amratians kept cattle, sheep, and pigs, and built reed boats with which to navigate the Nile.

IRRIGATION

The first agricultural communities in western Asia had developed in areas where there was ample rain to supply the growing plants with the water they needed. Along the Tigris-Euphrates and, particularly, along the Nile, people couldn't depend on the rain to water their crops. Instead, the water of the rivers had to be used.

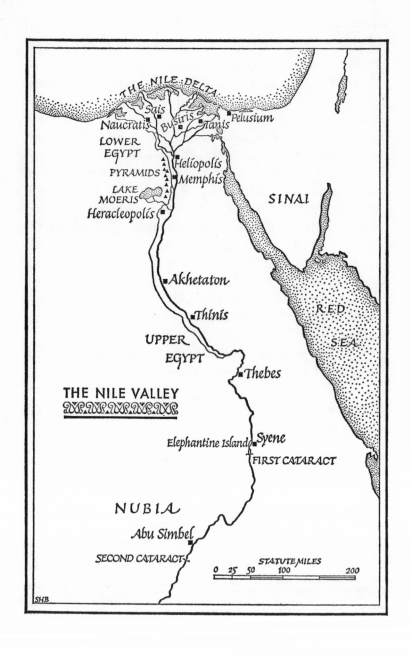

THE NILE DELTA

Sais
Busiris
Naucratis
Tanis
Pelusium

LOWER
EGYPT

PYRAMIDS
Heliopolis
Memphis

LAKE
MOERIS

Heracleopolis

SINAI

Akhetaton

Thinis

UPPER

EGYPT

THE NILE VALLEY

Thebes

Elephantine Island
Syene
FIRST CATARACT

RED

SEA

NUBIA

Abu Simbel

SECOND CATARACT

STATUTE MILES

0   25   50   100   200

SHB

At first, it was sufficient for the settlers along the Nile to wait for the floods to recede, and then to scatter seeds in the muddy soil. As the population grew, however, not enough crops could be grown in this way. Instead, it became necessary to cut passages through the river's banks to lead the water outward on either side. A network of canals (both along the Nile and along the Tigris-Euphrates) irrigated the land and kept it moist at times when, in the absence of floods, it would have dried hard.

This made things more difficult in one way because it was not easy to dig canals in the first place or to maintain them in working order afterward. It was hard labor, in fact, much harder than watching the rain fall. It had to be done in co-operation — in an even more elaborate cooperation than was required for ordinary agriculture.

Indeed, the necessity for this additional intensity of cooperation and for the development of advanced techniques for irrigated agriculture may have been the spur that led to the development of civilization to levels far higher along the rivers than was ever reached by the original farming communities in the highlands.

The towns along the rivers had to be particularly well organized. Those people who were clever enough and ambitious enough to be in charge of such work as canal building and maintenance naturally became dominant in each town. They usually established their prestige and power in the name of some local god.

Primitive men were always ready to believe that some supernatural being made the seeds grow and the earth bear fruit, and it was the job of the rulers of the city to develop the proper magical rites used to persuade the gods to be kind. They saw to it that those rites were carried out properly and exactly. The general population would believe firmly that on the knowledge and conscientiousness of those in charge of the rites, the prosperity of the town and the life of its people depended. The Nile Valley thus gained a priesthood which retained great power for thousands of years.

The difficulties of agriculture by irrigation were as nothing compared to the benefits that followed. The more men learned to cooperate with each other, the greater their achievements. It was necessary, for instance, to know exactly when the Nile flood would come each time, if maximum use were to be made of it. The priests in charge of irrigation carefully studied the height of the river from day to day and eventually discovered that, on the average, the flood came every 365 days.

The inhabitants along the Nile were the first, therefore, to develop a calendar based on a 365-day year. Each year consisted of twelve months as there are twelve complete cycles of change in the phases of the moon in a little less than a year, and the Nile people (like all others) had originally used a calendar based on the moon. Each month was set at thirty days long, and five additional days were added at the end of the year.

This calendar was much simpler and handier than any other calendar invented in ancient times. Historians are uncertain as to the date it was first adopted, but about 2800 B.C. seems a good guess. Nothing better was devised for nearly three thousand years, and when the better calendar came, it was still based on the Egyptian calendar with only slight improvements. Indeed, our present calendar is still based on the Egyptian calendar.

Then, too, the annual Nile floods wiped out landmarks that separated the holdings of one man from that of another. Methods had to be devised to redetermine what those holdings were. It is thought that this slowly gave rise to methods of calculation that we now know as *geometry* ("measuring the earth"). Other branches of mathematics were developed, too.

It became necessary to keep track of landholdings and crop quantities in the records. Some system of symbols had to be devised for different numbers, different people, different types of grain and produce, different events.

The people of the Tigris-Euphrates, some time before 3000 B.C., had invented a system of crude pictographs ("picture writing") that imitated the objects they represented. Such symbols must have been very simple at first, but gradually grew more and more complicated until they could represent anything men wanted to say.

The dwellers in the Nile Valley probably learned the concept of writing from news trickling toward them by way of traders and travelers from the Tigris-Euphrates. Quickly, the people of the Nile adapted the notion to their own uses and purposes. They invented symbols of their own, far more attractive than those developed along the Tigris-Euphrates. Writing along the Nile was fully developed shortly after 3000 B.C.

This system of writing was in the hands of the priests. Ordinary people could not read or write the complicated set of symbols any more than ordinary people today can make use of higher mathematics. The Greeks, who flooded into the land as tourists and soldiers centuries later, could not read this ancient writing, of course, but because they usually found it inscribed in temples, they assumed it had religious significance only and called it *hieroglyphics* ("sacred carvings").

SECURITY

The need for irrigation developed high civilizations in the Nile Valley and in that of the Tigris-Euphrates with an important difference in the two cases. The Tigris-Euphrates was exposed east, west, and north to wild, uncivilized tribes of the uplands. Subject to the constant terror of raids and rapine, the villages along the river built walls about themselves. They grew in size, developed weapons and armies, and trained themselves in military techniques and discipline.

In this way, the cities of the Tigris-Euphrates managed to hold off the barbarians most of the time. In periods of tribal quiet, though, what were the armed cities to do with their men and weapons of war? Kept idle, they could cause trouble for the cities that employed them. Naturally, then, the cities took to fighting each other.

Such fighting sometimes placed sizable areas under a single rule, forming "empires." On the other hand, such fighting also often destroyed the cooperation and the equipment on which agricultural prosperity was based, leading to the coming of a "Dark Age" in which civilization declined and prosperity lessened, so that the surrounding barbarians had their chance to take over temporarily.

The people along the Nile were spared all this for many centuries. To the east and west of their peaceful valley was desert, which armies could not cross easily. To the north was the Mediterranean Sea, and in early times there were no ships large enough and seaworthy enough to carry armies across it. To the south there was the First Cataract, which kept enemies from raiding down the Nile.

For a long time, then, the people of the Nile lived in almost complete security and isolation. Their villages remained unarmed and unaggressive. Few among them grew to any size and, indeed, some have described the Nile Valley as consisting of one long string of suburbs.

This meant comfort, but it also meant lack of change. Where the people along other rivers were forever facing new conditions, where invaders brought new ways or where they themselves were forced to learn new ways in defense, the men of

the Nile, for many ages, were not. The old ways were suitable
for generation after generation.

By the time strangers entered the Nile Valley and forced
their rule upon the native peoples, it was too late. The natives
had been so deeply ingrained by old custom that they had become the most conservative people in history (with the possible
exception of the Chinese).

Their system of writing remained very complicated, for instance, with numerous symbols, some of which represented individual words, some parts of words. About 1500 B.C. there
arose somewhere along the eastern shore of the Mediterranean
the practice of restricting the symbols to a mere couple of
dozen, each standing for a particular consonant. Any number
of thousands of different words could be built up out of such
an "alphabet," and the whole process of writing became much
easier to learn and use.

The dwellers along the Nile, however, proud of their ancient
civilization and tightly bound to their old ways, did not accept such an alphabet for nearly two thousand years. Stubbornly, they clung to their cumbersome system, so novel and
useful at first, but in the end nothing but a clog and a drag.
Such conservatism only served to help other people, more progressive, leap ahead of the Nile dwellers. (To this day the
Chinese will not abandon their own symbols, as complicated as
those of the Egyptians. Nor need we feel superior ourselves.
The United States will not abandon its foolish system of units
of measurement and adopt the much simpler and more logical
metric system used by almost all the rest of the world.)

As another example of conservatism, consider the calendar.
The priests along the Nile eventually discovered that the year
was 365¼ days long. Every fourth year ought to contain
366 days if the Nile flood was to remain at the same place in the
calendar. However, all efforts to have the people accept this
modification of the calendar were useless. The people clung to

the past and the old ways even though it meant that the calculation of the coming of the flood was made unnecessarily complicated.

THE TWO EGYPTS

The people of the Nile Valley called their land "Khem." This apparently means "black" in their native language. One guess is that this referred to the rich black soil left behind by the Nile flood, a soil that presented a strong color-contrast to the tawny sand of the desert on both sides.

The later Greeks called the land Aigyptos, which they may have derived, in distorted fashion, from the name of a large Egyptian city of later times, one with which they were familiar. We inherit that name and call the land Egypt.

In the earliest days of Egyptian civilization, the country was a collection of small towns or "nomes," each of which had its own god, its own temple and priests, and its own ruler, and each of which controlled a neighboring section of the farmland along the river. Communication from one town to the next was along the river and quite easy, since the river flowed one way and the winds usually blew the other. Without sails, one traveled north; with sails, south.

The people of each town cooperated among themselves, of course, but matters were made still easier if the towns cooperated with each other. Leagues would be formed in which groups of neighboring towns agreed to deal with common problems together. Eventually, some ruler would hold a loose sway over large sections of the river.

In general, the valley came to be considered as divided into two chief regions. There was the thin valley of the river itself, extending from the First Cataract to the region of Lake Moeris, a little over a hundred miles from the sea. This was a long, thin stringbean of a land, usually referred to as Upper Egypt.

North of Upper Egypt, the Nile River breaks up into a number of streams that fan outward in a large triangle about 125 miles on each side. The Nile enters the sea through a number of mouths, and all the land between and along those streams is rich farmland. This triangular area, "Lower Egypt," was manufactured by the Nile out of the silt it brought down over long ages from the distant mountains to the south.

On the map of Egypt, which moderns draw with north at the top, Lower Egypt is pictured as above Upper Egypt, and that looks queer. However, the reference is to the river. As one progresses with the current of a river toward its mouth, we say we go "downstream." The other direction is "upstream." If we consider that Upper Egypt is upstream from Lower Egypt, the names make sense.

In the Greek alphabet, one of the letters, "delta," is represented as an equilateral triangle, at least when it is written as a capital. The Greeks therefore referred to Lower Egypt as the delta of the Nile, because of its triangular shape. (Nowadays, any region of land about the mouth of a river which is built up by silt carried downstream by the current is called a delta, regardless of its shape. We speak of the Mississippi delta, for instance, which has a very irregular shape.)

2

ARCHAIC EGYPT

HISTORY

In general, our notion of the past history of mankind is obtained from three types of sources. First, there is the evidence of items left behind with no intention at all of serving as history. Examples are the tools and pottery of early man, remnants that cast a dim light backward some million years at least.

Such remains, however, do not tell a connected story. Rather, it is like trying to read a book by the light of an occasional lightning flash. But that is better than nothing at all, of course.

Second, there are the tales passed by word of mouth from generation to generation. These do tell a connected story but one which generally becomes distorted with the retelling. The results are myths and legends which can rarely be accepted as literal truth, though they sometimes contain important elements of fact.

Thus, the Greek legends of the Trojan War were passed down by word of mouth for many generations. They were accepted as sober history by the later Greeks and dismissed as mere fables by modern historians. The truth turned out to be something in between. Archaeological findings of the last century have indicated that many references in Homer are to actual fact (though Homer's tales of the gods' participation in the events may still be dismissed as fable).

Finally, there are written records, which, of course, may include legendary material. When these written records deal with events contemporary with the writer, or in his near past, we have something that is more satisfactory than any other historical source. It is not necessarily ideal, because writers can lie, or be prejudiced, or be honestly mistaken. Then, too, their writings, even when accurate, may become accidentally distorted in later copying, or be maliciously altered by propagandists. By comparing one historian against another, and all against archaeological findings, such errors or distortions can sometimes be caught.

Still, we have nothing more detailed than written records and, on the whole, when we speak of the history of man, we refer chiefly to the annals that have come down to us in written form. Events which took place before writing came into use in the particular area in question are "prehistoric," though not necessarily precivilized.

Thus, Egypt experienced two thousand years of civilization between 5000 and 3000 B.C., but that period of time is part of Egypt's "prehistory" because writing had not yet been developed.

Details concerning a nation's prehistory are necessarily dim and blurred, and historians are sadly resigned to this fact. How frustrating it is, however, when writing exists, but in a language that cannot be deciphered. The history book is there, at least in part, but it is sealed.

This was the case, even as late as A.D. 1800 for "historic Egypt" — that is, for Egypt after 3000 B.C. — and, indeed, for almost all other early civilizations.

In A.D. 1800, the only ancient languages that were thoroughly known were Latin, Greek, and Hebrew, and, as it happened, there were important ancient histories written in each of these languages, histories which survived in whole or in part into modern times. For that reason, the ancient history of the Romans, Greeks, and Jews was known quite well. In each case, the legends of their prehistoric past were also brought down to us.

The ancient history of the peoples of Egypt and of the Tigris-Euphrates was, however, not known to the men of 1800 B.C., save through the legends transmitted to them in the three languages they knew.

The Greeks, in their time, were almost as badly off as we were, as far as Egypt was concerned. They, too, could not read the hieroglyphic writing, and therefore remained ignorant of Egyptian history for some centuries.

In their time, however, Egyptian civilization was still alive and flourishing. There existed Egyptian priests who could read the ancient writing easily and who might conceivably have access to all sorts of annals dating back for thousands of years.

The curious Greeks, who swarmed into Egypt after 600 B.C. and stared with awed wonder at mighty evidences of an ancient civilization, inquired about it all, to be sure. But the Egyptian priests were suspicious and resentful of foreigners and preferred to be closemouthed.

The Greek historian Herodotus traveled in Egypt and questioned the priests closely. Many of his questions were answered, and he included the information he gained in the history he wrote. However, much of the information seems quite implausible, and one can't help getting the idea that the priests were sardonically pulling the leg of the Greek "greenhorn" who was so eager for information and so ready to accept all he was told.

Finally, about 280 B.C., at a time when the Greeks actually dominated Egypt, an Egyptian priest broke down and wrote a history of his land in Greek for the benefit of the new rulers, using priestly sources, no doubt. His name was Manetho (man'eh-thoh).

For a while Egypt after 3000 B.C. was truly "historic Egypt," even if we allow that Manetho was necessarily incomplete and may have told the story from a partisan Egyptian and priestly viewpoint.

Unfortunately, however, neither Manetho's history nor the sources he drew upon survived. "Historic Egypt" fell back into the darkness of human ignorance after the fall of the Roman Empire and remained so for some fourteen centuries. Not that the ignorance was absolutely complete, to be sure. Fragments of Manetho were quoted by other writers whose works survived. In particular, there survived long lists of Egyptian rulers which were quoted from Manetho's history notably in the works of an early Christian historian, Eusebius (yoo-see' bee-us) of Caesarea, who lived about six centuries after Manetho. But that is all, and it is scarcely enough. The king lists just whetted the historical appetite and made the surrounding darkness seem blacker than ever.

Of course, there were still hieroglyphic inscriptions all over the place, but no one could read them. Everything remained frustratingly mysterious.

Then, in 1799, a French army under Napoleon Bonaparte was fighting in Egypt. A French soldier named Bouchard or Boussard came across a black stone while a certain fort was being repaired. This fort was near the town of Rashid, on one of the western mouths of the Nile. To Europeans the name was Rosetta (roh-zet′uh), and the stone found by the soldier is therefore called the Rosetta Stone.

On the Rosetta Stone was an inscription in Greek, dating back to 197 B.C. It wasn't an interesting inscription in itself, but what made the stone fascinating was that it also contained inscriptions in two varieties of hieroglyphics. If, as seemed likely, it was the same inscription in three different forms of writing, then what one had was an Egyptian inscription with a translation into a known language.

The Rosetta Stone was tackled by men such as the English physician Thomas Young and the French archaeologist Jean François Champollion (shang-poh-lyone′). Champollion, in particular, used as a further guide the Coptic language, which still survived in his time in odd corners of Egypt. The language of Egypt today is Arabic, thanks to the Arabic conquest of Egypt thirteen centuries ago. Champollion maintained, however, that Coptic was a survival of the ancient Egyptian language that harked back to before the coming of the Arabs. Before Champollion died in 1832, he had prepared a dictionary and grammar of the ancient Egyptian language.

Apparently, Champollion was correct, because by the 1820's, he had cracked the secret of the hieroglyphics and, gradually, all the ancient inscriptions could be read.

The inscriptions aren't good history, of course. (Imagine trying to learn American history by reading the inscriptions on our public buildings and gravestones!) Even those which dealt with historical events were often inscribed merely to praise some ruler. They were official propaganda and not necessarily truthful.

Nevertheless, from what historians could gather from the inscriptions, and from other sources, including the king lists from Manetho, the history of Egypt gradually opened up to an extent no one would have dreamed prior to the finding of the Rosetta Stone.

UNIFICATION

Manetho begins his list of kings with the first man to unite both Egypts, Upper and Lower, under his rule. The traditional name for this first king is Menes (mee'neez), a Greek form of the Egyptian name Mena (mee'nuh). Before the unification, Menes had apparently ruled over Upper Egypt.

For a while, it was thought that Menes was purely legendary and that no such king had actually existed. However, some ruler must have been the first to unite all of Egypt, and if it wasn't Menes, it would have to be someone else.

Ancient inscriptions have been studied, but there is the complication that kings often take throne names when they begin to rule, names that differ from their given names. Sometimes they even get new names after they are dead. There are references on an ancient piece of slate, first unearthed in 1898, to a king named Narmer, who was shown first with the crown associated with rule over Upper Egypt, then with the crown of Lower Egypt. This seems a reference to a ruler who united the two parts of Egypt and perhaps Narmer and Menes are alternate names for the same person.

In any case, Menes or Narmer became king over all Egypt about 3100 B.C., just toward the end of Egypt's prehistoric period. One can't help but wonder how it was done. Was Menes a great warrior, a clever diplomat? Was it accident or design? Was a "secret weapon" involved?

For one thing, there are signs of a substantial Asian immigra-

tion into Egypt in the centuries preceding Menes' time. Perhaps Asians fled their own insecure, war-ridden lands for the
peace and lush fertility of the Nile Valley. (Down to the very
end of prehistoric times, even elephants could still be found in
the rich valley, so spacious was it, so fertile, and so lightly populated by men.)

Subtle Asian influences can be traced to this period. For
instance, certain Egyptian architectural and artistic techniques that appear after 3500 B.C. seem to show a definite relationship to typical techniques used in Asia at that time. The
Asian immigrants must also have brought with them the concept of writing from the civilization of the Tigris-Euphrates.

Upper Egypt seems to have been more under Asian influence
than Lower Egypt at this time, and it was Upper Egypt, therefore, that may have received the first kickoff into the upward
spiral of development.

On the other hand, this may only be an appearance that
arises out of archaeological accident. Lower Egypt is buried
deep in the silt of centuries, and it is much harder to find early
remains there than in the less extensively flooded regions of
Lake Moeris and of the upper Nile. We may be underestimat-
ing Lower Egypt for that reason only. Still, when Egypt was
finally unified into a single nation, it was from Upper Egypt
that the conqueror came.

Could the Asian immigrants have brought with them more
than a new art and the idea of writing? Could they have also
brought a tradition of war and conquest such as had not existed among the peaceful Egyptians of early times?

Could Menes himself have been of Asian descent, with a
family tradition that told of great armed cities whose soldiers
won dominion over their neighbors? Could he have wanted to
emulate his forebears and, like them, establish an Empire?

Somewhere in the centuries before Menes' time, men had
learned to smelt copper from stony ores obtained from the

Sinai Peninsula northeast of Egypt, and elsewhere, too. To be sure, silver, gold, and copper had been discovered much earlier as metallic nuggets that required no smelting. (A few copper objects, found in Badarian remains, may date back to 4000 B.C.) Even metallic iron was found, for this occasionally fell from the sky as meteorites. However, finds of free metal were always rare, and the metal so obtained was present in small quantities and could be used only as ornaments.

With the development of smelting, however, copper could be obtained from extensive copper ore deposits in quantities sufficient to be used for all sorts of purposes. Copper itself isn't hard enough to use for weapons and armor, but, mixed with tin, it becomes bronze, and that is hard enough. The period in which bronze became common enough to use for equipping armies is called the Bronze Age.

The Bronze Age didn't come into full flower until some centuries after Menes, but could enough crude bronze have been available to equip special corps of Menes' armies? Could it have been with these novel weapons that he forced his rule over all of Egypt? Perhaps we may never know.

According to Manetho, Menes' native city was Thinis (thigh' nis), which was located in Upper Egypt, roughly halfway between the First Cataract and the delta. Menes and his successors ruled from this city.

It may be, however, that Menes realized that if he were to keep his hold on Lower Egypt, he would have to appear as less of a foreigner to them and rule from a lesser distance. But he could not make himself a stranger to his own Upper Egypt, either. His solution was to build a new city on the border of the two lands — one that could be viewed as belonging equally to both — and to make this at least a part-time capital. (The United States chose a similar solution when its component parts were first united. After the Constitution was adopted, it seemed clear that the northern states and southern states were not entirely in sympathy with each other, and so a special capital city, Washington, was built where the two sections met.)

Menes' new city was built about fifteen miles south of the tip of the delta. The Egyptians may have named the city Khikuptah ("house of Ptah"), and it may be from this name that the Greeks got their "Aigyptos" and we our "Egypt." A later Egyptian name for the city was Menfe, so that the place came to be known to the Greeks as Memphis, and by that name it is known to history.

Memphis remained an important Egyptian city for some 3500 years, and it was the capital and the seat of royalty for much of the period.

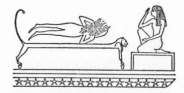

AFTERLIFE

Manetho divided the rulers of Egypt into *dynasties* (from a Greek word meaning "to have power"). Each dynasty consisted of members of a particular family who, in turn, ruled and had power over Egypt. Manetho listed thirty dynasties altogether over a period of three thousand years.

The dynasties include only the monarchs who ruled after the unification of the land, so that Menes is the first king of the First Dynasty. The period before Menes can be referred to as "predynastic Egypt," which is almost synonymous with "prehistoric Egypt."

The first two dynasties, all of whose kings were natives of Thinis, are called the Thinite dynasties. The period during which they ruled is referred to as the Archaic Period of Egypt and this lasted from 3100 to 2680 B.C. — more than four centuries.

The growing importance of Memphis, even in the early

times of Archaic Egypt, can be told from the evidence of the graves. And the particular usefulness of the graves to history arises in turn from the nature of the Egyptian religion.

The ancient religion of the Egyptians probably stemmed from the old hunting days when life depended upon finding animals and being lucky enough to slaughter them. As a result, there was a tendency to worship a kind of animal god, in the hope that propitiating this god would mean plenty of the particular animals this god controlled. If the animal were dangerous, worship of a god, shaped like that animal in part, would keep his beasts from doing too much harm. It would seem to be for this reason that, even in later times, Egyptian gods bore the heads of hawks, jackals, ibises, and even hippopotamuses.

But once agriculture became the chief way of life, new gods and new religious beliefs were grafted onto the old ways. There was the natural worship of the sun which, in cloudless Egypt, was a powerful force and very clearly the giver of light and warmth. What's more, the flooding of the Nile always came at a time when the sun reached a certain position among the stars, so that the sun could be thought of as controlling the life-giving cycle of the river and, therefore, as the giver of all life. Under various names, the Egyptians worshiped the sun for thousands of years. The best-known of the names of the sun-god was Re, or Ra.

Perhaps sun worship led naturally to the thought of the cycle of life, death, and rebirth. Each evening the sun set in the west and each morning it rose again. The Egyptians visualized the sun as an infant rising in the east, maturing rapidly, reaching full growth at noon, then aging as it declined to the west and setting as a dying old man. But then, after making a dangerous journey through caverns of the underworld, it returned to the east, where it rose again the next morning as a fresh young child, its life renewed.

In agricultural communities, one could not help but notice

that grain followed a similar, though slower, cycle. It ripened and was cut down, apparently dying; but from its kernels new grain could be grown the following planting season.

Eventually, such a cycle of birth, death, and rebirth, was embodied in the Egyptian religion. It centered on a god of vegetation, Osiris (oh-sigh′ris), who was always shown in full human form with no animal attributes. According to the myth, it was he who taught the arts and crafts to the Egyptians, including the practice of agriculture. In other words, he was civilization personified.

In the legend, Osiris was killed by his younger brother, Set. (Perhaps Set was a personification of the dry and arid desert, which was always waiting to kill the vegetation if ever the Nile flood failed for any reason.) Osiris's loyal and lovely wife, Isis (eye′sis), also pictured in completely human form, recovered his body and restored it to life, but it had been torn into fragments by Set, and one fragment remained missing. Incomplete, Osiris could no longer rule over living men and descended to the underworld, where he ruled over the realm of men's souls, which descended there after death.

Horus (hō′rus), the son of Osiris and Isis (usually pictured as a hawk-headed god, so he may represent the incorporation of a fragment of older myth into the new agricultural legend), completed the vengeance by slaying Set.

The story fits into the cycle of the sun, too. Osiris might represent the setting sun, killed by night (Set). Horus is the rising sun that, in his turn, kills night. The dying sun descends into the underworld, as Osiris does.

Naturally, it was tempting to associate such cycles with humanity. Few people welcome death, and almost anyone would be delighted at the thought that life could somehow continue beyond death, or be rekindled after death, as is true of grain and of Osiris.

To insure such rebirth for man, the gods (especially Osiris), who had utter power over such matters, had to be carefully worshiped and propitiated.

The Egyptians kept careful records of the various rituals, prayers, hymns, chants to be said and sung in order to insure the survival of the soul in the afterlife. Such rituals accumulated over the centuries, of course, but in essence they dated back to Archaic times and even, perhaps, to predynastic Egypt.

A document containing a list of such formulas — a rather heterogeneous collection with no more interconnection or order than is found in the Biblical book of Psalms — was published in 1842 by a German Egyptologist, Karl Richard Lepsius. It had been sold to him by someone who had found it while looting an old tomb.

The document is usually called the Book of the Dead, though that is not the name given it by the Egyptians. The core of the book is the list of formulas and incantations that will carry the soul safely into and through the hall of judgment. If acquitted of evil (and the Egyptian idea of good and evil is very much like that of any decent man today), the soul entered into eternal bliss with Osiris.

Safety in the afterlife seemed also to require the physical presence of the dead body. Perhaps this notion arose because, in the dry soil of Egypt, bodies decayed only slowly, so that the Egyptians came to think of the stretched-out survival of the physical shape of the body as natural and even desirable and learned to take measures to extend it still further.

Thus, the Book of the Dead contained directions for the preservation of dead bodies. The internal organs (which decayed most easily) were removed and stored separately in stone jars, although the heart, as the very core of life, was restored to the body.

The body was then steeped in chemicals and wrapped in bandages which were smeared with pitch to make them waterproof. Such embalmed bodies came to be called *mummies* from a Persian word for pitch. (Why Persian? Well, the Persians ruled over Egypt for a period in the fifth century B.C., and passed their word on to the Greeks, who passed it on to us.)

The Egyptian concern with mummification may have been the result of superstition, but it had certain very useful results. It gave the Egyptians the incentive to learn about chemicals and their behavior. Much practical knowledge was gained in this way and there are some who even try to derive "chemistry" from "Khem," the ancient Egyptian name for their country.

If preservation failed or the mummy were misappropriated, other methods of imitating life were used as "backup" devices. Statues of the dead individual were placed in the tomb; and many items of the sort used by the individual in life — tools, ornaments, little models of furniture and servants, even food and drink — were placed there.

Then, too, the walls would be covered with inscriptions and paintings representing scenes from the dead man's life. It is from these inscriptions and scenes that much knowledge is gained of the daily life of the ancient Egyptians. Hunts involving elephants, hippopotamuses, and crocodiles are shown, for instance, and a graphic example is given of the greater richness of the Nile Valley in ancient times.

There are scenes of feasting that tell us about the Egyptian diet. Intimate touches of family life and children at play are shown. We see that there was warmth and love in family life; that women held a high position in society (much higher than among the Greeks); that children were sometimes indulged and spoiled. It is rather ironic that we owe so much knowledge of Egyptian life to the Egyptian concern for death.

The whole practice of insuring life after death became very elaborate and expensive. Perhaps this was because, at first, it applied to the king only. The king (as was often the case in early societies) was viewed as the representation of all the people in their relationship to the gods and thus gained the attributes of divinity himself. If he dealt with the gods according

to the proper formula, the Nile rose and crops grew while dis-
ease and human enemies kept their distance. The king was all
because the king was Egypt.

Naturally, when the king died, no elaboration of ritual and
beauty was too great, for it was all Egypt that was being
buried, and it was all the Egyptians who had died during his
reign who would gain eternal life with the king.

As time passed, however, and Egypt's wealth grew, the various important court functionaries and provincial rulers — the
nobility — aspired to similar treatment. They wanted tombs
and mummification, too; a personal survival and not one that
was merged in the survival of the king. This gave the religion
a broader base but helped, eventually, to shunt a dangerously
high percentage of the Egyptian national effort into a rather
sterile concern for entombment. It also increased the power of
the nobility to occasionally dangerous heights.

As the rich and powerful were entombed, there was a natural
tendency to "keep up with the Joneses." Each tried to outdo
others, and families tried to gain status by the munificence
with which they buried a dead member.

The wealth buried in the tombs in the form of precious metals naturally attracted grave robbers. The best methods of
guarding these treasures, of concealing them, of blocking them
up, of guarding them with the power of the law and the in-
visible threat of the vengeance of the gods, did not keep those
treasures safe, and very few tombs have survived reasonably
intact to this day.

Our first impulse, naturally, is to recoil from such grave robbers with horror; first, because theft for personal gain is wrong,
and theft from the helpless dead particularly despicable; and
second, because archaeologists have been deprived of priceless
evidence concerning ancient Egypt.

On the other hand, we must realize that Egyptians, in fool-
ishly burying quantities of gold in an age when the substitute
of paper money did not exist, were needlessly crippling their

own economy. Grave robbers, whatever their motives, served to keep the wheels of Egyptian society turning by restoring the gold and silver to circulation.

It is the evidence of the tombs, then, that tells us of the growing importance of Memphis in Archaic times. It is a matter of sheer numbers, for there is a tremendous set of early tombs honeycombing the limestone of a desert ridge that borders the Nile Valley west of what was once the site of Memphis. At present, a village named Saqqarah (suh-kah'rah) is found near the site, and the graveyards are known by this name.

The earliest tombs were oblong structures, shaped something like the rectangular benches built outside Egyptian houses. These benches are known as *mastabas* in modern Arabic, and the name is given to the ancient tombs as well.

The ancient mastabas were built out of brick. The burial chamber, containing the dead body in a protective coffin, sometimes made out of stone, was below, and was usually stopped up for safekeeping. Above it was a chamber open to the public where the pictures of the dead man's life could be seen and where people could come to make ritual prayers for the dead.

Some of the oldest tombs at Saqqarah are thought to belong to several kings of the First and Second dynasties. If so, that shows that Memphis was their capital at least part of the time.

3

THE OLD KINGDOM

IMHOTEP

Very little detail is known concerning the political history of
the first two dynasties. We have the names of nearly twenty
kings in Manetho's lists, but not much more than that. There
are legends that Menes ruled for sixty-two years, that he led
armies against the tribes who controlled coastal areas west of
Egypt, and that he was finally eaten by a hippopotamus, but it
is difficult to take any of this seriously, especially the last since
hippopotamuses are vegetarians.

Nevertheless, the Archaic period must have seen a gradual
increase in Egyptian prosperity and, therefore, an increase in
the power of the divine king, who controlled and guided that
prosperity in the eyes of the people.

Naturally, the kings must have been eager to capitalize on
this self-interested devotion of the people. For one thing, it

must have pleased them to be so highly regarded and to be treated as godlike. For another, there was a "feedback" in such matters. The more magnificent the king's way of life and death, the more the people were convinced of the king's divinity, and the more securely he ruled.

The necessity for gaining such security would naturally occur whenever a new dynasty arose. We rarely know the manner in which an old dynasty came to an end and a new one began. Presumably, a series of weak rulers of one dynasty would allow power to slip from their hands. Some strong general might seize control; or some capable court official might first become the adviser of the king, then the power behind the throne, and then finally a new king himself, while the old one was either retired or quietly executed. Or it might be that the old line ran out of male members and a general or official married a daughter of the old line and himself became the first member of a new dynasty.

The nation might be expected to welcome a vigorous new monarch in place of a weak ruler, an enfeebled dotard, or a helpless child of the old line. And yet the reverence for a divine family is not always an easy thing to replace, and the monarch of the new dynasty might feel it important to demonstrate to the people his own divinity by some startling display of power that outdid all that had gone before.

This may be what happened when the Third Dynasty came to the throne. The evidences of power supplied by that dynasty are so remarkable that the period beginning with this dynasty is known as the Old Kingdom. (The reason for the adjective is that there were later periods of kingly magnificence and power in Egyptian history which received the names of Middle Kingdom and New Kingdom.)

The first (or possibly the second) king of the Third Dynasty was Zoser (zoh'ser). He began his rule about 2680 B.C., and he was fortunate indeed in having as a counselor a wise man named Imhotep (im-hoh'tep).

Imhotep is the first scientist in history whom we know by name. As the centuries passed, all sorts of legends clustered about him. He came to be known as a great doctor, with almost magical powers of healing. Indeed, many centuries later, he was made into the Egyptian god of medicine. He was also supposed to have guided Egypt successfully through years of drought by wisely hoarding grain in advance — so that the Biblical story of Joseph may be based, in part, on the Imhotep legend.

Quite apart from his legendary fame as a physician, scientist, and wonder-worker, however, Imhotep was certainly the first great architect. He undertook to build a mastaba for Zoser that was to be the biggest ever built and, what's more, to be of stone rather than brick. That would satisfy Zoser's urge to impress the Egyptians with the power of the kings of the new dynasty.

Imhotep built this mastaba at Saqqarah, making it 210 feet long on each side and about 25 feet high. It was the first large stone structure anywhere in the world, but in many details it shows a typical human conservatism, for the stone is so carved as to imitate the wood and reed of earlier and simpler structures.

Zoser was not, apparently, satisfied with his mastaba; or perhaps Imhotep himself regretted his own moderation and decided to do even better. Whatever the reason, Imhotep extended the mastaba on all sides until its base was about 400 feet by 350 feet. Then he placed a second, smaller mastaba on top of it, followed by a third, still smaller mastaba on top of that, and so on. In the end, he had six mastabas of decreasing size, one on top of another, reaching a total height of nearly 200 feet.

What's more, it had smaller structures all about it, of which some traces still exist, and the whole was surrounded by a high wall made of elaborately designed panels of limestone. The enclosure was 1800 feet long by 900 feet wide.

All the finer aspects of the original magnificence are gone, but the central edifice — battered and in bad disrepair — still stands, 4600 years after it was built. It is not only the first large stone structure ever built, but it is the oldest man-made building of any kind still to exist on the face of the globe.

Moderns have been astonished at the multiple mastaba of Zoser and at the still larger and more elaborate structures that followed shortly thereafter. As far as nineteenth-century archaeologists could tell, they came out of nowhere. It seemed that Egypt had first been a Neolithic land of villagers, no further advanced than what we would today call "primitive tribesmen" and then, suddenly, with no warning, began to produce monuments that have been the wonder of all succeeding ages — even of our own magnificently technological one.

To be sure, Zoser was of the Third Dynasty and Manetho spoke of a first and a second, but there were no records of those first two dynasties, and many nineteenth-century archaeologists suspected that Manetho's lists of those ancient kings were mythical.

It is no wonder that to romantics and mystics Egyptian civilization seemed to spring full-blown out of nothing, to have been brought, perhaps, to the Nile from elsewhere. A "logical" source seemed to be the Atlantis of which the Greek philosopher Plato wrote a century before Manetho's time.

According to Plato, the tale had first come from Egyptian priests who spoke of a very ancient land, far out to the west, which had reached a high level of civilization and had been destroyed by an earthquake that had caused it to sink beneath the ocean. Why not suppose, then, that refugees, fleeing from this disaster, came to Egypt and established a high civilization there (evicting the primitive tribesmen who had lived there earlier, or enslaving them) after all traces of their origin had been destroyed? Of course, this is all poppycock. There never was an Atlantis, and Plato was merely writing a fable to point a moral.

Besides, as the twentieth century opened, archaeologists (particularly the Englishman Sir Flinders Petrie) found increasingly important remains of the first two dynasties. It was possible to trace a steady growth of culture and architectural technique from primitive times to the great structure of Imhotep.

There is no question but that Imhotep's building of Zoser's multiple mastaba was a tremendous feat, an amazing advance for its time, and something never to be sufficiently admired — but it did not come out of nowhere. It did not spring full-blown out of the efforts of refugees from Atlantis. It was built by Egyptians working on the basis of a slow and painful development of technique over many centuries.

Nor did the Old Kingdom develop in the direction of grandiose monuments only. By the time of Zoser, Egyptian writing had been perfected. (Imhotep, to whom all advances were later attributed, was supposed to have made improvements in writing as well as in architecture.) The hieroglyphic symbols were no longer merely cartoons of objects, but were pressed into service to express abstractions and the full range of human thought.

The papyrus reeds (the word "papyrus" reaches us from the Greek, and is of unknown origin) that grew along the banks of the Nile served as the material to write upon. The pith was extracted, glued together in separate layers, soaked, and then dried. The result was an admirably light and reasonably long-lasting surface on which to write with brushes or with pens made out of other reeds. No other nation in ancient times had so convenient a writing material. In the Tigris-Euphrates, bulky clay bricks were used, and symbols had to be punched into them. Such clay writing was adequate for the purpose, but it lacked the convenience and beauty of the Egyptian writing.

Papyrus was used in the Greek and Roman civilizations until the supply of reeds dwindled to the point where it was no

longer economical to use. In modern times, we manufacture a
similar writing material from wood, and we still call it *paper,*
though it no longer comes from papyrus reeds.

The use of a convenient and cheap writing surface is an important contribution to the advance of knowledge. It becomes easier to write down instructions, rather than be forced
to rely on the less certain method of passing them on by word
of mouth. This is particularly important when the instructions
are elaborate and when mistakes can be serious — as in the case
of surgical techniques.

Perhaps it is no accident that among the oldest papyrus
treatises that have been discovered (either dating back to the
Old Kingdom, or copies of treatises that date back so) is one
called the Edwin Smith Papyrus that deals with the treatment
of injuries such as fractures.

THE PYRAMIDS

The building of gigantic tombs caught the fancy of the land.
Succeeding kings of Egypt had to have similar tombs, but even
larger and more magnificent ones. The architectural techniques improved rapidly under the pressure of that desire. Imhotep had used small rocks in building his structure, rocks imitating the mud bricks used earlier. This is wasteful of effort
since it is much harder to place a hundred rocks into accurately
spaced rows and columns than to move one large hewn rock
into place. The larger the rocks, the less time it takes to put
them together, provided the rocks can be handled at all.

As it happened, the Egyptians learned to handle very large
rocks by utilizing sledges, rollers, large quantities of oil to re-

duce friction, and very liberal use of human muscle. The tremendous stone monuments which were built over the next two centuries, as a result, have remained the wonder of all succeeding ages, and serve as the "trademark" of the Old Kingdom and, indeed, of Egypt generally.

Two thousand years later, when the curious Greeks swarmed into Egypt, they gaped in awe at structures that were already age-old in their time. They called them *pyramides* (singular, *pyramis*), a word of uncertain origin. We inherit the word and make "pyramid" the singular.

Zoser's multiple mastaba is the only one of its kind that remains. It must have struck later kings that it would be neater to have the sides of the pyramid slope smoothly upward to a point rather than to recede in stages. (Zoser's structure has come to be called a "step pyramid" because of its stages.)

The innovation came about after 2614 B.C. when a new dynasty, the Fourth, ascended the throne of Egypt. Under it, the Old Kingdom reached its cultural peak.

Perhaps the first monarch of the line, Sneferu (sneh'fuh-roo), wanted to demonstrate the divinity of himself and his line by outdoing his predecessors of the Third Dynasty. He did this by building a step pyramid larger than Zoser's — one that had eight stages. He then filled in the indentations between the stages until the sides sloped upward uniformly. The whole was covered, finally, with a smooth white limestone facing that must have shone brilliantly in the bright Egyptian sunlight and far outstripped in splendor and beauty anything that had gone before.

Unfortunately, the limestone facing has long since been stripped away by succeeding generations for use elsewhere (as was true of the limestone facing of other pyramids). Some of the fill between the stages has also fallen away so that the pyramid seems built of three uneven steps.

Sneferu also built another pyramid in which each layer of

stone is slightly smaller than the one below so that the pyramid is not in stages at all, but slopes uniformly, even without fill. Partway up, however, the slope was changed and made flatter so that the point was reached more quickly. Perhaps Sneferu was getting on in years, and the architects wished to finish more quickly in order to have the tomb ready for the monarch when he died. It is called the Bent Pyramid.

After Sneferu's time, all pyramids (some eighty survive altogether) were true pyramids, sloping smoothly upward.

The luxury of the Fourth Dynasty, as expressed in its pyramids and, no doubt, in the splendor of the castles it must have built for its living monarchs, encouraged trade. Egypt's accumulating wealth could be well spent abroad to obtain materials and products not available at home.

The peninsula of Sinai was occupied by Egyptian garrisons for the sake of its copper mines — copper that could be used at home and for ornaments to exchange abroad.

One desirable import could not be obtained so close to home. This was the logs one could obtain from tall straight trees; logs that could serve as strong and attractive pillars, and which would be much easier to handle for nonmonumental structures than would stone, which is so heavy and so difficult to carve. The proper sort of trees did not grow in the Nile Valley, where the vegetation was semitropical, but they did grow on the mountain slopes along the eastern shore of the Mediterranean, just north of the Sinai Peninsula.

This area has a variety of names. To the ancient Hebrews, it was Canaan (kay'nan) along the southern portion of the coast, Lebanon (leb'uh-nun) a little farther north. The "cedars of Lebanon," which were the sort of trees the kings of the Fourth Dynasty coveted, are mentioned many times in the Bible as the most magnificent and beautiful of all trees.

The Greeks, in later centuries, called the east Mediterranean coast Phoenicia (fee-nish'ee-uh) and the area behind the coast Syria. These names are quite familiar, and I will use them.

The kings of the Fourth Dynasty might have sent trading parties overland through Sinai and then northward to where the cedars could be obtained. However, this would have meant a trip of some 350 miles each way, and land travel was difficult and arduous in those days. What's more, to drag back huge logs all that distance would have been completely impossible.

The alternative was to reach Phoenicia by sea. Unfortunately, the Egyptians were not a seagoing people (and never became one). Their experience was with the mild and gentle current of the Nile. This they handled well. Indeed, under Sneferu, ships as long as 170 feet traveled up and down the Nile.

But ships that were suitable for river navigation were not very likely to survive the rougher waters of the Mediterranean Sea in a storm. Nevertheless, under the lash of desire for timber, Sneferu sent out fleets of as many as forty ships to the cedar forests. Such Egyptian ships, strengthened somewhat, crawled out of the Nile into the Mediterranean and then, hugging the coast, made their way to Phoenicia. There they loaded themselves with huge logs and other desirable products and felt their cautious way back.

No doubt some ships were lost to storms (as they are in all ages, even our own) but enough survived to make the trade most profitable. The Egyptians ventured out also into the smaller Red Sea, which lies to the east of the land, and maneuvered their way down that body of water, too, reaching southern Arabia and the Somali coast of Africa. From there, they could bring back incense and resins.

Expeditions were even sent up the Nile beyond the First Cataract into the mysterious forest to the south, and ivory and animal skins were brought back. (By the time of the Fourth Dynasty, the growing population of the valley, and its increasingly intense devotion to cultivation, was already having its effects on the larger animals, and elephants had been driven southward past the First Cataract.)

THE GREAT PYRAMID

Sneferu's successor was Khufu (koo'foo). With him, pyramid-building reached its climax, for he built the greatest one of all. This was about 2580 B.C., just a century after Imhotep had started the fashion. So rapidly (for those times) did Egyptian technology advance.

Khufu had his monster pyramid built on a rocky plateau a few miles north of Saqqarah near where the town of Giza (gee'zuh) stands today. When the pyramid was finished, its square base was 755 feet on each side so that it covered an area of thirteen acres. The walls sloped upward to a point 481 feet high. This "Great Pyramid" is solidly composed of slabs of rock — 2,300,000 of them, it is estimated, with an average weight of 2½ tons apiece. Each had to be brought some six hundred miles (by water, of course — on ships carried downstream by the current of the Nile) from the quarries near the First Cataract.

In among these granite slabs are carefully engineered sets of passages, leading to a chamber near the center of the huge pile in which the king's coffin, his mummy, and his treasures were to be contained.

Considering the state of engineering at the time and the fact that the structure was built practically with bare hands (even the wheel was not used), the Great Pyramid is certainly the most magnificent achievement of architecture in the world — except possibly for the Great Wall of China.

Men have never ceased marveling at the Great Pyramid, the largest single building ever erected by man; a building never surpassed in the 4500 years since it was built. The Greeks referred to it and neighboring pyramids as among the "seven wonders of the world," and of the seven they listed, only the pyramids still remain for modern men to view. They may even remain after modern nations have gone the way of ancient Egypt and ancient Greece.

The Great Pyramid naturally attracted the attention of Herodotus, and he asked the Egyptian priests for information concerning it. They told him some pretty tall tales that we need not accept, but some of the information seems reasonable. They told Herodotus that it took twenty years to build the Great Pyramid and that a hundred thousand men worked at it. This may very well be so.

They also told Herodotus the name of the king who had built it, but Herodotus translated the strange Egyptian name into something that sounded more Greek and customary to his ears, so Khufu became Kheops (Kee'ops). We are more familiar with this Greek version in its Latin spelling as Cheops. (In general, Greek versions of Egyptian names are known to us most familiarly in Latin spelling, and I will give the Latin spelling henceforward without explanation.)

It is fashionable to imagine that the hundred thousand pyramid-builders were slaves, groaning under the lash of heartless overseers. Many, from their reading of the Biblical book of Exodus, had even thought that the builders were the enslaved Israelites. However, the Great Pyramid and its sister structures were built a thousand years before the Israelites entered Egypt, and in any case they were probably built by free men who worked gladly and were well treated.

We must remember that in the Egyptian culture of the time, there was a good and accepted reason for such pyramids. They were built to please the divine king and the gods, and to insure peace and prosperity for the people. The builders probably approached the task in the same spirit that medieval men did in building their cathedrals or modern men do in building their great hydroelectric dams. In fact, some historians have suggested that the building season for pyramids came at a time when the Nile flood made agricultural labor impossible so that one of the purposes of the project was to make work and keep people busy.

Interest in the Great Pyramid in the last century has often been based on mystical suggestions. Because the structure is so huge and so precisely built (the sides of the square base are oriented almost exactly north–south and east–west) some people have imagined that the Egyptians actually had access to great knowledge and science and that certain measurements embodied the values of mathematically important quantities. There were thoughts that minor features of the internal passages were oracles predicting the future in intimate detail and that the end of the passages gave the date of the end of the world (not too far in our present future). Some even considered it significant that the Great Pyramid was built near the place where the 30° North Latitude line crosses the 30° East Longitude line, as though the Egyptians knew that the earth was spherical, that 360 degrees marked off a circumference, and, most important of all, that many thousands of years in their future, the Prime Meridian would be established as passing through the city of London!

Still others have suggested that the Great Pyramid was an astronomical observatory, and one man once wrote a book (shown me in manuscript) maintaining that the structure was really a launching base for spaceships.

Alas, all such speculations are completely groundless. Egyptologists have shown quite conclusively that the Great Pyramid is exactly what it is supposed to be — an elaborate tomb. Moreover, it failed its chief function, that of protecting the body and treasures of the dead Khufu. Despite the fact that the coffin was placed in the center of the greatest single

stone pile ever erected and despite the fact that the passages
to it were camouflaged and stopped up — thieves broke in.
When modern explorers finally made their way to the center,
they found nothing but a lidless sarcophagus in an empty
chamber.

Khufu's pyramid was the acme. From then on, it was all
downhill as far as that form of architecture was concerned.

Khufu was succeeded by an elder son, then by a younger
son. The younger was Khafre (kaf'ray), whom Herodotus
reported as Chephren (kef'ren). He built a considerably
smaller pyramid, about 2530 b.c., than his father had. He
cheated by building it on a higher eminence, so that its peak
rises above that of Khufu. Much of its original limestone facing
remains near the top.

Khafre's son and successor was Menkure (men-koo'ray) or,
to the Greeks, Mycerinus (mis''uh-righ'nus). He built a third
pyramid, the smallest of the three, about 2510 b.c.

These three pyramids are grouped together at Giza and
represent a silent testimony of the greatness of the Old Kingdom forty-five centuries ago. We cannot, of course, see them as
they were originally. It is not only a matter of the lost limestone
facing. Each was surrounded by smaller pyramids and mastabas for other members of the royal family. There were temples, causeways, statues, and so on. Along the causeway to
Khafre's pyramid, for instance, there were no less than twenty-
three statues of the king. What were built were not merely
pyramids but pyramid complexes.

One object, not a pyramid, that was built during the Fourth
Dynasty rivals even the pyramids in fame. This is a huge carving of a recumbent lion built near the causeway to Khafre's
pyramid and only 1200 feet southeast of the Great Pyramid.
It is a natural outcropping of rock, the shape of which may
have suggested a crouching lion, and the sculptor's chisel did
the rest.

The head of the lion is that of a man wearing the royal headdress. It is thought to represent a portrait of Khafre, and the whole represents the power and majesty of the king.

The Greeks in later centuries invented myths concerning monsters with the body of a lion and the head of a human being (a woman rather than a man, though) which may have been inspired by Egyptian sculptures. The Greeks may have viewed the monsters as a danger to men, for they called a lion-woman a *sphinx*, from a Greek word meaning "one who chokes someone." The most famous myth concerning a Greek sphinx has it posing riddles to passersby and killing those who cannot answer. For this reason any person who cultivates an air of mystery is called "sphinxlike."

The Greeks applied the same name to the Egyptian carvings of human-headed lions, of which there were thousands in the land. There was only one huge one, however, and that was the one built by Khafre. That is the "Great Sphinx," and its silent brooding over the desert reinforces the notion of mystery that surrounds the word. The face of the Great Sphinx is now badly damaged because Napoleon's soldiers were criminal enough to think it fun to use it as target practice for their guns.

Even the pyramids of the following dynasties, smaller and cruder than the great products of the Fourth, are useful to us since the inner walls are scribbled over with hymns and spells designed to make easier the entrance of the king or queen into the afterlife. These so-called Pyramid Texts are valuable guides to Egyptian religious thought. Indeed, they, and the Book of the Dead, are the oldest religious documents we have.

DECLINE

The Fourth Dynasty came to an end about 2500 B.C., only a few years after the death of Menkure and after a successful century of tremendous feats. Was this because of the premature death of Menkure's successor and the lack of a male heir? Was there a successful revolt? We have no way of telling. Even legend is silent.

To be sure, we can guess that there were factions. Egypt had been under a single rule for five centuries before the coming of the Fourth Dynasty, but that did not completely remove the separate traditions of the various cities and the rivalries between them. These rivalries were expressed religiously since each city had its own particular god, as a carryover from the old days of disunity. A change of dynasty often meant a change in the character of religious worship, and various sets of priests may have intrigued for a change of dynasty at the first sign of weakness in the king upon the throne.

Thus, the kings of the Fourth Dynasty worshiped Horus in particular and considered him to be the royal ancestor. Since the patron god of Memphis was Ptah, the creator of the universe, according to the Memphite tradition, and the patron of the arts and crafts, he, too, was especially honored.

Thirty miles north of Memphis, however, was Onu (on'oo), where the sun-god, Re, was held in particular eminence. The city remained faithful to Re for thousands of years, in fact, and to the Greeks, in a later century, the city came to be known as Heliopolis (hee''lee-op'oh-lis) or "city of the sun."

The priesthood of Re was powerful; indeed, powerful enough so that even the great kings of the Fourth Dynasty saw fit to flatter the priests by incorporating the name of the sungod into their throne names, so that we have Khaf*re* and Men-k*u*re.

But when the Fourth Dynasty grew weaker — for whatever reason — after Menkure's death, the priests of Re saw their chance and somehow managed to place one of their own upon the throne to initiate the Fifth Dynasty. This lasted a century and a half and was succeeded by the Sixth Dynasty about 2340 B.C.

Pyramid building declined under the Fifth and Sixth dynas-.

ties. No monsters were erected; only small ones. Perhaps the Egyptians had grown tired of sheer size, once the novelty wore off. Perhaps it simply consumed too much of the national effort and had become an obvious weakening factor in the land.

The arts continued to flourish, however, and in military power, Egypt actually advanced. A military peak was reached in the reign of Pepi I (pay'pee), the third king of the Sixth Dynasty, who were natives of Memphis. Pepi I left more monuments and inscriptions than did any other monarch of the Old Kingdom, and there is a small pyramid at Saqqarah that is his.

He had a general named Uni (oo'nee) who is known to us from an inscription he left behind (one in which, we trust, he did not exaggerate too greatly). From a position as an obscure court official he rose to lead an army. He fought off the desert nomads to the northeast five times, to retain and strengthen Egypt's hold on the metal-rich Sinai Peninsula and even penetrated Asian territories northeast of Sinai. He also supervised expeditions south of the First Cataract.

But perhaps these military adventures — together with the accumulated effect of pyramid and temple building — overstrained the Egyptian resources of the time, and helped institute a decline in Egyptian prosperity. For one thing, the wider the realm and the greater the works of the kingdom, the more the monarch had to delegate power, and the stronger the officials, generals, and provincial leaders grew. And in proportion as they grew stronger, the power of the king grew weaker.

The demands of the aristocracy for separate mummification and burial and to a separate claim on the afterlife grew ever stronger in this period. In a way it might be looked upon as progressive, since it led the way toward the notion of individual salvation for all, however humble, based on the personal acts and behavior of each individual, rather than allowing all people automatic afterlife as part of the kingly soul. It was only by such democratization of religion that a high ethical content could be inserted into it.

On the other hand, when nobles grow powerful, they quarrel among themselves, and the energy so expended is withdrawn from the common problems of the nation. The people as a whole suffer.

A younger son of Pepi I succeeded to the throne in 2272 B.C. as Pepi II, but he must have been a mere infant at the time. We know this because in one way his reign was unique in history. It lasted, according to all the evidence we have, for ninety years! This is the longest reign in recorded history.

The very length of the reign was disastrous to Egypt.

In the first place, during the first decade or so of his reign, such an infant king cannot rule, and power must be in the hand of some regent or courtly official. Such regents can never hold the full respect given a king, and there are bound to be continual palace squabbles over who is to hold the office. A child on the throne for many years (as we know from modern history) is bound to accelerate a general trend toward the shift of power from the king to the nobility.

It certainly did so in the time of Pepi II. The tombs of the aristocracy grew steadily more elaborate, and although Egyptian trade flourished, it was in the hands of individual nobles rather than those of the central government.

By the time Pepi II became king in his own right, the nobility was too strong to handle easily, and the king had to walk warily. Then, in his final decades, when he was old and weak — perhaps even senile — his feeble fingers must have let go the reins altogether. He could have been nothing more than the shadow of a monarch sitting in his palace and waiting to die. The nobles lent him lip service and waited for that death.

Pepi II died in 2182 B.C., and within two years Egypt fell apart. No one king could any longer exert power over the squabbling nobility. The Sixth Dynasty and with it the Old

Kingdom came to an end after nearly five centuries, and all the benefits of unification were lost to Egypt, which sank into a splintered anarchy.

A papyrus has survived from (possibly) the end of the Sixth Dynasty. Its author, Ipuwer, laments the disasters that are befalling the land as a result of anarchy and apathy. His cries are probably poetically exaggerated, but even allowing for that, it is a graphic description of a decaying land and a suffering people.

So graphic is Ipuwer's description of misery* that the Israeli writer Immanuel Velikovsky, in a book published in 1950, *Worlds in Collision*, maintained that Ipuwer's words described the Biblical plagues given in the book of Exodus, plagues that arose through a gigantic astronomic catastrophe.

This, however, is pure fantasy. Velikovsky's astronomic catastrophes are scientifically impossible, and Ipuwer (whose poetic exaggerations can scarcely be taken as literal descriptions) wrote of a period nearly a thousand years before the most reasonable date that can be assigned to the Biblical Exodus.

* He says in part: ". . . laughter hath perished and is no longer made. It is grief that walketh through the land, mingled with lamentations. . . . The land is left over to its weariness . . . corn hath perished everywhere. . . . The storehouse is bare and he that kept it lieth stretched out on the ground. . . ."

4

THE MIDDLE KINGDOM

THEBES

A century of obscurity follows, a "Dark Age" of civil war, unrest, and contending pretenders for the throne. During this period, every one of the magnificent tombs of the great pyramid-building pharaohs was rifled.

Virtually no details are known of the history of the various fragments of Egypt in this period. The petty rulers needed all their strength to survive and had no energies left over for elaborate monuments and inscriptions.

Manetho lists four dynasties during this interval, but the individual kings are shadowy figures who cannot have had much status. They were probably local chieftains who claimed kingship but had very little power outside their immediate home bases.

The Seventh and Eighth dynasties operated from Memphis and probably rested their claims on the prestige of the capital city of the Old Kingdom. The Ninth and Tenth dynasties were based on Heracleopolis (her"uh-klee-op'oh-lis) — the later Greek name — a city on Lake Moeris.

Undoubtedly, had Egypt been any other country in the world at that time (or had it even been a later century), this period of fragmentation would have proved an unbearable temptation for surrounding nations. The country would have been invaded and occupied for who can tell how long. It was Egypt's good fortune that her weakness came at a time when no neighbor nation was in a position to take advantage of it.

Salvation came at last from a city far to the south — 330 miles south of Memphis, in fact, and only 125 miles north of the First Cataract. The chief god of the city was Amon (ay'mun), or Amen (ay'men) a fertility god who was completely obscure in the time of the Old Kingdom, but who was growing more important as the city gained strength during this period of weakness. It called itself Nuwe, meaning "the City" (that is, "the City of Amon"), and from this comes the Biblical name, No, used for it.

When the Greeks arrived, centuries later, the city had grown large and great with magnificent temples. The Greeks called it, therefore, Diospolis Magna (digh-os'poh-lis-mag'nuh) or "great city of the gods." The name of one of the city's suburbs sounded to Greek ears like Thebes (theebz), the name of one of their own cities. They therefore applied that name, too, to the Egyptian city. It is as Thebes that the city is best known to history and to us, and although that is an inconvenient name because of the chance of confusion with the Greek city, it is the one that must be used.

Thebes must have prospered during the Fifth and Sixth dynasties with the growth of the trade routes past the First Cataract. It was spared the worst of the disorders that whittled down the power of Lower Egypt as Memphis, Heliopolis, and Heracleopolis fought bitterly among themselves for power.

A line of capable governors of Thebes came to power in 2132 B.C., about midway through the century of darkness, and these brought increasing sections of Upper Egypt under their control. Manetho lists them as the Eleventh Dynasty. For eighty years they fought against the Heracleopolitan kings and finally, about 2052 B.C., the fifth of the line, Mentuhotep II (men″too-hoh′tep), completed the conquest.

Once more, 130 years after the death of Pepi II, Egypt was under the control of a single monarch. The period of the "Middle Kingdom" can be said to have begun. This new period was reflected in religion, too, for the Theban god Amen was now so powerful (since his city was the home of the ruling dynasty) that the priests of the great Re were forced to recognize the new god as a second aspect of their own. Egyptians began to speak of the god Amen-Re as the greatest of the gods.

In this time, also, Thebes began to grow large and prosperous, and tombs and monuments began to enrich it. It even survived its dynasty. A little over half a century after the founding of the Middle Kingdom, the Eleventh Dynasty fell upon hard times. The last of the Mentuhoteps (either the IV or the V) had a capable vizier named Amenemhat (ah′men-em-hat′), who was also of Theban family, as one can tell from the fact that the god Amen forms part of his name.

The details are unknown to us, but Amenemhat must have rebelled and in 1991 B.C. established himself on the throne as Amenemhat I, first king of the Twelfth Dynasty. He removed the capital from Thebes, which was too far south to enable him to be sure of maintaining effective control of the turbulent north, and he established his capital at Lisht, about twenty-five miles south of Memphis. Momentum, nevertheless, carried Thebes onward. It was to serve as capital again in later

centuries and was to remain one of the great cities of the world
for about fifteen hundred years.

NUBIA

A reunited Egypt began to hum with activity. Pyramid
building continued, and both Amenemhat I and his son were
buried in pyramids built near Lisht. Amenemhat I maintained
Egyptian power in Sinai, continued trade with the south, and
brought the nobles to heel. It was almost as though all the evils
of the century of darkness were undone, but it would seem that
nothing is ever really undone. The kings of the Middle Kingdom never had the complete power of the kings of the Old
Kingdom. The nobles of the Middle Kingdom were never completely tamed.

Yet the Twelfth Dynasty, like the Fourth Dynasty, was a
"golden age," and if the pyramids were smaller, art was more
sophisticated. Some jewelry in Middle Kingdom tombs managed to escape the robbers and remained to be discovered by
moderns and proved to be delicately lovely in its intricate detail. Miniature, painted wooden models were placed in tombs
to represent the life of the dead man three-dimensionally, and
an intact cache of these was discovered in a tomb at Thebes in
1920. In many ways, the refinement of small works of art is
more satisfying than the sometimes oppressive grandeur of
enormous monuments.

The literary works of the Middle Kingdom also reached new
heights. Indeed, later ages in Egypt looked back upon the
Twelfth Dynasty as the classical period of literature. Very little

survives to this day, of course, and heaven knows how what does survive (through the accidents of history) compares to what did not.

For the first time, secular fiction (as distinct from myths and religious literature) was written. Or at least, for the first time, such material has survived to be read by us, giving us the oldest known literature of the sort.

There are exciting adventure stories with touches of fantasy as, for instance, in the tale of a shipwrecked sailor who encounters a monstrous serpent. There is "The Tale of Two Brothers," which sounds rather like a tale from the Arabian Nights and which may have inspired some parts of the Biblical tale of Joseph. And there is the "Tale of Sinuhe," which survives almost intact and which tells of an Egyptian exile and of his life among the nomad tribes in Syria. Its interest lay, no doubt, in its exotic locale, and in its description of customs strange to the Egyptians.

Science also advanced. At least, a document called the Rhind Papyrus has been uncovered, which is a copy, apparently, of an original written in the time of the Twelfth Dynasty. It explains how to handle fractions, how to calculate areas and volumes, and so on. Egyptian mathematics was very matter-of-fact, and seems to have consisted of a mere expression of rules given for individual cases (like recipes in a cookbook) without the beautiful generalization developed, thirteen centuries later, by the Greeks. Of course, though, we are handicapped by knowing only the Rhind Papyrus. What might have been included in documents forever lost, we cannot say.

Then, too, there appeared examples of what later came to be called Wisdom Literature, collections of wise sayings and maxims intended to guide youngsters through life. The example with which we are most familiar is the Biblical book of Proverbs. There are Egyptian equivalents, however, which are at least a thousand years older. One set is attributed to

Amenemhat I himself and is supposed to be a set of instructions to his son, teaching him how to be a good king.* In it, Amenemhat makes some bitter remarks that may arise out of an attempt on his own life by some court officials.**

It is possible that Amenemhat I was assassinated, but if he was, it heralded no change in dynasty, for he was succeeded by his son, Senusret I (sen-us'ret), for whom, according to the legend, he had written his collection of wisdom sayings. The new monarch, who reigned from 1971 to 1928 B.C., is far better known to us by the Greek version of his name, Sesostris (seesos'tris).

Sesostris I turned the energies of the Middle Kingdom outward and became the first Egyptian king to engage in important conquests abroad.

A logical place for expansion was southward, to the land centered about the reaches of the Nile River, upstream from the First Cataract. The Egyptian kings had been trading there since the time of Sneferu, seven centuries earlier, but undoubtedly such trade had been periodically interfered with by hostile tribes. Sneferu had had to raid southward to protect the trade and so had Pepi I of the Sixth Dynasty.

To Sesostris it seemed that by conducting a full-scale conquest of the land and placing it under complete Egyptian control, trade could be made simple and the wealth and prosperity of Egypt enhanced.

With Sesostris's move, the land south of Egypt enters a brighter glare of history than it had enjoyed hitherto (though that is probably poor compensation for having to endure an invasion). To the Egyptians, and to the Biblical writers, this southern land was known as Cush. To the Greeks, however, it came to be known as Ethiopia, possibly from words meaning

* "Act better than thy predecessors, maintain harmony between thy subjects and thyself lest they succumb to fear."
** "Be on guard against subordinates . . . trust not a brother, know not a friend, and make not for thyself intimates."

"burnt face," which referred to the Negroid coloring of its people. (The name may, on the other hand, be from a distortion of the same word that gave rise to "Egypt").

But "Ethiopia," though commonly used for the region by modern historians of Egypt, is a particularly misleading name, for in modern times it has come to be applied to a nation well to the southeast of the ancient Ethiopia of the Greeks. The nation which, in modern times, occupies the section of the Nile south of the First Cataract is Sudan (an Arabic word for "black," so that the inspiration of that name is the same as that of Ethiopia). Modern Sudan, however, stretches over large areas beyond the ancient districts we are discussing.

The best name, then, and the one I will use, is Nubia. This applies directly to the region in question and no other and is not confused by any modern use of the name for some contemporary nation. The word is derived from a native term meaning "slave," which indicates perhaps the fate to which the population was subjected by early invaders of the region.

Sesostris I, if he were to begin a career of conquest, needed an army, but he did not have much of one. Egypt, thanks to its security, had no military tradition. The army of the Old Kingdom was small and simply armed, scarcely more than a royal bodyguard and the equivalent of a local police. That was sufficient to maintain control over the ill-organized and primitive tribes that occupied Sinai. Even in the Middle Kingdom, the armies — which had been increased in numbers and improved in training as a result of the civil strife during the century of anarchy — would not have been a match for the armies of the Asian powers that existed to the east beyond the Egyptian horizon. Nubia, however, was occupied by primitive peoples who were in no position to fight off even armies as unimpressive as those of Egypt.

Sesostris I was therefore able to pass the First Cataract in force, to line the Nile with forts, and to place occupying contingents all the way to the Second Cataract, two hundred miles upstream from the First. Later kings of the dynasty penetrated still farther south, and trading posts were established eventually at the Third Cataract, still another two hundred miles beyond.

Undoubtedly the Egyptians took pride in this exhibition of power over a neighboring people unequipped to fight them off. (On the national level, there seems to be great credit attached to beating up someone weaker than yourself.) Fifteen centuries later, when Herodotus was visiting Egypt, the Egyptians were smarting under their own weakness, and the priests could only take refuge in a mythical past. They exaggerated the deeds of their conquering monarchs of the past and pretended that they had conquered the whole known world. And what name did they give this mythical conquering Egyptian? Why, Sesostris.

THE LABYRINTH

Under Amenemhat II, son and successor of Sesostris I, trade with a land called Punt flourished. We know little about Punt except that it was reached by the Red Sea and probably represented one of the coasts of the southern stretches of that body of water. It was either the area now known as Yemen, in southern Arabia, or Somaliland on the African coast opposite. In any case, gold was obtained from Punt which could be used to trade with the Canaanite cities along the shores of Syria. Egyptian power, carried partly by its merchants and partly by its army, spread into Syria for the first time in force. It was not to be the last time.

The arts of peace were not neglected, and the kings of the Twelfth Dynasty made it their care to develop Lake Moeris.

It had shrunk badly from the time, twenty-five centuries before, when Neolithic villages had flourished along its shores,
and it no longer maintained connection with the Nile.
Amenemhat I had ordered the channel to the Nile widened,
deepened, and freed of silt. Water poured in, the lake was restored to its earlier size, and the fertility of the region was
restored.

It was also the notion of the Middle Kingdom pharaohs to
use the channel to Lake Moeris as a device for producing a
natural reservoir for the Nile flood. By blocking or unblock-
ing the channel, the lake could be used to regulate the flow of
water, draining the Nile when it rose too high, conserving water
when the rise was too low.

Considering the Egyptian labors in this respect, it is no wonder that Herodotus, inspecting the site some fourteen centuries
later, thought that the lake was an artificial project altogether.

The Twelfth Dynasty reached its peak of power and prosperity under the reign of Amenemhat III, who ruled for nearly
half a century, from 1842 to 1797 B.C. Under him, Egyptian
rule stretched from the Third Cataract well into Syria, a distance of nine hundred miles. The population, some scholars
guess, may have been about one and one-half million at this
time. Never, however, did the personal power of even the
greatest of the kings of the Middle Kingdom attain to that of
the pyramid builders of the Old Kingdom.

(It was perhaps in the reign of Amenemhat III, or one
of his immediate predecessors, that the legendary patriarch
Abraham dwelt in Palestine. If the stories in the Bible can be
accepted, it would seem that Abraham traveled freely between
Canaan and Egypt, and this would indicate that both regions
were under the same rule at the time.)

Amenemhat III signified the strength of his reign, architec-
turally, by building two pyramids about 240 feet high. More
than that, he constructed colossal statues of himself, together
with a complicated group of palaces, all surrounded by a single

wall, along the shores of Lake Moeris. These served in part as tombs. Sheer weight and power had failed to preserve the mummies of the pyramid builders, so Amenemhat III tried to use craft — to confuse the potential grave robber by intricacy rather than bar him by mass.

Herodotus marveled at this palace complex, considering it to outrank even the pyramids as a wonder. He speaks of its thirty-five hundred chambers, half above ground and half below. (He was not allowed into the lower chambers, which were, of course, burial rooms.) He also describes its many intricately winding passages.

The Egyptians called the structure by a word meaning "the temple at the entrance to the lake." The Greeks made this Egyptian phrase into *labyrinthos* and in English this becomes "labyrinth." The word is now used for any complex maze of passages.

The size of the Egyptian labyrinth, its careful workmanship, its white marble, its rich adornment, all make it a pity that it has not survived intact for the admiration of our own age. Nevertheless, it must be admitted that not all the ingenuity of the Middle Kingdom architects served the purpose. The tombs it contained were, in the end, all rifled by the persevering ingenuity of the grave robbers.

Very few, to be sure, have heard of this Egyptian labyrinth of the Middle Kingdom, but many have heard of the labyrinth spoken of in Greek myths. This mythical labyrinth is placed in Knossos, the capital of the island of Crete (about four hundred miles northwest of the Nile delta). In it, the myths say, there dwelt a "minotaur," a bullheaded man, who was slain by the Athenian hero Theseus (thē'seus).

The Greek myths concerning Crete were found, at the opening of the twentieth century, to have a basis in fact. An ancient civilization, not much younger than that of Egypt itself, existed on this island, and all through the period of the Old Kingdom there had been trade between the two nations. (The

Egyptians weren't seagoing, but the Cretan islanders were. Crete established the first naval empire in history, in fact.)

The Cretan palaces at Knossos began to be elaborate indeed about the time of Egypt's Middle Kingdom. They may have been strongly influenced by tales of the Egyptian labyrinth, and a Cretan imitation may have sprung up. It was the Cretan imitation that entered the Greek myths. (The minotaur undoubtedly arose out of the fact that bulls — as symbols of fertility — played important parts in Cretan religious rites.)

Nor did the Twelfth Dynasty forget its Theban origin. That southern city was beautified, and a number of temples and other structures were built in it, although these were to be dwarfed by the activities of a later Theban dynasty.

But after the death of Amenemhat III, something happened. Perhaps a weak ruler mounted the throne, and the nobility seized the chance to quarrel among themselves. Perhaps the labyrinth had overstrained Egyptian prosperity as the pyramids might have done centuries before.

Whatever the reason, within a very few years after the death of the great king, all the glory and prosperity of the Middle Kingdom came to an end. It had lasted two and a half centuries, only half the length of time that the Old Kingdom had endured.

Once again, the realm broke up into fragments, ruled by quarreling nobles. Once again, shadowy monarchs claimed the throne.

Manetho speaks of two dynasties, the Thirteenth and the Fourteenth, who must have ruled at the same time, so that neither could properly claim lordship over the land. Indeed, the work of Menes was once again temporarily undone, and the two Egypts were separated. The Thirteenth Dynasty ruled over Upper Egypt from its base at Thebes, while the Fourteenth ruled Lower Egypt from Xois (zoh'is), a city in the very middle of the delta.

Again, for a century, there was chaos and a second Dark

Age. This time, however, the quarreling dynasties did not have a chance to fight it out in isolation until one or another managed to regain control over a united nation. Instead, something happened that had never taken place before in the history of civilized Egypt. The land was invaded by foreigners who were ready to take advantage of Egyptian weakness.

The Egyptians, who already had a history of fifteen hundred years of civilization, who had a land in which the oldest pyramids were already a thousand years old, scorned foreigners. They had traded with them, to be sure, but always from a position of wealth, bartering ornaments and cleverly made gadgets for mere raw material — lumber, spices, lump metal. Where Egyptian armies had moved outward, whether into Nubia or into Syria, they had been able to establish rule over peoples far less wealthy and technologically developed than themselves. They must have felt about themselves as Englishmen felt about Great Britain in Queen Victoria's day, or as we feel about the United States today.

How did it come, then, that a bunch of miserable foreigners could sweep into Egypt — even a divided Egypt — and take it over without a fight?

THE HYKSOS

Later Egyptian historians, thoroughly ashamed of this episode, seem to have done their best to wipe all records of the period out of their history books, with the sad result that we know virtually nothing about the period or about the invaders.

Indeed, we barely know the name of the conquering

invaders. In the first century A.D. the Jewish historian Josephus
quotes Manetho to the effect that the invaders were called Hyksos (hik'sohs), and this is usually translated as "shepherd
kings." The implication is that they were nomads, whose live-
lihood depended upon herds of animals such as sheep, a form
of life which the civilized Egyptians, long wedded to agriculture, considered barbarous.

This may well have been so, but it is now thought not to be
the derivation. It is believed, instead, that the word comes
from the Egyptian *hik shasu*, meaning "rulers of the uplands"
or even merely "foreign rulers."

It is certain, moreover, that the Hyksos flooded into Egypt
from the northeast, across the Sinai Peninsula; that they were
Asians and the product of the comparatively sophisticated
military might of that continent. Egypt had, in the past, penetrated short distances into Asia, and Asia was now returning
the dubious compliment.

Until 1720 B.C. the people of the Tigris-Euphrates, the most
militarily advanced in Asia, had not impinged directly on
Egypt. There had been trade and cultural borrowings, but no
military interactions. The nine hundred miles that separated
the two river civilizations had acted as an effective insulator
through all the early period of their histories.

During Egypt's Archaic period and in the first centuries of
the Old Kingdom, the cities of the Tigris-Euphrates remained
disunited. They fought each other ceaselessly, built walls
about their cities in defense, and then developed the arts of
siege warfare to break down and through those walls. They
were far too busy with themselves to engage in foreign adventures.

About 2400 B.C., however, a ruler named Sargon of the city
of Agade (ah-gah'deh) established his power over the entire
area, setting up an empire that eventually may have reached,
briefly, Syria and the Mediterranean Sea. Egypt was strong at

the time, though, and the Fifth Dynasty was ruling in peace. Neither Sargon nor his successors ventured to stretch their precarious line of communications to the point where they could attack the land of the Nile.

The empire of Sargon declined and vanished in less than two centuries and when Egypt's Old Kingdom disintegrated into chaos, the Tigris-Euphrates was once again merely a collection of quarreling cities and could in no way take advantage.

At just about the time when Egypt's Middle Kingdom was coming into power, a group of nomads called Amorites established themselves in the Tigris-Euphrates. They made their capital a town (till then unimportant) on the Euphrates River, a town named Bab-ilu ("the gate of god"). To the Greeks, the name of the town became Babylon (bab'ih-lon), and it is by that name it is best known to us. Babylon became a great city under the Amorites and remained one for fifteen centuries afterward. For that reason, the area of the Tigris-Euphrates is most commonly referred to as Babylonia when the period of ancient history is under discussion.

About 1800 B.C., the Babylonian king Hammurabi (hahm''-oo-rah'bee) ruled over an empire almost as large as Sargon's. By that time, though, Egypt's Middle Kingdom was riding high, and once again the Asians, in a period of power, did not attempt to cross swords with Egypt, or even intrude upon Egypt's outward-pushing tendrils in southern Syria.

The pulse of rise and fall of empire in Egypt and Asia had synchronized well, and Egypt was most fortunate in this. The period of fortune was soon to end, however.

In all the fighting that went on in Asia over relatively wide areas, an important war-weapon had been developed: the horse and chariot. The horse had been tamed somewhere in the great grasslands that stretched across Europe and Asia north of the civilized centers in Babylonia.

Nomads had always drifted downward from the north, but usually there was a reasonable chance of fighting them off. The nomads had the advantage of surprise, and they were more inured to fighting. The cityfolk were generally unwarlike, but they did have organized armies and city walls. They could hold their own. The Amorites infiltrated Babylonia but established themselves in small towns first and took the large cities only as they adopted Babylonian civilization.

After the time of Hammurabi, however, the nomads came down from the north with the new weapon. Horses, each dragging a light two-wheeled chariot, formed the van of the army now. On the chariot stood two men, one handling the horse, and the other concentrating on wielding a spear or handling a bow and arrow. Their weapons designed to be used during rapid travel were longer, stronger, and more far-reaching than those which sufficed the slow-moving foot soldiers.

The effect of a racing cloud of cavalry upon a group of footmen who had never encountered them can well be imagined. The wild horses, with hoofs thundering and manes tossing, were fearsome sights. No foot soldier, unused to withstanding cavalry, could face the speeding animals fearlessly. And if the soldiers broke and ran, as they usually did, the horsemen could round them up in no time, reducing a retreat to an absolute rout.

Nomad horsemen conquered everywhere they penetrated, in the period after Hammurabi, unless their intended quarry was quick enough to join them, to adopt the horse and chariot himself, or to seek refuge within walled cities.

The cities of Babylonia held them off for a while, but a certain tribe, known to the Babylonians as Kashshi and to the Greeks as Kassites, advanced continually. By 1600 B.C. they had established an empire over Babylonia that was to last four and a half centuries.

To the west, the more poorly organized cities of Syria did not hold out against the northern horsemen as long as did those of Babylonia. The nomads took over Syria. Some of the Canaanite cities were taken; others joined them as allies.

A mixed horde of nomads and Canaanites descended on Egypt. They were not a unified people or tribe, and they did not call themselves Hyksos. The name was given to them by the Egyptians, and a single name does not imply a single people.

Nor were the Hyksos the advancing front of a conquering empire. They were anything but that. They were, rather, a raggle-taggle horde of raiders. *But* they had the horse and chariot — and a bow and arrow better than anything the Egyptians had.

The Egyptians had no horses. They used slow-moving donkeys for transport. They had no chariots. Perhaps a capable king might have managed to adopt the enemies' weapons quickly, but Egypt was divided against itself at this time. It was a mere congerie of principalities. Egypt's luck had run out.

In came the horsemen; away ran the Egyptian foot soldiers. The land fell without a battle in 1720 B.C., less than eighty years after the death of the great Amenemhat III.

But not all of Egypt fell. The Hyksos were not a numerous troop, and they dared not spread themselves too thin along all the length of the Nile. Rather they let the distant south go and concentrated on the rich delta and the areas immediately surrounding. They ruled over an empire consisting of Lower Egypt plus Syria.

They established their capital at Avaris (uh-var'is) at the northeastern edge of the Nile delta, a central location for a realm that had one foot in the delta and the other in Syria.

Two lines of Hyksos kings ruled over Egypt, and Manetho refers to them as the Fifteenth and Sixteenth dynasties. (It is important to remember that foreign rulers are listed among the dynasties, too.) Virtually nothing is known of these dynasties, for the later Egyptians preferred to turn their faces away and not to include them in their writings. When they are mentioned at all in inscriptions, it is only with extreme hostility.

The notion has grown up, therefore, that the Hyksos were extremely cruel and tyrannical and devastated Egypt mercilessly. This, however, does not seem to be true. They ruled with reasonable decency.

What really offended the Egyptians was that the Hyksos kept their own Asian customs and paid no attention to the Egyptian gods. The Egyptians, who, for thousands of years, had followed their own customs as the only decent way of life, and who knew virtually nothing of foreigners, could not get it through their heads that other peoples had other ways that seemed as right to themselves as Egyptianism seemed to Egyptians. The Hyksos were, to the Egyptians, a completely godless and sacrilegious folk, and for that, there could never be forgiveness.

As a matter of fact, the rulers of the second Hyksos dynasty, the Sixteenth, seem to have grown quite Egyptianized. Perhaps they did not carry through such Egyptianization with sufficient thoroughness to win the hearts of the Egyptians, but did so sufficiently to alienate the Asians. This may have been an important factor in weakening Hyksos rule.

It may have been during the period of Hyksos domination that Asian immigrants entered Egypt from southern Syria (Canaan) in large numbers. Under native Egyptian rule, such immigrants would have been viewed with grave suspicion, and their entry would not have been encouraged. The Hyksos kings, on the other hand, would have welcomed such immigrants as fellow Asians upon whom they could rely in their program to keep the native Egyptians under control.

In fact, the Bible story of Joseph and his brethren may be a reflection of this period of Egyptian history. Surely, the kindly Egyptian monarch who made Joseph his prime minister and welcomed Jacob and assigned the Hebrews a place in Goshen (in the delta east of Avaris) could not have been a native Egyptian. He must have been a Hyksos king.

Indeed, the historian Josephus, who was intent on proving the past greatness of the Hebrew nation, gave them a conquering history by maintaining that the Hyksos *were* the Hebrews and that they conquered Egypt in this period. This, however, is certainly not so.

5

THE RISE OF EMPIRE

THEBES AGAIN

While the Hyksos ruled in the north, Thebes, with its memories of the glorious Middle Kingdom, remained under the rule of the priests of Amen. Gradually, these consolidated their power, grew accustomed to having no higher authority to whom they need defer—at least in Upper Egypt — and began to plan for more.

By about 1645 B.C., seventy-five years after the coming of the Hyksos, the rulers at Thebes claimed the title of king and, indeed, considered themselves to be the rightful kings of all Egypt. In this way a line of rulers begins which Manetho lists as the Seventeenth Dynasty, one which existed concurrently with the Sixteenth Dynasty of the Hyksos.

The situation of the Theban "kings" could not have been

particularly impressive at first. The rich north was ruled by invaders. The Nubian fortresses had been burned and destroyed. All they had was their own city and the thin stretch of the Nile a hundred miles or so to the north and to the south. To this, though, they held on grimly.

Two things worked in their favor. If a warlike people, used to living in rude simplicity, conquer and occupy a civilized region, they soon grow used to comfort and luxury and are increasingly reluctant to trouble themselves with the difficulties and hardships of the military life. In short, they cease to be warlike. (Often, writers on historical events tend to consider such a loss of willingness to fight as a sign of "decadence," as though there were something despicable about not being a bully and not being willing to engage in mass murder. Perhaps we ought to feel instead that to cease to be warlike means to begin to be civilized and decent.)

However that may be, though, the Hyksos did settle down and grow "soft." The rulers and leaders among them, in particular, became Egyptian in culture and manner, and were not as formidable in battle as they had been.

The second factor was that "secret weapons" don't remain secret after they are used. The Egyptians of the south began to learn to use the horse and chariot themselves and were able to meet the Hyksos more nearly on equal terms.

The kings of the Seventeenth Dynasty fought against the Hyksos and slowly began to make headway. They extended their power northward, and the region subject to the invaders shrank. By the time of Kamose (kay'mose), the last of the kings of the dynasty, the Hyksos had been forced back to the territory immediately around their capital.

Neither Kamose nor the Seventeenth Dynasty endured to witness the final victory. What happened we don't know. Presumably Kamose died and had no son to succeed him. We might suppose some unrelated individual then took power, but there seems reason to believe that it was a brother who took the throne. If so, that would scarcely seem excuse enough to start a new dynasty. However, we can't tell what criteria Manetho may have used in marking off his dynasties. Perhaps he felt that Egypt was making a new start with the final expulsion of the Hyksos and deserved a new dynasty, whether the family relationships called for it or not.

The Eighteenth Dynasty (Theban, like the Seventeenth) was destined to be the greatest in Egyptian history. It came to power in 1570 B.C., and its first representative was Ahmose (ah'mose), who completed the work of his predecessor and, possibly, brother, Kamose.

In a final battle in the delta, Ahmose completely defeated Apophis III (ap'oh-fis), the last of the Hyksos kings, and drove him out of Egypt. He even followed the retreating Hyksos into Palestine and defeated them there again.

Thus, the Hyksos, having suddenly entered the pages of history and ruled a rich empire for a century and a half, seem as suddenly to disappear from those pages, dropping out as silently and as mysteriously as they had entered. This is an illusion, however; it is only the name — not the people — which appears and disappears. The Hyksos were a loose alliance of Semitic tribes gathered out of Syria and neighboring regions, and to those regions they now returned. As Hyksos they no longer existed, but as Semitic tribes — Canaanites, Phoenicians, Amorites — they remained to dispute the eastern shores of the Mediterranean with Egypt for a long time.

Having dealt with the Hyksos, Ahmose went on to reestablish Egyptian power in northern Nubia and to clamp a firm hand upon the nobles. The Hyksos interlude had taught the Egyptians one lesson at least and the turbulent nobility bent in subjection to the throne. The world had become too dangerous for games of ambition. The situation in Egypt thus returned very much to what it had been under the great Fourth Dynasty, so that the rule of Ahmose marks the beginning of a new period of power, after a two-century hiatus. The portion of Egyptian history that follows is therefore often called the New Kingdom.

No doubt some of the Asians who had entered Egypt during the period of Hyksos rule, remained after native Egyptians had taken over once more. These Asians could scarcely have been looked upon with affection by Egyptians, who considered themselves to have been wickedly tyrannized over for five generations. It would have been quite according to the general custom of the period to enslave the remnant of the hated, once-feared, and now-defeated foreigners.

One could even argue a logical excuse. If Asians ever attempted to invade Egypt again, those Asians remaining within Egyptian territory would serve as a natural "fifth column." For security reasons, therefore, the Asians would have to be deprived of all power. It is this that may have given rise to the later tales of the Israelites concerning their period of enslavement in Egypt, after the rise of a pharaoh who "knew not Joseph."

But the New Kingdom was different in one important respect from the Old and Middle kingdoms. Egypt had learned the facts of life. Egyptians had discovered they did not exist alone in the world — Egypt was not the one civilized power, surrounded by inferior beings. There were other military powers who were dangerous, and whom Egypt must smash if it were not to be smashed.

Egypt now had its chariotry; it had its tradition of victory over a powerful foe. Monarchs arose who took pride in leading their armies to conquest beyond Egypt's borders. The king was now not only a priest and god; he was also a great general. Somehow this made the king even more exalted to the people, and made him an even greater and more effective symbol of power. As a god, his bringing of good crops was quiet and unspectacular; as a general, the trophies, spoils, and prisoners he brought back were loudly triumphant evidence of deeds that served to enrich himself, his soldiers, and his people.

In the New Kingdom, the Egyptian king gained a new title. People have always felt reluctant to refer to a monarch directly. His position seems too exalted to be sullied by ordinary treatment. In modern times, it is common to say "Your Majesty" and "His Majesty" rather than "you" or "he" in speaking to or of a king. Even in democratic America, one would scarcely presume to address the President by any ordinary form of address. It is "Mr. President." And often one says, "The White House feels that — " when one really means that the President feels that way.

Similarly, the Egyptians took to referring to the king by *his* place of residence, his huge palace, which they called *per-o* ("the big house"). Our version is "pharaoh."

Strictly speaking, the title should not be applied to the kings who came before the Eighteenth Dynasty, but this is commonly done, thanks to the influence of the Bible. The early books of the Bible are based on legends that were reduced to writing after the period of the New Kingdom. The title "pharaoh" used in this period was applied, anachronistically, to the early kings — to the king of the Twelfth Dynasty with whom Abraham dealt, and to the Hyksos king whom Joseph served.

EXPANSION

Amenhotep I (ah″men-hoh′tep), the son and successor of Ahmose I, came to the throne in 1545 B.C. (Some Egyptologists prefer the name Amenophis [am″eh-noh′fis], for while there is usually no disagreement on the meaning of Egyptian words, there is often disagreement on the pronunciation.)

Under Amenhotep I, the new mood of Egypt was made clearly manifest. His armies plunged deep into Nubia, establishing Egyptian power as far as ever it had reached in the days of Amenemhat III, three centuries before. He strengthened the Egyptian posture beyond Sinai as well and, in addition, struck westward from the Nile.

To the west of Egypt lay the Sahara Desert, but even in the time of the Middle Kingdom it was not yet as dry and unpopulated as it is today. The coastal areas remained fertile enough to support considerable population. There were vineyards, olive orchards, and cattle in plenty in areas now too dry to support much beyond scrub and some goats. There were, in those days, even inland oases about which people could cluster — oases more extensive than any today.

In later centuries, the Greeks colonized parts of the African coast west of Egypt. From the name by which a particular native tribe called itself, the Greeks obtained the word "Libya" and applied this to all of northern Africa west of Egypt. The inhabitants of the oases and coasts west of Egypt are therefore referred to as Libyans in our history books. (The region is still known by that name and, since 1951, has formed the independent kingdom of Libya.)

The Libyans, while racially similar to the Egyptians and speaking a similar language, remained far behind culturally. The guaranteed agricultural return of the Nile floods had supplied enough wealth to allow the growth of an immense civilization. Nothing of the sort could take place in the far more nearly marginal economy of Libya, where herdsmen were loosely organized into tribes and where what civilization existed was largely a diluted reflection from the land of the Nile.

The Libyans found it profitable to mount an occasional raid eastward into the peaceful agricultural communities along the Nile. If those communities were caught by surprise, the pickings were rich, and any punitive expeditions sent into the desert by the smarting Egyptians were easily evaded by men who, after all, knew every foot of the desert.

Such raids would naturally increase in number and effectiveness whenever Egypt was disunited and at war with itself, for it would then be impossible for the Egyptians to maintain an effective system of outposts to watch for encroaching Libyans. During the Hyksos period, when Egypt, whether being conquered or in rebellion, was in greater confusion than it had ever been, the Libyan raids were most painful.

Amenhotep I saw that the most effective stopper would be a systematic move westward. The oases west of the Nile as well as strong points on the coast must be permanently occupied by Egyptian army contingents. Libyan raiders, if they were to come at all, would have to come from outposts farther west. They would have a greater distance to travel to reach their prey and to return, and they would have to run a dangerous Egyptian gauntlet. The risks would become too great to make such attempts profitable.

Amenhotep I carried through the plan successfully so that the New Kingdom spread Egyptian power in every direction and over broader areas than the Old and Middle kingdoms had. Egypt ruled over Nubians to the south, Libyans to the west, and Canaanites to the northeast. It is therefore fashionable to refer to the New Kingdom as the period of the "Egyptian Empire."

The successor of Amenhotep I was not his son or even, apparently, of the royal family. Yet it is unlikely that he was a usurper, for Manetho does not begin a new dynasty with him but continues both the new king and his successors as part of the Eighteenth Dynasty. Perhaps Amenhotep had no son and it was a son-in-law who succeeded, a son-in-law whose legal status and whose membership in the dynasty were fixed by virtue of his wife.

However that might be, the successor was Thutmose I

(thut'moze), a name often given as Thothmes (thoth'meez). Coming to power in 1525 B.C., Thutmose I pursued Amenhotep's policy vigorously. He penetrated still farther southward, reaching the Fourth Cataract so that, under him, Egypt dominated some twelve hundred miles of the Nile — an immense stretch for that day.

The new pharaoh's greatest feats, however, were to the northeast where the easternmost shores of the great Mediterranean Sea were now made part of the Egyptian sphere of power for three centuries.

The Canaanites, living in the land later known to the Greeks as Syria, had built up a considerable civilization. Jericho, just north of the Dead Sea, was one of the oldest cities in the world and may date back, as an agricultural community, to 7000 B.C. at which time even the Nile and the Tigris-Euphrates had not felt the touch of civilization.

The Canaanite cities did not, however, have a convenient river-highway binding them together and were never effectively united. They remained separate "city-states" to the end of their history. For that reason, they could never compete with the unified empires of Egypt on the one side and Babylonia on the other. Except in those rare cases where both Egypt and Babylonia were simultaneously weak, they could not maintain their independence for long, let alone build an empire of their own.

Egyptian armies had been in Syria before. Amenemhat III, at the height of the Middle Kingdom, had captured a city that some identify with Shechem (shee'kum), a hundred miles north of the limits of the Sinai Peninsula. Ahmose I had penetrated Syria in his pursuit of the Hyksos, and Amenhotep I had won victories there.

Thutmose I intended to do more. He led a large army into Syria and took it northward to Carchemish (kahr'kuh-mish) on the upper Euphrates, four hundred miles north of the Sinai

Peninsula. There he planted a stone pillar testifying to his presence.

The Egyptian soldiers, sons of the cloudless land of the Nile, were fascinated when they encountered rain — "a Nile falling from the sky." They were amazed, too, at the direction of flow of the Euphrates. The Nile flowed north, so that "north" meant "downstream" to them, but here was the Euphrates, a river which "in flowing north flowed south."

Under the New Kingdom, a new style of grandiose architecture came into fashion. Gone were the pyramids of the Old and Middle kingdoms. Not one new pyramid was ever built. Instead, the pharaohs bent their efforts toward gigantic pillars and colossal statues.

The ornamentation went on most spectacularly at Thebes, the capital of the pharaohs of the Eighteenth Dynasty. At this time, there was no tendency to run toward the delta or Lake Moeris as had been the case with the Theban Eleventh and Twelfth dynasties. Perhaps Lower Egypt had lost prestige somehow because it had been under Hyksos domination while Thebes had remained free and had eventually spearheaded the liberation. Then, too, the long stretch of Nubian territory now under Egyptian domination made Thebes more centrally located than it had seemed to be in earlier centuries.

Thutmose I and his successors built huge temples in Thebes. Each pharaoh attempted to outdo his predecessor in quantity of stone and elaborateness of ornamentation. For his part, Thutmose I enlarged the temple to Amen in the northern quarter of Thebes, a place on which the modern village of Karnak stands. In the southern quarter of Thebes, occupied now by the village of Luxor, another huge and magnificent temple was eventually to be built.

Thebes was on the eastern bank of the Nile. On the western bank, a vast royal cemetery grew up. It was still necessary to hide the corpse of the king in order that the treasures buried with him might be safeguarded. Previous methods for accomplishing this had failed, and Thutmose I therefore tried something else.

Instead of building a mountainous pyramid and placing the tomb in the middle, natural masses of rock were used. Shafts were sunk deep into the earth through the rock of a cliffside. Labyrinth-like corridors were designed to baffle would-be grave robbers, and the tombs with their treasures were placed in chambers made as secure as possible behind every kind of false trail and dead end. One tomb was eventually placed 320 feet underground and was reached by tortuous passages 700 feet long.

Thutmose I was the first to be buried within the cliffside, but after his time about sixty pharaohs imitated his action. The ridge became, virtually, a city of the dead.

But this, too, was all for nothing. The winding tunnels, the clever false scents, the hidden entrances, the powerful spells — all failed. Every grave but one was rifled within mere decades of burial. The one that remained intact till modern times escaped only through the sheerest accident. The rubble from a later grave covered and hid its entrance, and for thirty-five centuries no one thought of looking past that rubble.

From the reign of Thutmose I onward, over a period of several centuries, Thebes became the greatest and most magnificent city in the world — the wonder of all who beheld it. Nor must we dismiss such beautification as mere vainglory (though that was an important part of it). An enormously elaborate capital not only fills the people of a nation with pride and with a feeling of power, but it also correspondingly disheartens prospective enemies who judge power by magnificence. Beautified cities can therefore be looked upon as presenting an important "image" and as playing a role in psychological warfare. In modern times, Napoleon III beautified Paris for this reason, and quite recently the western powers have deliberately promoted the prosperity of West Berlin as a blow, and a successful one, at East German morale.

THE GREAT QUEEN

Thutmose I was followed by an even more remarkable monarch. This was not Thutmose II, his son and successor. Thutmose II ruled in conjunction with his father toward the end of Thutmose I's reign, and ruled in his own name for a very short period, if at all.

Rather, the true successor was a woman, the daughter of Thutmose I and the wife of Thutmose II.

It was quite usual for Egyptian princes to marry their sisters, a custom which to us seems strange. All sorts of reasons can be advanced. It may be that inheritance of land was originally through the daughters, a procedure dating back, perhaps, to a primitive period before the idea of fatherhood had been established. Or it dated back to a time when women conducted agricultural labors (while men continued to hunt) and therefore owned the land. The old-fashioned and ultraconservative Egyptians may have clung to this antique notion and may have felt that the king's son was never truly king until he had married the king's daughter, who was the real inheritor.

It could also be that Egyptian princes felt it necessary to marry only their equals — a snobbish attitude often encountered in royal houses. Such an attitude was certainly common in European royalty and is maintained to this day. The European royal marriages frequently involved first cousins, or uncles and nieces. This was not allowed by Church dogma for people generally, but the limited supply of royalty made it necessary, and the Church allowed special dispensations.

For the Egyptian royal house, however, there was no other of equal rank, through all its days of glory. Snobbishness would dictate then the marriage of brother and sister — or half sister, if the father had more than one wife, as was usually the case. Thutmose II had married his half sister Hatshepsut (hat-shep'soot). When Thutmose II died, in 1490 B.C., his young son by a concubine (not by Hatshepsut) was, in theory, the new pharaoh under the name of Thutmose III. But Thutmose III was too young to rule, and Hatshepsut, his aunt and step-mother, acted as his regent.

She was a most forceful woman and very soon assumed the full powers of a pharaoh. In the monuments which she had built, she always had herself represented in masculine clothes, and in the form of a male — even to omitting breasts and in-cluding a false beard. She is the first important woman ruler, known to us by name, in history.

A false beard did not accomplish everything, of course. She could not very well lead an army and expect the generals (or even more, perhaps, the common soldiers) to obey a woman. Perhaps she did not even have any particular desire to do so. Her reign represents a peaceful interval in the warlike history of the dynasty, and she took to enriching the country by in-dustry rather than loot. She was particularly interested in the Sinai mines, for instance, and she tried to expand Egypt's trade.

She built a beautiful temple across the river from Thebes, and on its walls she carefully depicted scenes from a trading expedition to Punt which she sponsored. The products im-ported are carefully and even beautifully drawn and include a panther and a number of monkeys. (Did Hatshepsut want them for pets or was there a royal zoo?) The scenes also show the great queen supervising the transport of two obelisks from the quarries near the First Cataract.

Obelisks are structures which were originally set up to honor Re, the sun-god. They are long, thin, slightly tapering stone pillars, set upright, and topped by a pyramidlike point, originally plated in gleaming metal to capture the rays of the sacred sun. (Could they have served to cast a shadow that would serve as a sundial to tell the time of day?)

The name "obelisk" is from a Greek word meaning "needle," a term used by the later Greek tourists as a kind of humorous understatement.

Obelisks had first been erected during the Old Kingdom, and they weren't particularly tall then. The Egyptians hewed them out of single pieces of red granite, and such pieces were increasingly difficult to handle properly as they became longer. Whether they were used first as sundials or as grave monuments, obelisks ten feet in height were considered high enough.

During the Middle Kingdom, however, when smaller pyramids were built, more effort could be put into obelisks. They came to be placed before temples, one on each side of the door, and eventually nearly every temple had these rather impressive objects at the entranceway. Heliopolis was particularly rich in them. They rose in scores there, each with deeply incised hieroglyphs running down the face, giving the name and title of the pharaoh under whom they were built, together with whatever boastful self-praise that pharaoh wished to include. One obelisk from the Middle Kingdom was 68 feet high.

In the New Kingdom, when pyramids disappeared altogether, it became almost a fad to erect enormous obelisks. Thutmose I set up one that was 80 feet high, while the two set up by Hatshepsut were 96 feet high.

The tallest obelisk to survive to this day is 105 feet high and now stands in Rome. Another obelisk, about 69 feet high, originally built in the reign of Hatshepsut's successor, was transported to New York's Central Park in 1881. There it is popularly known as Cleopatra's Needle, after Egypt's most famous queen, who reigned, however, almost 1500 years after the obelisk was built. There is another "Cleopatra's Needle" in London.

Three and only three of all the obelisks that were built remain standing in Egypt today, one at Heliopolis and two at the site of Thebes. Of the latter, one is from the time of Thutmose I and the other from that of Hatshepsut.

The obelisks supply moderns with an interesting puzzle. They are extremely heavy, the largest weighing over 450 tons. How could a single piece of stone that heavy be placed on end without the brittle structure breaking, considering the limited tools possessed by the ancient Egyptians? Methods for doing so have been worked out, but not all Egyptologists are agreed on the details. (The same problem faces us in connection with the early Britons who upended the huge flat rocks at Stonehenge — which were erected, by the way, at just about the time that Hatshepsut sat on the throne of Egypt.)

While the Egyptian pyramids have not been imitated, let alone surpassed, by later cultures, their obelisks have been. The best-known by far of all modern obelisks is the Washington Monument, completed in 1884 in memory of George Washington. As befits the advance in technology and power since the time of the Eighteenth Dynasty, the Washington Monument is far larger in size than anything the Egyptians could manage. It is 555 feet tall, and its square base is 55.5 feet on each side. (And all those fives are not merely coincidental.)

However, we cheated. The Washington Monument is not built out of a single huge rock, but out of ordinary masonry, and we were never put to the task of having to upend a long brittle piece of stone as the Egyptians had to.

AT THE PEAK

Queen Hatshepsut died in 1469 B.C., by which time Thutmose III was about twenty-five years old and aching for a chance to show his mettle. From what he accomplished later on, it is hard to realize that he had remained completely under the thumb of his overbearing aunt-stepmother while she was alive. We can recognize what a woman she must have been to have dominated the kind of man Thutmose III showed himself to be once he was free of her.

There is no mistaking the new pharaoh's bitter resentment of her and of his long oppression by her. He repaid it by a systematic desecration of the monuments left behind by Hatshepsut. Her name was cut away from every place it was safe to do so, and his own, or that of one of the earlier Thutmoses, substituted. He even left her tomb uncompleted, the utmost act of revenge he could take upon her in the light of Egyptian thought.

What's more, he determined to shine in the one area in which Hatshepsut had been wanting — the military. This was not merely a matter of vanity, either, but one of necessity. The situation in Syria had deteriorated badly since the great days of his grandfather, Thutmose I. A new power had arisen.

Two centuries before, a non-Semitic people, the Hurrians, had come down from the north. It might have been their pressure which set the Semitic tribes of Syria into motion and sent them southward against Egypt to establish the Hyksos domination. Indeed, there may even have been Hurrian contingents included with the Hyksos.

Chiefly, however, the Hurrians remained north of the upper Euphrates, and there they slowly consolidated a strong kingdom known as Mitanni, which stretched across the upper reaches of the Tigris and Euphrates rivers. Their sphere of influence reached almost to the Syrian outposts of the Egyptian Empire, and they represented a new and great danger to Egyptian influence in that area.

A vigorous Egyptian king might have struck northward in a kind of preventive war to keep this from happening, but Hatshepsut's peaceful policy, however beneficial for Egypt itself, did encourage potential trouble at the distant boundaries of the empire.

When Thutmose III came to the throne, the Canaanite princes of Syria felt the time was ripe to break the Egyptian overlordship. The new pharaoh's past history as a puppet king dominated by a woman gave them every reason to think he would be incompetent in battle. Then, too, behind them, undoubtedly encouraging them with money and with promise of military help, was the bright new realm of Mitanni, fresh from recent conquests.

But Thutmose III reacted at once and violently. He marched into Syria and faced the coalition army of the Canaanite cities at Megiddo (meh-gid'oh), the Biblical "Armageddon," which was about fifty miles north of the city that was eventually to become world-famous as Jerusalem. There, Thutmose won a great victory, and then began a systematic and tireless effort to complete the job once and for all.

The city of Kadesh (kay'desh), about 120 miles north of Megiddo, which was the heart and soul of the coalition, fought grimly on. Though it took Thutmose III six campaigns to do so, in the end he reached and took Kadesh in 1457 B.C.

Beyond Kadesh lay the still greater threat of Mitanni itself. Thutmose III fought eleven more campaigns, pushed his way to the Euphrates as Thutmose I had done (but against far stronger opposition), crossed it, as his grandfather had not done, and invaded the Mitannian realm. Successful as always, he placed Mitanni under tribute.

It was the high point of Egypt's military prestige, and Thutmose is sometimes called Thutmose the Great, or the Napoleon of Egypt. If military proficiency were all, Thutmose might be dismissed merely as a capable general. However, the home administration was firm and efficient, and Egypt was prosperous as well as militarily great. Thutmose III may therefore be considered the greatest of the pharaohs.

Thutmose III died in 1436 B.C., having reigned thirty-three years on his own. The impetus he gave Egypt kept it going at its magnificent peak for three quarters of a century, and its population might have reached a peak of about five million.

Amenhotep II, Thutmose IV, and Amenhotep III were the son, grandson, and great-grandson of Thutmose the Great, and they successfully preserved the heritage of the great Pharaoh. They made no attempt to enlarge the empire still further, and it probably would not have been wise to do so since the Egypt of the time was very likely extended as far as it could safely be. The lines of communication would not have endured further stretching.

Thutmose IV pursued a deliberate policy of peace with Mitanni and tried to make that peace stable by departing from Egyptian exclusivism to the point of marrying a Mitannian princess. He also finished the last obelisk planned by Thutmose III, the monster which now stands in Rome.

Under Amenhotep III, the son of the Mitannian queen of Thutmose IV, Egyptian prosperity reached its highest point. Amenhotep III, who came to the throne in 1397 B.C. and reigned for thirty-seven years, preferred luxury at home to fighting abroad, and Egypt enjoyed it with him. His predecessors had been constantly beautifying Thebes and enlarging the temple to Amen. He continued that, making use of the tribute money that came from all corners.

He was apparently deeply in love with his queen, Tiy (tee), also from Mitanni. He associated her with himself in his monumental inscriptions, and built a mile-long pleasure-lake for her on the western bank of the Nile.

A splendid temple was built in his honor after death and its gateway was flanked by two great statues of him. The northern one of the pair had the ability to emit a high note shortly after sunrise. Undoubtedly, there was some internal arrangement set up by the priests of Amen to impress the unsophisticated. And, to be sure, worshipers were impressed, including the later Greek tourists.

Indeed, rumors of these amazing statues must have reached the Greeks quite early, for it may have inspired one of their myths. Among the Greek legends concerning the Trojan War (fought a century and a half after the time of Amenhotep III) was that concerning a king of Ethiopia, a name that might well have been used in referring to Thebes and the far southern stretches of the Nile which were then under Egyptian domination. This king, named Memnon, fought on the Trojan side, and he was supposed to be the son of Eos, goddess of the dawn. He was killed by Achilles, and the northern statue of Amenhotep III is supposed to be "the singing Memnon" who greets his mother with a cry each morning.

6

THE FALL OF EMPIRE

THE RELIGIOUS REFORMER

All of Egypt's glory was compromised by Queen Tiy, wife of Amenhotep III and mother of the new pharaoh, Amenhotep IV. She was a Mitannian woman and, apparently, not in sympathy with the infinitely complex Egyptian religious system. She preferred her own simpler rites.

Her doting husband (half Mitannian himself) may have listened fondly and even sympathetically. Yet he could do nothing, for he could not very well be expected to oppose the powerful priesthood who had ruled the pious Egyptians for many centuries now with an accumulated force that even a pharaoh could not surmount.

But Tiy must have made some converts, for the breath of a new religion was making itself felt in the last years of Amenhotep III. Of course, Tiy's chief convert was her own son, and others may have followed the lead out of consideration for the benefits they would gain by being of the "right religion" when the new pharaoh sat on the throne.

While Amenhotep III lived, his son could do little, but when the old king died in 1370 B.C., the new king (three-quarters Mitannian by descent) began to put into action the newfangled ideas he had received from his mother and had, perhaps, gone on to develop on his own.

He even abandoned his name, Amenhotep IV, since that memorialized Amen (meaning "Amen is pleased"), one of the Egyptian gods he despised as mere superstition. His own god was the glorious sun, worshiped in a new non-Egyptian fashion. He worshiped it as no god at all, in the usual sense of visualizing a human or animal form for it. Rather it was the disk itself he adored, the gleaming round sun which he pictured as giving forth rays that ended with hands — hands that showered the blessings of light, warmth, and life upon the earth and its inhabitants. (From a modern scientific view, this isn't such a bad notion.)

The disk he called Aton, and he renamed himself Ikhnaton (ik-nah'ton), meaning "pleasing to Aton."

Ikhnaton, as he is known to history, had every intention of imposing his beliefs on the Egyptians. He was the first "religious fanatic" known by name in history, unless we count Abraham, who, according to Jewish legend, broke the idols in his home city of Ur out of religious convictions, some six centuries before Ikhnaton.

Ikhnaton built temples to Aton and prepared a complete ritual for his new god. There is even a beautiful hymn to the sun, found carved on the tomb of one of his courtiers. Tradition ascribes it to the Pharaoh's own creative mind, and it is a hymn which sounds almost like a Biblical psalm.*

Indeed, such was Ikhnaton's enthusiasm for Aton that he was not content merely to add him to Egypt's gods or even to make him the chief of Egypt's gods. He decided Aton must be the *only* god, and all others must be eliminated. He is thus the first monotheist in history known to us by name, unless, again, we accept the monotheism of Abraham.

Indeed, there are some who argue that the Biblical Moses lived in the time of Ikhnaton, and that the Egyptian Pharaoh picked up a kind of distorted version of Judaism from the great prophet. However, this is certainly not so, for Moses could not possibly have lived in Ikhnaton's time but, if he lived at all, must have lived at least a century later. With that in mind, there are even some who maintain that Moses adopted the monotheistic notion from Ikhnaton and then added his own refinements.

But whether Ikhnaton taught Moses or not, he certainly did not succeed in teaching the Egyptian people. The Theban priesthood recoiled in horror from a man they could only consider an atheist and a vile desecrator of all that was holy; a pharaoh, more foreign than Egyptian, who was on a par with the Hyksos themselves.

No doubt, they carried the people with them. The Egyptians had grown up loving the beauty and magnificence of the temples and the awesome ritual devised by the priests. They would not have this replaced by some unheard-of mishmash about a sun disk.

* Part of the hymn reads, in translation:

"Thou art in my heart
And there is no other that knows thee
Save thy son. . . .
The world came into being by thy hand . . .
Thou art lifetime thy own self
For one lives only through thee. . . .
Since thou didst found the earth
And raise them up for thy son,
Who came forth from thy body:
The king . . . Ikhnaton . . .
And the Chief Wife . . . Nefertiti . . ."

Ikhnaton had to seek consolation in the sun worship within his own court, on the part of his family and his loyal courtiers. The chief consolation may have been that of his wife, Nefertiti (neh″fur-tee′tee). She is better known to most men than her royal husband — entirely through a single piece of art. Art itself, you see, had also been revolutionized under the rule of this "heretic king." Since the days of the Old Kingdom, Egyptians had used a certain stylized method of portraying themselves. The head had to be in profile, but the body itself was seen from the front with the arms held stiffly down the sides, and the legs and feet in profile again. Expressions were of nothing more than calm dignity.

With Ikhnaton there came a new realism. Ikhnaton and Nefertiti are seen in informal poses, in moments of affection, in play with their children. No effort is made to mask the fact that Ikhnaton was quite an ugly man, with a lantern jaw, a potbelly, and fat thighs. (All this "modern art" must have shocked the conventional Egyptians quite as much as the queer religious views propounded by their pharaoh.) Perhaps Ikhnaton suffered from a glandular malfunction, for he died while still fairly young.

But the finest piece of art is a portrait bust of painted limestone, found in 1912 in the remains of a sculptor's workshop in the ruins of what had once been Ikhnaton's capital. It is now in a museum in Berlin.

It is presumed to be of Nefertiti and is certainly one of the most exquisitely beautiful surviving products of Egyptian art. It has been imitated and photographed innumerable times, and vast numbers of people have seen some form of reproduction at one time or another. It has almost fixed itself in the human mind as the ideal representation of Egyptian beauty. This is rather ironic since Nefertiti was probably still another Asian princess.

It is rather sad, by the way, that the seemingly idyllic marriage of Ikhnaton and Nefertiti appears not to have been lasting. Toward the end, Nefertiti incurred the royal displeasure and was divorced or banished.

Upset and disheartened by the obdurate resistance of the Thebans, Ikhnaton made the rather desperate decision to abandon the great royal city. With his family and with those courtiers whom he had converted, he decided in 1366 b.c. to build himself a new capital, a pure one that would be dedicated to the new worship from the start. He chose a spot on the eastern bank of the Nile about halfway between Thebes and Memphis and built there Akhetaton ("the horizon of Aton").

In this city, he built temples and palaces and villas for himself and his loyal nobility. The temple to Aton was a most unconventional building, for it was roofless. The sun he worshiped could blaze down freely into the temple built in its honor.

There in Akhetaton, Ikhnaton retired from the real world. He surrounded himself with an artificial one in which his version of religion had won out, and devoted himself to persecuting the old priesthood, to ordering the name "Amen" cut out of monuments, and to deleting references to "gods" in the plural.

Ikhnaton's monomania deprived him of all interest in anything but religion, and he neglected military affairs and foreign problems. These were pressing, for nomad raiders were advancing on Syria from the east. Message after message came to Ikhnaton from his generals and viceroys in Syria, reporting the dangerous situation and pleading for reinforcements.

Apparently, Ikhnaton ignored all such pleas. Perhaps he was an honest and convinced pacifist who would not fight. Perhaps he felt that the only real battle was the religious one and that all else was secondary. Perhaps he even felt that if Egypt suffered, it was a deserved suffering for their rejection of what he considered the true faith.

Whatever the reason, Egyptian prestige abroad experienced a disastrous decline, and all that had been gained and held in the previous century by Thutmose III and his successors was lost. It was during Ikhnaton's reign, apparently, that various Hebrew-speaking tribes formed nations on the outskirts of Syria. These were Moab, Ammon, and Edom, so familiar to us from the Bible.

More important than these small groups of desert tribesmen, who could be nothing more than irritations to mighty Egypt, was the emergence of a new great power to the north.

In eastern Asia Minor, a people speaking an Indo-European tongue (the family to which the common European languages of today belong) had gradually formed a strong nation. They are the Hatti, according to Babylonian records, but are called the Hittites in the Bible, and it is the latter name by which they are usually referred to.

During the time when Egypt lay under the Hyksos yoke, the Hittites enjoyed a period of power under able kings. This is the period of the Hittite "Old Kingdom," from 1750 to 1500 B.C. The rise of Mitanni, however, brought on the decay of this Old Kingdom, and in the time of Hatshepsut, the Hittites were tributaries of the Mitanni.

When Mitanni's power had been broken by Thutmose III, the Hittites had their chance again. They recouped their lost dominance, gaining ground as Mitanni lost.

In 1375 B.C., a king with the liquid-sounding name of Shubbiluliu came to the Hittite throne. Carefully, he reorganized the land, establishing a centralized power and strengthening the army. When Ikhnaton came to the Egyptian throne and began to occupy himself, and Egypt, with religious controversy, Shubbiluliu had his chance. He began a strenuous campaign against Mitanni, which at that time was existing as an Egyptian ally and, indeed, puppet.

Mitanni relied on help from Egypt, but that help never came. She declined rapidly and within a century had disappeared from history. Left in her place was the powerful Hittite "New Kingdom" that now faced Egypt threateningly.

REFORM DEFEATED

Ikhnaton died in 1353 B.C. and left behind six daughters but no sons. Two of his sons-in-law reigned briefly after him, and even in the course of these short periods of time, the attempted accomplishments of the reformer began to crumble and vanish as though they had never been, except for the irreparable damage the religious controversy had done Egypt.

The converts to Ikhnaton's religion soon unconverted themselves. The city of Akhetaton was gradually deserted, dismantled, and allow to crumble to dust as an abode of wicked demons.

The priests of the old religion steadily regained their power and reversed everything. Tutankhaton, Ikhnaton's second reigning son-in-law, who was pharaoh from 1352 to 1343 B.C., changed his name to Tutankhamen, as official pharaonic testimony that Amen was back on the job as chief god.

And yet, an echo of Ikhnaton remained to survive into modern times. On the site of long-vanished Akhetaton there now exists the village of Tell-el-Amarna. In 1887, a peasant woman happened to dig up a cache of about three hundred clay tablets inscribed in cuneiform symbols (the writing of Babylonia, which was by then well understood by archaeologists). They turned out to be messages from Asian kings of Babylonia, Assyria, and Mitanni to the royal court of Egypt — and also from vassal princes in Syria asking for help against the pressure of invading nomads.

In a few years, careful excavations began in the area. Because Akhetaton had been built from scratch on virgin territory and because it had been abandoned permanently after Ikhnaton's death, so that no later construction blurred its contents, it proved to be a find of inestimable value for determining the content of Ikhnaton's attempted religious reform, to say nothing of the details of the diplomacy and of military events of the time.

In fact, so complete was the priestly desire for vengeance and so thorough their industry in wiping out all traces of Ikhnaton from the monumental structures of Egypt, that if we had not found the records, we might have ended knowing very little, if anything, about this important epoch in the history of Egypt and of religion. The "Tell-el-Amarna letters" were the greatest find in Egypt after the Rosetta Stone.

Ikhnaton's son-in-law, Tutankhamen (toot"ahnk-ah'men) supplied another great treasure trove — this time, literally. In himself, he was a completely unimportant pharaoh. He was only twelve when he came to the throne, and he was scarcely more than a teen-ager when he died. Nevertheless, upon death, he received the usual sumptuous burial.

His grave was at once robbed but, for a wonder, the robbers were caught in the act and forced to return the loot. Perhaps the word was put out that the grave had been looted while the story of the forced return was withheld, so that the grave was not bothered thereafter. Then, two centuries later, while a grave was being excavated for a later pharaoh, the stone chips were disposed of in such a way as to cover up the entrance to Tutankhamen's tomb.

It remained covered up and intact. By 1000 B.C., every known pyramid, every known rock tomb, had been rifled. Not one set of treasure remained in place — except that of Tutankhamen.

In 1922, a British archaeological expedition, under Lord Carnarvon and Howard Carter, accidentally discovered the tomb and uncovered the treasure, sumptuous and magnificent. Aside from its impressiveness and its usefulness to the study of the culture of ancient Egypt, the chief interest in the discovery lies in the way it gave rise to the myth of the "Pharaoh's curse." Lord Carnarvon died less than half a year after the discovery as a result of an infected mosquito bite complicated by pneumonia. Sunday supplements at once took notice and raised a fearful row about it, but it is quite unlikely that the death had anything to do with any pharaoh's curse.

After Ikhnaton's disastrous failure, the Eighteenth Dynasty, which had brought Egypt two centuries of glory, petered out to a whimpering finale. Tutankhamen was succeeded by a pharaoh named Ay, who attempted to maintain some semblance of Ikhnaton's beliefs, but that was a completely hopeless task.

The final liquidation of Aton-worship was entrusted, by the relentless priests, to a general. Generals are usually a conservative force who can be relied on to oppose social change. In this case they may well have been exasperated by the decline in Egypt's military prestige.

A general named Horemheb (hoh'rem-heb") became pharaoh in 1339 B.C., succeeding Ay, and under him the old ways returned in full force. He was not a member of the Eighteenth Dynasty really, but is usually included as the final member of that group since he had been an important official under Ikhnaton and since he did not found a ruling family of his own.

Order was restored, and Egyptian expeditions were sent to reestablish the empire in Nubia. Nothing, however, was ventured in Syria. Shubbiluliu had died in 1335 B.C., but he had left behind a Hittite power that Horemheb preferred not to tangle with.

Horemheb died in 1304 B.C., and one of his generals ascended the throne as Ramses I (ram'seez) or Rameses I (ram'-

uh-seez). He was quite old, and he reigned only about a year. However, he established a line of successors and is therefore considered the first king of the Nineteenth Dynasty.

His son, Seti I (seh'tee), succeeded in 1303 B.C., and at last Egypt saw a return to full vigor. He invaded Syria and made Egyptian power felt in the area once more, but he came up hard against the Hittites, and agreed to a compromise peace. He also won victories over the Libyans. At home, he built elaborate temples in Thebes and at Abydos, a city about a hundred miles downstream from Thebes. He also built himself an elaborate tomb on the cliffside where the kings of the Eighteenth Dynasty slept (or would have slept if their tombs had not been rifled).

It was like old times; or rather, it would have been like old times if it hadn't been for one heritage that yet remained from the unsettled period under Ikhnaton. The Hittites were still there and would have to be dealt with. That was to be a problem for the son and successor of Seti I, a pharaoh who was to be by all odds the most flamboyant ever to sit on the Egyptian throne.

THE GREAT EGOTIST

That son was Ramses II, who succeeded to the throne in 1290 B.C. as a young man and proceeded to reign for sixty-seven years, the longest reign in Egyptian history save for that of Pepi II.

This reign was characterized by extraordinary self-praise. Ramses' power was absolute, and he filled Egypt from end to end with monuments in his own honor, all inscribed with boastful accounts of his victories and greatness. He had no hesitation, even, in inscribing his name on older monuments and appropriating the deeds of his predecessors.

He extended the already vast structures at the huge temple complex in Thebes (at what is now Karnak), raising obelisks and colossal statues to himself. When he was done with it, the temple complex reached essentially its final form and was the greatest temple (in terms of sheer size) ever built, then or since. One hall, the Hypostyle Hall, is the largest single chamber of any temple in the world, covering 54,000 square feet. Its roof was supported by a virtual forest of giant pillars — 134 of them. Some of them were 12 feet thick and 69 feet high.

Under him, Thebes reached its peak, spreading over both sides of the Nile, with a circuit of walls fourteen miles long and an accumulated wealth drawn from all the civilized world. Other peoples, who viewed it or heard rumors concerning it, were left in wondering awe.

Thebes is mentioned, for instance, in the *Iliad*, the epic poem in which the Greek poet Homer (who composed it perhaps three centuries after the time of Ramses II) sang of the Trojan War, which was fought not long after the death of Ramses.

In it, Homer has Achilles say, when he is refusing all bribes to return to the wars, that no amount of money would induce him to do that. "Not if he offered me . . . all that goes into Egyptian Thebes, the world's greatest treasure-house — Thebes with its hundred gates, where two hundred men issue forth from each gate with horses and chariots . . ."

But time conquers all, and Thebes is long since gone, and the magnificent temple at Karnak is in ruins — impressive even in what remains, but in ruins nevertheless. One of the statues of Ramses, the largest ever built in Egypt, is now broken and fallen. It was this fallen head (or reports concerning it) which inspired the English poet Percy Bysshe Shelley to write his chillingly ironic poem "Ozymandias":

I met a traveller from an antique land
Who said: Two vast and trunkless legs of stone
Stand in the desert . . . Near them, on the sand,
Half sunk, a shattered visage lies, whose frown,
And wrinkled lip, and sneer of cold command,
Tell that its sculptor well those passions read
Which yet survive, stamped on these lifeless things,
The hand that mocked them, and the heart that fed:
And on the pedestal these words appear:
"My name is Ozymandias, king of kings:
Look on my works, ye Mighty, and despair!"
Nothing beside remains. Round the decay
Of that colossal wreck, boundless and bare
The lone and level sands stretch far away.

Nor was Karnak the only place where Ramses II exercised his enormous self-love. Far to the south, 120 miles upstream from the First Cataract, where Egyptian monument-makers ordinarily did not venture, he constructed a notable temple.

In modern times, the village of Abu Simbel is on the spot, drowsing through the centuries of forgetfulness. There the great relic of the past was discovered in 1812 by the Swiss explorer Johann Ludwig Burckhardt. In a recess in the cliff he found four enormous seated representations of Ramses II, each 65 feet high. They are accompanied by smaller statues of other members of the royal family. They are part of the temple built in honor of Re (or Ra), the sun-god. The sun-god was Ramses' favorite deity, and the Pharaoh's name itself means "son of Ra." The temple is so oriented that the rising sun penetrates the interior and falls on the statues of Re and (who else?) Ramses in the center.

In the 1960's, a huge dam was under construction near the

First Cataract, and a long and large lake will be formed up-stream from that dam. The temple and colossal statues at Abu Simbel would be covered with water if nothing were done. Tremendous efforts are being made, at enormous ex-pense, to transport as much as possible of the complex to higher grounds. If the spirit of Ramses were watching, it would un-doubtedly be very gratified at this.

So impressive is Ramses' adoration of himself and so effi-cient his propaganda in his own favor that he is sometimes called Ramses the Great. In my opinion, it would be more accurate to call him Ramses the Egomaniac.

Militarily, Ramses II gives the impression of having restored the great empire of Thutmose III, but the impression is a false one. To be sure, Nubia was under Egyptian control again to the Fourth Cataract, and the Libyans remained subdued, but there was still Syria, and to the north of Syria there was the Hittite power.

Early in his reign, Ramses II marched against the Hittites and, in 1286 B.C., met them in a great battle at Kadesh, the city which, a century before, had led the Canaanite coalition against Thutmose III.

The course of the battle is obscure. The only account we have of it is the official version in Ramses' inscriptions. Ap-parently, the Egyptian army was caught unprepared and was in danger of being cut to pieces by the hard-slashing Hittite cavalry. The retreat had already begun, and Ramses II and his personal bodyguard were themselves under attack. Sud-denly Ramses II, throwing caution to the winds, determined to conquer or die, charged the enemy single-handed, and held them off with mighty strokes until reinforcements fought their way to his side. Heartened by this fantastic courage of their pharaoh, the army rallied and, turning imminent defeat into victory, smashed the Hittites.

We may be excused if we refuse to believe that. Ramses was perfectly capable of telling all sorts of lies about himself, and we need not take seriously the picture of Ramses in the role of a Hercules or a Samson, alone against an army. Nor need we think the battle of Kadesh was truly a great Egyptian victory. It could scarcely have been that, since the Hittite realm was as strong afterward as before and since Ramses had to fight against them for seventeen years more.

In all likelihood, the battle of Kadesh was a drawn battle or, if anything, a narrow Hittite victory. Despite all of Ramses' frantic boasting, Egypt was glad to sign a treaty of peace in 1269 B.C., one in which Hittite domination south of the Euphrates River was recognized and in which Egyptian rule was restricted to that portion of Syria nearest Egypt. Ramses was content to include a Hittite princess in his harem as a means of sealing the contract, and the remainder of his reign was peaceful.

So although it *seemed* as though Ramses II was Thutmose III all over again and that Egypt was restored to its maximum strength, it was not so. Thutmose III had, to the north, a defeated and tributary Mitanni; Ramses II had there a powerful and undefeated Hittite Empire.

Nevertheless, the long and bloody war between the two powers was fatal for both of them. They appeared strong, but their inner vigor had been utterly sapped by protracted warfare, and each was ready to collapse under blows that might be given it by some new and freshly strong foe.

There is a tradition that Ramses II is the "Pharaoh of the Oppression," the pharaoh referred to in the Biblical book of Exodus as having enslaved the Israelites and subjected them to harsh tasks. One of the reasons for that is the comment that the Israelites "built for Pharaoh treasure cities, Pithom and Raamses." (Exodus 1:11.)

This is quite possible. The Nineteenth Dynasty seems to have stemmed from the eastern section of the delta, where the Israelites, according to Biblical legend, lived in Goshen.

Ramses paid a natural attention to his home territory, building a temple in Tanis, a city near the easternmost mouth of the Nile, and constructing within it a 90-foot colossus of (naturally) himself. And he did build the elaborate palaces and storehouses (not "treasure cities" as mistranslated in the King James Version) referred to in the Bible. The storehouses were probably necessary to supply his armies during the Syrian campaigns against the Hittites. No doubt Ramses made use of local forced labor for all this.

The very length of the reign of Ramses II, like that of Pepi II, was bad for Egypt. Ramses' vigor declined; he craved rest. The nobility gained power, and the army decayed. More and more, Ramses was willing to fill the army ranks (or allow them to be filled) with mercenaries, foreigners who served for pay rather than out of any feeling of duty and patriotism.

This has been a trap into which wealthy and secure nations have fallen repeatedly in history. The citizens, prosperous and comfortable, see no use in suffering the hardships of army life when there are noncitizens eager to do so for pay. It is simpler to give them a little money, of which there is plenty, than to take of one's own time and comfort, of which there seems not enough. To the rulers, mercenaries may even seem preferable to native soldiers, since the former can more surely and mercilessly deal with internal unrest.

But all possible advantages are wiped out by two great disadvantages. In the first place, if the nation falls on hard times and cannot pay its mercenaries, those soldiers will cheerfully loot whatever is nearest, and prove a greater terror and danger to the homeland than an invading foe would be. Secondly, when the ruler begins to depend on mercenaries to conduct his wars and guard his person, he becomes the tool of those mercenaries, can make no move of which they disapprove and, in the end, is reduced to a puppet or, for that matter, to a corpse. All this has happened over and over again in history.

THE END OF GLORY

Ramses II finally ended his long reign in 1223 B.C., dying at an age that was close to ninety. His death seemed to come at a high point. The empire remained wide as ever, and its only important enemy began unexpectedly to fade. This was through no direct effort of Egypt's; rather it came about through the effects of internal unrest and civil war. Egypt itself, on the other hand, was wealthy, prosperous, and at peace. Ramses himself, having had numerous wives, left behind a veritable crowd of sons and daughters.

Merneptah (mer'nep-tah), the thirteenth son of Ramses, succeeded him. Merneptah, already about 60 years old, attempted to carry on his father's policies. He suppressed rebellions in that portion of Syria under Egyptian control and, in doing so, he records the name of Israel for the first time in historical records.

Apparently, as in the time of Ikhnaton, desert nomads were swarming toward the Canaanite cities from the east. The nomads were, this time, the people who later entered history as the Israelites. They found the Canaanite cities rimmed by the kingdoms of Ammon, Moab, and Edom, founded, by people kindred to the Israelites, in Ikhnaton's time. Blood was not thicker than water, and the established kingdoms opposed the newcomers. Apparently, Merneptah's army took part in the fighting and won a victory, for Merneptah's inscription gloried in the fact that "Israel is desolated and has no seed." Her manpower, in other words, was wiped out. This was obviously an exaggeration of the kind customary in official war bulletins.

Merneptah apparently also conducted successful campaigns

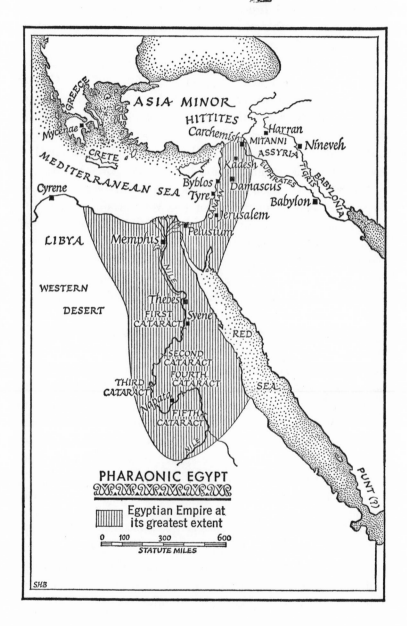

PHARAONIC EGYPT

Egyptian Empire at
its greatest extent

0   100   300   600
STATUTE MILES

SHB

in Lydia — but then the lightning struck and from a completely unexpected direction. Invaders plunged in upon Egypt from a place which had been assumed secure for thousands of years — from the sea itself.

The Egyptians were never a sea people, and they had always remained at peace with the seafaring Cretans. The Cretan civilization had, however, spread its rays over the European mainland to the north, that portion of the land that is known to us as Greece. During the time of the Hyksos domination over Egypt, Greek-speaking peoples had built elaborate cities of their own on the mainland, and had adopted Cretan ways.

Whereas Crete itself had always followed the way of peace, depending upon a monopoly of the Mediterranean trade for wealth, not so the Greek tribes on the mainland. They fought among each other violently and felt always in danger of renewed incursions of tribes from the north. They built cities with enormously thick walls, the chief of which was called Mycenae (migh-see′nee). This early period of Greek history is referred to, therefore, as the Mycenean Age.

The Myceneans, engaged in continuing warfare, developed military techniques to a high point, and once they learned how to build ships and venture out to sea, Crete itself could not stand before them. While Egypt was enjoying its period of power at the height of the Eighteenth Dynasty, the Mycenean sea-rovers completed their conquest and occupation of Crete.

But they were distant, beyond what seemed to the Egyptians to be a vast and untraversable stretch of salt water. No one worried in the confident Egypt of its imperial days.

And Egypt remained secure from these northerners for two centuries after the Mycenean capture of Crete. That situation might have continued longer, but the Myceneans were themselves under pressure from the north. In the north there were other, more primitive Greek-speaking tribes which had not yet felt the softening impulse of Cretan civilization. What they felt, instead, was the hardening impulse of iron.

For two thousand years armor had been made of bronze, although iron was known to make harder shields, sharper and more durable points, and keener cutting edges. The trouble was that iron was an exceedingly rare metal, available only in very occasional meteor finds. Iron could be obtained out of rocky ores, as copper could, but not as easily. Hotter flames were needed and a more complicated technique.

It was the Hittites, apparently, who first worked out a practical method of smelting iron ore. Knowledge concerning the technique spread, and small supplies of iron weapons began to find their way into armies. The primitive Greek tribes, called the Dorians, possessed some iron weapons, and their pressure against the Myceneans was multiplied by this fact.

The Myceneans, finding affairs in the north constantly more difficult, found relief in spreading eastward and southward. The Trojan War was fought in the days of Merneptah, or shortly after, and may represent a Mycenean push eastward. Other bands of sea rovers traveled southward and landed on the Libyan coast. With the eager assistance of the Libyan tribesmen, they began to raid the rich Egyptian lands. (Greek legends tell us that Menelaus, king of Sparta, while returning from the Trojan War, spent some time in Egypt — a dim memory perhaps of ancestral exploits on the African shores.)

In fact, the whole eastern rim of the Mediterranean was aflame. The Phrygians, a people in western Asia Minor, pushed eastward into a torn and bleeding Hittite nation, which was almost a suicide as a result of civil war. The Phrygians completed the job, and by 1200 B.C., the Hittite kingdom, which for a while had disputed the mastery of the civilized world with Egypt, came to an end and disappeared as an important force in history. (Hittite towns lingered on, however, in Syria, and one of the soldiers in the army of King David of Israel, two centuries later, was Uriah the Hittite.)

Egypt was in chaos as a result of the raids of these "Peoples from the Sea" — the only name the dumfounded Egyptians could give them. Unlike the Hittite kingdom, Egypt survived, but it was wavering and glassy-eyed as a result of the efforts required to beat off the sea peoples. It was never to be the same again.

According to one tradition, Merneptah was the "Pharaoh of the Exodus," the one upon whom the plagues had descended at the call of Moses and who was then drowned in the Red Sea.

There may be something to this, for the story of the plagues may be the result of the dim memory of the unexpected catastrophe that struck Egypt when the sea rovers landed and ravaged it.

Indeed, during the disorders, some of the Asian slaves in the land may well have seized the opportunity to leave and join the kindred contingents who were trying to storm Canaan.

While many people accept the Biblical stories literally, it nevertheless remains a fact that nowhere in the known Egyptian archives is there any mention of enslaved Israelites, of Moses, of the Biblical plagues. There is certainly no mention of any pharaoh being drowned in the Red Sea.

But if the Biblical details are considered as legendary growths that come with the recounting of stories from generation to generation, the basic core — that Asians entered Egypt during the Hyksos period, were enslaved during the New Kingdom, were particularly harshly treated under Ramses II, and escaped in Merneptah's time to join the Israelites battering at the Canaanite cities — may well be so.

Indeed, one can even wonder if perhaps Ikhnaton's cult of Aton had even yet survived through the century and a half that had passed since the time of the heretic king. Did a religious minority live on, scorned and persecuted, too lowly and despised to be mentioned in the official annals and inscriptions? Did they find a hearing among the Asian slaves, likewise scorned and persecuted? And when the Asians left, did they carry the notion of a single god and no other with them, a notion that was to take root among the Israelites and, through them, spread to hundreds of millions of people in all the long centuries since? Who can tell?

Merneptah died in 1211 B.C., and for the next twenty years there followed a group of weak and shadowy monarchs.

Yet one more time, an Egyptian rose to the occasion; one more time Thebes seemed as though it might be the healthy core of another rebirth. The governor of Thebes, claiming descent from Ramses II, seized the throne in 1192 B.C. and founded the Twentieth Dynasty. He beat down the nobles and established his rule over all of Egypt, leaving a reunited land to his son Ramses III, who ascended the throne in 1190 B.C.

Ramses III reigned for thirty-two years and represented a last breath of native vigor. He was much needed, too, for Egypt found it had to face another invasion of the Peoples from the Sea. This time the invaders included a group called Peleset in the inscriptions, who, it seems almost certain, are the "Philistines" of the Bible. This contingent landed on the southern coast of Asia Minor to begin with, and may have come from Cyprus, an island only seventy miles south of that shore.

They marauded their way down the eastern coast of the Mediterranean, entering Egypt from Syria as once the Hyksos had done. Ramses III was ready for them, however, and defeated them utterly. He had scenes of the battle carved on temple walls in commemoration. One shows Egyptian ships battling those of the Philistines — one of the earliest representations of a naval battle ever produced.

The discomfited Philistines were forced to settle down on the coast northeast of Egypt. The victory over them, however, was Egypt's last gasp and the end of its glory. She fell back on the Nile exhausted, her empire gone. The New Kingdom was at an end after four centuries of power, and there was never to be a native "Newer Kingdom" of equal power.

With Egypt helpless, the Israelites broke across the Jordan

River and began to subdue the Canaanite cities. For two centuries, Israelites and Philistines were to contend for domination at the very doorstep of Egypt, and Egypt was unable to move a finger to interfere in one way or the other.

7

FOREIGN DOMINATION

THE LIBYANS

Ramses III died in 1158 B.C., and succeeding him were a dim line of kings, all named Ramses (Ramses IV to Ramses XI), all unimportant, all weak. Together they are the Ramessids.

It was during the eighty-year period of these Ramessids (1158–1075 B.C.) that all but one of the tombs at Thebes were ransacked. Even the burial treasures of Ramses II himself were stolen. It was on the occasion of the burial of one of these Ramessids — Ramses VI in 1138 B.C. — that the tomb of Tutankhamen, who had ruled two centuries earlier, was effectively covered over, enabling it to remain intact until modern times.

As the power of the pharaoh declined, that of the priesthood increased. The victory of the priesthood over Ikhnaton had been a shadow over the pharaoh's crown ever since. Even Ramses II must have had to tread warily in respecting the priestly rights. Throughout the Nineteenth and Twentieth dynasties, more and more land, peasantry, and wealth had come under their power. Since the power of a long-established religion tends to be conservative and inflexible, this was by and large a bad thing for the nation.

The Ramessids were puppets in the hands of the priesthood, who probably remembered that, under the Hyksos domination, the priests of Amen ruled over Thebes and Upper Egypt. When Ramses XI finally died in 1075 B.C., no direct successor mounted the throne. Instead, the high priest of Amen, who happened also to be the leader of the army, made obvious what was actually the fact and declared himself ruler of Egypt. He did not, however, become ruler of a united kingdom.

A second set of rulers developed in the delta, with a capital at Tanis, the home city of Ramses II. It is the line of Tanite rulers that are called by Manetho the Twenty-first Dynasty.

Egypt was now weaker than ever, for it was divided, and Menes' work two thousand years ago again seemed undone.

About the only thing clearly known concerning the Egypt of the Twenty-first Dynasty is a single offhand Biblical mention which, in itself, highlights the low estate to which the mighty land of Thutmose III and Ramses II had fallen.

During the period of the Twenty-first Dynasty, the tug-of-war in Syria had ended. The Israelites found their leader in the Judean warrior David, and under him the Philistines were completely defeated, and the surrounding small nations brought to heel. It was one of those rare moments in history when the civilizations along the Nile and along the Tigris-Euphrates were *both* going through a period of feebleness. David therefore had his chance, and he founded an Israelite empire that reached from the Sinai Peninsula to the upper Euphrates River, taking in virtually all the eastern shore of the Mediterranean. Even the coastal Canaanite cities (the Phoenicians), while maintaining independence, were carefully subservient allies of David and of his son Solomon.

Under the reigns of David and Solomon, Israel was stronger than the fragment of Egypt ruled by the monarchs of the

Twenty-first Dynasty. Egypt was glad to make an alliance with Israel, and the pharaoh donated a daughter to Solomon's harem (1 Kings 3:1). The name of the particular pharaoh is not given in the Bible, but Solomon's rule endured from 973 to 933 B.C., and this coincides quite closely with the reign of Psusennes II (soo-sen'eez), the last king of the dynasty.

Psusennes II had his difficulties. The army, during the generations of Egyptian weakness, had grown to depend more and more upon mercenaries and, in particular, upon Libyan chieftains to lead it. It is almost in inevitable progression that an army made up of mercenaries is going to be docile only under the command of a mercenary; and that mercenary generals will invariably dominate the government and sometimes subvert it.

In the reign of Psusennes II, the Libyan leader of the army was Sheshonk. His support was absolutely necessary to Psusennes, who was forced to agree to marital alliances between the two families. The pharaoh's daughter married Sheshonk's son — a fatal sign, for it clearly showed that the general had designs on the throne. Perhaps Psusennes gave another daughter to Solomon in the hope that he would be able to count on Israelite support against the encroachment of the general.

If so, he was disappointed. In 940 B.C., when Psusennes II died, Sheshonk calmly took the throne. With his mercenary army in control of Tanis, who was to object?

The new pharaoh reigned as Sheshonk I, first monarch of the Twenty-second Dynasty. This is sometimes called the Libyan Dynasty, but it is rather misleading to do so. There was no true Libyan conquest of Egypt, and the Libyan soldiers who reigned were thoroughly Egyptianized.

Sheshonk made his capital at Bubastis (byoo-bas'tis), about thirty-five miles upstream from Tanis. He once again united the Nile Valley by bringing Thebes under control. After a century and a quarter of division, Egypt was a single power again. Sheshonk tried to tie Thebes to the delta by making his own son high priest of Amen.

He then turned his attention to Israel, whose alliance with his predecessor he probably had resented. He attempted no direct attack at first but resorted to intrigue. Northern Israel resented the rule of a Judean dynasty and attempted a rebellion. It was crushed, but its leader, Jeroboam, found ready asylum with Sheshonk. Once Solomon died, in 933 B.C., Sheshonk sent Jeroboam back to Israel, and a new rebellion succeeded.

The short-lived empire of David and Solomon broke up forever. The larger and richer northern portion retained the name of Israel and was ruled by monarchs not descended from David. In the south was the smaller kingdom of Judah, centered about Jerusalem, and there the Davidic dynasty was to retain power for more than three centuries.

Sheshonk found himself facing a shrunken Judah, badly shaken by the revolt, and he felt it safe to indulge in a foreign adventure. Like Thutmose III and Ramses II, he marched beyond Sinai. But it was not to face a powerful Mitanni or Hittite kingdom this time. Egypt would not have dared do so at this stage in its history. It was only tiny Judah it tackled. In 929 B.C., Sheshonk invaded that land with results that are recorded in the Bible (where the monarch is referred to as Shishak). He occupied Jerusalem, looted the Temple, and no doubt placed Judah under tribute for a period of time.

He felt himself a conqueror as a result and erected a monument in Thebes on which his conquests were enumerated. Indeed, he further enlarged the temple complex at Karnak, and it may have been in his reign that the final touches were placed upon the tremendous Hypostyle Hall.

Sheshonk was, however, not only the first king of his dynasty, but also the only one to show any vigor. His successor, Osorkon I (oh-sawr'kon), mounted the throne in 919 B.C. and found Egypt fairly wealthy and prosperous but could do no more than hold his own. After his death in 883 B.C., the inexorable decline began again.

The army was unruly, and its generals were intent on seizing what they could. Thebes pulled loose once more in 761 B.C., and its rulers were counted by Manetho as the Twenty-third Dynasty.

Such was the low state of Egypt now that, for the first time in its history, the tide of conquest flowed from Nubia northward rather than from Egypt southward.

THE NUBIANS

Under the New Kingdom, Nubia had been virtually a southern extension of Egypt. All the archaeological finds from that period are completely Egyptian in character.

For some centuries afterward, though, during the period of Egyptian decline, Nubia seems to disappear from our sight. Undoubtedly, with Egypt in fragments most of the time and with competing governments in Thebes and in the delta, there could be no chance of the pharaohs dominating the long stretches of the Nile beyond the First Cataract. Native elements must have taken over in Nubia.

Apparently they established the center of their power at Napata (nap'uh-tuh), just below the Fourth Cataract. This town represents the virtual limit of Egyptian penetration (Thutmose III had left an inscribed pillar there); it had felt the softening influence of Egyptian civilization, and yet was far enough from Egypt to be secure under all but the most extreme instances.

Nubia remained Egyptian in culture, however. When Sheshonk had taken over Thebes, a body of priests of Amen sought refuge in Napata and were made welcome there. No doubt they functioned as a kind of "government in exile" and urged the native Nubian princes to invade Egypt and to restore the loyal priesthood to power.

112 THE EGYPTIANS

Indeed, under the priestly influence, Nubia became more thoroughly Egyptian in religion than Egypt itself, more orthodox in its Amen-worship. To the natural desire of its native kings to win glory through conquest was added the notion that it would be pious to seek that glory. By 750 B.C., the Nubian push northward was under way.

Conquest was not difficult, for a disorganized Egypt was an easy prey. The Nubian ruler, Kashta, conquered Thebes almost at once, and the descendants of the exiled priests were restored. Kashta's successor, Piankhi (pyang'kee), pushed farther north, deep into the delta, about 730 B.C. and is considered the first king of a new dynasty (often termed the Ethiopian Dynasty, from the Greek name for his native land). For a while a pair of Egyptian rulers held out against him in portions of the delta. Manetho counts the Egyptians as the Twenty-fourth Dynasty and the Nubian conquerors as the Twenty-fifth Dynasty.

Piankhi's brother, Shabaka (sha'buh-kuh), succeeded him in 710 B.C. and moved his capital from Napata to the far greater and more prestige-encrusted city of Thebes.

Again, it would be a mistake to think of the Ethiopian Dynasty as representing foreign rule. To be sure, the monarchs were native to regions outside Egypt proper, but like the Libyan Dynasty, they were thoroughly Egyptian in culture.

But a new empire was arising in western Asia, one that was to put the older lands of Mitanni and the Hittities quite in the shade, and was to establish new records for ruthlessness.

THE ASSYRIANS

The empire was that of Assyria.

Assyria had its origins on the upper Tigris during the time of the Egyptian Old Kingdom. It borrowed its culture from the city-states of the lower Tigris-Euphrates and established a prosperous trading nation.

For some centuries it remained under the domination of neighboring nations that were more military minded. It was tributary to the Mitanni, for instance, and shared in the discomfiture of that nation by Thutmose III. A century later, it was dominated by the Hittites.

After the fall of the Hittites, in 1200 B.C., things were fairly difficult for Assyria for a while since the anarchy precipitated by the migrations of the Peoples from the Sea produced a kind of Dark Age that affected all of western Asia.

But then an odd and, eventually, spectacular thing happened. The Assyrians had picked up the secret of smelting iron from the Hittites, as other peoples of the time did, but were the first really to see that the new metal ought to be used to the full.

They began to equip their army not merely with odds and ends of iron, as was true of the Dorians who invaded Greece, for instance. Instead, they gradually became the first completely "ironized" army in history. The effect once again was that of a "secret weapon," as in the case of the horse and chariot a thousand years before.

The Assyrians had a preliminary taste of military victory when their king, Tiglath-Pileser I (tig'lath-pigh-lee'zer), led armies westward all the way to the Mediterranean about 1100 B.C., when the Ramessids were ruling over Egypt.

Assyria was hurled back, however, when new nomadic invasions swept over the west Asian area. This time it was Aramean tribes who eventually set up a kingdom north of Israel and Judah. This kingdom was known as Aram to themselves and to the Israelites, but in the King James Version of the Bible the kingdom is given the Greek name of Syria.

At about the time that the Libyan Dynasty was ruling over Egypt, Assyria recovered. Its army was equipped with hitherto unprecedented engines of war, such as massive battering rams, designed for laying siege to walled cities. By 854 B.C., Assyrian armies were invading Syria and were just barely held off by a Syrian-Israelite coalition.

But the weakness in the river civilizations that had made the empire of David and Solomon possible was over and done with. The end of the small kingdoms on the Mediterranean coast was in plain sight.

In 732 B.C., while the Nubians were taking over Egypt, the Assyrian king, Tiglath-Pileser III, destroyed the Syrian kingdom and took its capital, Damascus. Ten years later, a successor, Sargon II, destroyed Israel and took its capital, Samaria. By 701 B.C., Sargon's son and successor, Sennacherib (seh-nak'-uh-rib), was placing Jerusalem itself under siege.

The Nubian pharaohs, newly established in the delta, sought desperately to deflect the Assyrian menace. Nothing like this had happened since the time of the Hyksos. The Mitanni and the Hittites had remained near the Euphrates, but the Assyrians were coming right down to the borders of Egypt. What's more, they carried on their warfare with a deliberate sadistic cruelty that was very effective (in the short run) in paralyzing the will to resist and in filling even distant hearts with foreboding.

Egypt knew there was little chance in attempting a confrontation with the dreaded, ironclad Assyrians. The Nubian pharaoh, Shabaka, endeavored, instead, to urge the Syrians, Israelites, Judeans, and Phoenicians to resist. His emissaries scattered money and honeyed words where they would do the most good and did their best to stir up any trouble they could behind the Assyrian lines. Egypt carefully hoarded its own strength and hoped that somehow Assyria would meet disaster, or find itself so busy with one thing or another as never to have time for Egypt.

Finally, when the Assyrian army was besieging Jerusalem, Shabaka felt he had to fight, and he sent the Egyptians under his nephew Taharka (tuh-hahr'kuh) to face Sennacherib. The

Egyptians were defeated, but it was a hard fight, and Sennacherib, faced with a perceptibly weakened army and the news of revolts within his empire, decided to retire for a while and fight another day. Egypt was saved and so was a jubilant Jerusalem, which had thus gained another century of life.

Sennacherib was assassinated in 681 B.C. after he had succeeded in quelling all disorders and had savagely reduced the Assyrian Empire to the quiet of terror.

His son, Esarhaddon (ee″sahr-had′on), could afford to look abroad again. It seemed elementary good sense to do something about Egypt. As long as she was allowed to use her wealth in anti-Assyrian intrigue, Assyria would be fighting one revolt after another. He therefore marched his army westward.

By now Taharka was on the throne as the Egyptian pharaoh, and Esarhaddon may have welcomed a chance to cross swords with the very man who had blunted the earlier Assyrian thrust westward.

Taharka and his Egyptians fought with the courage of desperation. In 675 B.C., they actually defeated the Assyrians in one battle, but that only delayed the inevitable end. Esarhaddon, having corrected an earlier overconfidence, returned to the fight more purposefully in 671 B.C., took Memphis and the delta, and forced Taharka to flee southward.

But Taharka was not done. He prepared a counterattack and swooped downstream most effectively. Esarhaddon died in 668 B.C., before he could organize another expedition, but his son Asshurbanipal did so in his place. He not only retook Memphis but did something that the Hyksos themselves had never done. He tracked Taharka to his place of refuge in Thebes.

In 661 B.C., he took and sacked Thebes, putting an end to the Nubian line of pharaohs. They continued to reign in Nubia for a thousand years more, but their civilization declined, and their brief century of greatness was gone forever.

8

SAITIC EGYPT

THE GREEKS

The second Semitic occupation of Egypt (the Assyrian) came a thousand years after the first (the Hyksos). The Assyrian invasion was deeper, for it reached Thebes, but it was not as intense. The Assyrians were content to rule through Egyptian deputies known to be hostile to the Nubians. Their choice was a prince of lower Egypt named Necho (nee′koh). He had remained an Assyrian prisoner of war long enough to appreciate who his masters were, and he agreed to serve as their Egyptian viceroy. This he did loyally, dying at last on the side of Asshurbanipal's armies in the fight against the Nubians.

His son, Psamtik (sam′tik) — called Psammetichos (sa-met′i-kos) by the Greeks — succeeded to the rule.

He waited cautiously for a chance to break with Assyria, for its great days were patently passing. Asshurbanipal was beset by an immense host of troubles. Babylonia was in apparently perpetual revolt. The independent nation of Elam, east of

Babylonia, fought doggedly against Assyria. A new wave of nomads, the Cimmerians, swept down into Asia Minor from the lands north of the Black Sea and devastated the land like a tornado.

The capable Asshurbanipal managed to handle it all. He wiped out the Elamites in two campaigns and destroyed a twenty-century-old kingdom so thoroughly that virtually nothing is known of them today. He crushed the Cimmerians as well. But all was at a price. For one thing, even Asshurbanipal could not be everywhere. He could not hold Egypt while so busily engaged elsewhere.

Psamtik, feeling his way cautiously, cast himself adrift of the conqueror. He hired mercenaries from across the Mediterranean in western Asia Minor, where the kingdom of Lydia had just been founded on the ruins left by the marauding Cimmerians. Like Egypt, Lydia was on the western fringe of Assyrian power and, like Egypt, she was eager to be free.

Lydian mercenaries fought alongside Psamtik, and by 652 B.C., the last of the Assyrian garrisons was driven out of Egypt, only nine years after the sack of Thebes. The whole Assyrian episode had lasted but twenty years and, on the whole, Egypt, having united in the face of the external danger, emerged stronger than before and Psamtik ruled as Psamtik I. Egypt had a native pharaoh again.

Psamtik founded the Twenty-sixth Dynasty, by Manetho's reckoning. He made his capital at Sais (say'is) on the westernmost branch of the Nile, about thirty miles from the sea. As a consequence, Psamtik's line is sometimes spoken of as "the Saitic Dynasty" and the Egypt of the period as "Saitic Egypt."

Psamtik was a capable monarch, and under him Egypt experienced not only an economic revival but an artistic renaissance. There was a deliberate return to ages past, as though Egypt were anxious to shake the dust of a confusing world off its feet — a world in which Asian empires were stronger than she, and in which barbarians across the sea were needed to people her armies. She would return instead to the great days when only Egypt existed and when the rest of the world could be ignored.

The times of the pyramid builders were extolled, the spells and religious rituals that marked those ancient tombs were studied once more, the literary classics of the Middle Kingdom were revived, the damage done to Thebes by the Assyrians was repaired. In all this, indeed, the Saitic Dynasty was following the orthodox religious lead of the Nubian pharaohs that had preceded.

And yet the contemporary world could not really be ignored. If Psamtik was to keep Egypt safe, he would have to come to terms with it in some fashion.

The most important new factor in the world were the Greeks. The Greeks had come through the Dark Age that followed hard upon the Trojan War and emerged in growing glory. They were increasing rapidly in power and in culture, and they had inherited from their predecessors, the Myceneans and the Cretans, two things that the Egyptians found very valuable indeed.

Constant warfare against invaders and among themselves had taught the Greeks military techniques of a kind that made them unequalled as soldiers, man for man. Then, and for some five centuries afterward, they made the best mercenaries in the world and no non-Greek army was so huge as not to be better for a few Greek contingents to form a cutting edge. This was particularly so since the Greeks had developed the heavily armed infantrymen who, in comparison with the usually lightly armed Asian or Egyptian soldier, was virtually a walking tank.

Secondly, the Greeks loved the sea. They had a maritime tradition that was surpassed only by that of the Phoenicians. Through their Dark Age, the Greeks had been moving from

Greece itself across the Aegean Sea to Asia Minor and founding there cities that outrivaled those they had left behind. Then, in the eighth century B.C., while Egypt was sunk in decay, Greek sailors spread out into the Black Sea and westward to Sicily and Italy.

Psamtik was aware of all this, and he decided to take advantage of it. To do so required daring, but Psamtik was the most unorthodox of all the pharaohs since Ikhnaton, and, unlike Ikhnaton, he had a feeling for what was possible and what was not.

Psamtik had made use of Greek mercenaries in his troops and had stationed them in strong garrisons east of the delta to take the brunt of any invasion that might approach from the east.

But that was moderately cut-and-dried. Why not use Greek talents in peace as well as in war? Egyptians could trade as well as Greeks could, to be sure, but Egyptians lacked the ships (or the will to build and use them) to carry that trade far overseas. About 640 B.C., therefore, Psamtik encouraged the Greeks to enter Egypt as settlers (undoubtedly to the horror of the conservative Egyptians, who always held to their suspicion of foreigners).

A nucleus of Greek traders grew up only ten miles southwest of Sais, and there they founded the trading post of Naucratis (noh'kruh-tis), a name meaning "ruler of the sea."

On their own, about 630 B.C., the Greeks carried through the colonization of the Libyan coast. About five hundred miles west of Sais, well outside the Egyptian sphere of influence, Greeks founded a city they called Cyrene (sigh-ree'nee) which was to serve as the nucleus of a prosperous Greek-speaking area for many centuries.

Psamtik ruled for fifty-four years, dying in 610 B.C. It was the longest Egyptian reign and the most successful one since that of Ramses II six centuries before. Psamtik had lived to see the utter destruction of Assyria — and yet the close of the reign was darkened by new troubles abroad.

THE CHALDEANS

Asshurbanipal, who had briefly dominated Egypt, had died in 625 B.C., and for the first time in a century and a quarter, Assyria was left without a strong king. Babylon, still uncrushed and still rebelling, seized its chance.

The city and the region about it was under the control of the Chaldeans, a Semitic tribe that had entered the area about 1000 B.C. In Asshurbanipal's last year, the Chaldean prince Nabopolassar (nab''oh-poh-las'er) ruled over Babylonia as an Assyrian viceroy. Like Psamtik, he was determined to strike out for himself when Assyrian strength had declined sufficiently to make that safe and, like Psamtik again, he looked for allies abroad.

Nabopolassar found them among the Medes. These were a group of people speaking an Indo-European tongue, who settled in the area east of Assyria about 850 B.C. when Assyria was beginning its climb to empire. While Assyria remained at its height, Media remained a tributary to it.

About the time of Asshurbanipal's death, however, a Median chieftain named Cyaxares (sigh-ak'suh-reez) had succeeded in uniting a number of the tribes under himself and had formed a strong kingdom. It was with Cyaxares that Nabopolassar formed an alliance.

Beleaguered Assyria found itself facing the Medes on the east and the Babylonians on the south. Almost as a reflex action, the Assyrian armies reacted, but their strength, spent prodigally for two centuries with scarcely a pause, was gone. They cracked, collapsed, and caved inward.

In 612 B.C., Nineveh, the Assyrian capital, was taken, and a cry of joy went up from the subject peoples who had so long suffered under its rule. (Not the least of these triumphant outcries was from a Judean prophet named Nahum, whose poem of joy is included in the Bible.)

It was only two years after that climactic event that Necho I (named for his grandfather) succeeded his father on the Egyptian throne. Necho found the situation dark. A weak Assyria was ideal for Egypt. To have it replaced by new, vigorous, and empire-hungry powers would be bad.

It seemed to Necho, however, that all was not yet lost. Even after the fall of Nineveh, fragments of the Assyrian army fought on. One Assyrian general had retreated to Harran, 225 miles west of Nineveh, and there had held out for several years.

Necho decided to do something about that. He could dash up the eastern coast of the Mediterranean, following the routes of the great Thutmose III. It was, it seemed to him, a doubly wise policy, for even if he was not in time to relieve Harran, he would at least secure the east coast of the Mediterranean and hold the Chaldeans — these new empire builders — at arm's length and far away from Egypt.

In Necho's path, however, was the small state of Judah. It was four centuries now since David had established his short-lived empire, and its remnant, Judah, still existed, and was ruled by Josiah, a descendant of David. Judah had survived the fall of the northern kingdom of Israel, had withstood the armies of Sennacherib and had, indeed, managed to outlast Assyria.

And now it faced Necho. Josiah of Judah could not very well allow Necho to pass unopposed. If Necho were then to be victorious, he would dominate Judah; if he were to be defeated, the Chaldeans would sweep south in a search for revenge over a Judah that had let him pass. Josiah therefore led out his small army.

Necho was most reluctant to waste time on Judah, but he had no choice. In 608 B.C., Necho met Josiah at Megiddo, on the site where Thutmose III had overthrown the coalition of Canaanite princelings nearly fifteen centuries before. History repeated itself. Again the Egyptian won — and Judah's king was slain. For the first time in six centuries, Egyptian power was dominant in Syria.

However, the Chaldeans were on the move also. By now, they controlled the entire Tigris-Euphrates. Nebopolassar was old and sick, but he had a capable son named Nebuchadrezzar (neb''yoo-kad-rez'er), who led the Chaldean armies westward. Josiah had been beaten and killed by Necho, but he had delayed the Egyptian army just long enough to allow Nebuchadrezzar to reach Harran and place it under siege. In 606 B.C., he took the city, and the last bit of Assyrian power vanished. Assyria disappeared from history.

That left the Chaldeans and the Egyptians face to face. They met at Carchemish, where once Thutmose I had raised a marker to testify to the first occasion when Egyptian armies had stood on the bank of the Euphrates.

If the spot held some magical powers in consequence, however, it was not in favor of Egypt. Necho could defeat Judah's small army, but Nebuchadrezzar's mighty host was something else again. The Egyptians were smashed, and Necho went tumbling out of Asia something faster than he had entered. Necho's dream of restoring Egypt's imperial position ended in less than three years, and he was not to try again.

In fact, Nebuchadrezzar, a most vigorous campaigner, might well have pursued Necho into Egypt and taken the land if Nabopolassar had not died at this moment and Nebuchadrezzar had not had to dash back to Babylon to secure the succession.

Left in relative peace by this lucky event, Necho had a chance to mature plans for the benefit of Egypt's internal economy. His mind turned toward the question of waterways.

Egypt was the land of a river and thousands of canals, but it also abutted on two seas, the Mediterranean and the Red. Along the shores of each, Egyptian ships had carefully ventured for two thousand years or more, to Phoenicia in the first case and Punt in the second.

It had occurred to Egyptian monarchs now and then that it would be most convenient if a canal could be dug from the Nile River to the Red Sea. Trade could then extend from sea to sea, and ships could ply from Phoenicia to Punt.

In the dawn of Egyptian history the section between the Nile and the Red Sea was better watered than it was to be later, and certain lakes were present at the Sinai border that are not there now. Probably a canal of sorts, using those lakes, existed in the Old and Middle kingdoms, but it required constant care, and when Egypt was in turmoil, it silted up and was gone. Its restoration, with the increasing aridity of the climate, became progressively more difficult.

Ramses II considered reconstructing it but failed, perhaps because he spent too much of his energies on foolish statues of himself. Necho also dreamed of doing so, and he failed, perhaps because his Asian venture had taken too much of his.

Apparently, though, he had another idea. If the Mediterranean and Red seas could not be connected by an artificial waterway, perhaps they were connected by the natural waterway of the ocean. According to Herodotus, Necho determined to find out if one could travel from the Mediterranean to the Red Sea by circumnavigating Africa. For the purpose, he hired Phoenician sailors (the best in the world), and they succeeded in accomplishing the task in a voyage that lasted three years. Or, at least, so Herodotus was told.

Yet Herodotus, although he repeats the story, says flatly that he doesn't believe it. His reason for skepticism is that, according to reports, the Phoenician sailors were supposed to have seen the noonday sun to the north of the zenith when they passed the southern tip of Africa. This, Herodotus states, was impossible since in all known regions of the world, the sun was to the south of the zenith at noon.

Herodotus' lack of understanding of the earth's shape misled him here. To be sure, in the north temperate zone, the noonday sun is always south of the zenith. In the south temperate zone, however, the sun is always north of the zenith.

The southern tip of Africa is, indeed, in the south temperate zone. The fact that the Phoenician sailors would report the noonday sun to the north, something that seemed so improbable in the light of "common sense," is strong evidence that they had actually seen the phenomenon and had, therefore, actually circumnavigated Africa. They would not have told so silly a lie, in other words, if it were not the truth.

Nevertheless, the circumnavigation, even if successful as an adventure, was a failure as a guide to a practical trading route. The journey was too long. Indeed, it was not until two thousand years later that the voyage around Africa was practical.

THE JEWS

Nebuchadrezzar remained a threat to Egypt throughout his forty-four-year reign. After Carchemish, however, Egypt never dared issue forth to meet him. Instead, Necho and his immediate successors followed the policy of the Nubian pharaohs against Assyria. With money and words they encouraged the petty nations of the Mediterranean coast to keep up a constant turmoil of intrigue and rebellion in order to keep the dreaded Chaldean off balance.

This policy, a century earlier, had kept Egypt free for a while but had cost Syria and Israel their existence. Judah, which had survived the Assyrian Empire, had not learned from the fate of its northern neighbors. Preferring weak Egypt to strong Chaldea, it was ready to play Egypt's game and to beard the Chaldeans on the poor promise of Egyptian help.

In 598 B.C., Judah refused tribute to Nebuchadrezzar, and Jerusalem was placed under siege. It had to capitulate, and a number of its most important men, including the king, were carried off into exile in Babylonia.

Under a new king, however, the old game was still carried on, despite the eloquent appeals of the prophet Jeremiah, who demanded the nation refuse to listen to Egypt but come to an accommodation with the Chaldeans. A decade later, Judah revolted again, and this time Nebuchadrezzar took Jerusalem, destroyed the Temple, and carried off virtually the entire aristocracy into exile. The Judean kingdom came to an end and so did the Davidic dynasty.

Even then, Nebuchadrezzar was not free to turn against Egypt. The Phoenician city of Tyre still held out against him, and he did not think it wise to move southward as long as that powerful city remained as an enemy in the rear.

The Jewish prophet Ezekiel, in Babylonian exile, preached confidently that Tyre would be destroyed and that Egypt would then be harrowed from end to end (we have his words in the Bible), but the prophet's predictions did not come true.

Tyre, a city built on a rocky island off the Phoenician shore, with a strong fleet bringing in food, and with a population capable of fighting with an endurance that seemed to be characteristic of Semitic populations, held Nebuchadrezzar at bay for thirteen years! From 585 to 573 B.C., Nebuchadrezzar held on to the throat of the city with a Semitic doggedness of his own and yet could not deliver the final throttle. By the time the matter ended wearily in a compromise settlement in which Tyre ended its anti-Chaldean policy but retained its self-government, Nebuchadrezzar had had enough of war.

We have few records concerning the latter half of his reign, and there are some indications that he attempted a halfhearted invasion of Egypt, but if he did, it failed. Egypt's policy had saved its independence for the time — but at a high cost to its cat's-paws.

Necho had died in 595 B.C., while Jerusalem still existed, and had been succeeded by his son Psamtik II. Nebuchadrezzar's involvement with Judah made it possible for Psamtik to turn at least part of his attention in another direction — the south. In Napata, the Nubian kings still ruled, and there was always the chance they would remember that their ancestors had ruled Egypt a century before and might feel the urge to return. There was also the question of Egyptian pride; it was necessary to punish the Nubians for their presumption.

Psamtik II therefore sent an army southward into Nubia in a successful expedition that may even have reached Napata. However, he made no attempt to stay here. The Egypt of the Twenty-sixth Dynasty was not the Egypt of the New Kingdom. The invasion in itself was enough, and the Nubian monarchs, having been taught a certain humility, might then be left in peace.

The expedition is best known to us today because of an oddly human event that took place on the way back. The Egyptian expeditionary army contained in its ranks a number of Greek mercenaries. Returning, the army, with those mercenaries, seems to have encamped for a while in the neighborhood of Abu Simbel where, six and a half centuries before, Ramses II had set up his elaborate temple to himself and the sun-god (in that order of importance, I'm sure) together with the four seated statues.

The Greeks lacked the Egyptian awe of these monuments of the past, and a number of them carved their names here and there on the pillars in antique Greek script. Modern archaeologists are fascinated by the light this sheds on the development of the Greek alphabet, and humans generally must be amused at this evidence that a certain childishness unites all men, past and present.

Psamtik II also took a wise precaution against any Nubian attempt at a reprisal raid. The First Cataract placed difficulties in the way, but these difficulties were not, in themselves, insurmountable. Psamtik therefore set up a permanent garrison on Elephantine, an island in the Nile River just downstream from that cataract. It served as Egypt's southern line of defense.

The garrison at Elephantine consisted very largely of Jewish mercenaries. Judah's misadventures with Nebuchadrezzar led to a constant drizzle of Jewish refugees into Egypt. They were tough fighters, and Psamtik was glad to employ them.

In 1903, a cache of documents was discovered on Elephantine and with it a great deal of interesting information about the development of the Jewish way of life during the two centuries after the establishment of the garrison. In Judah, the descendants of the men carried off into Babylonian exile had returned in installments, beginning about 538 B.C. A new Temple was built by 516 B.C. The Jews at Elephantine were out of touch with these developments. Judaism had developed into its modern form during the Babylonian Exile, and in the new Temple this form took root and became an elaborate orthodoxy. The Jews in Elephantine, insulated from all this, used their own traditional rituals and set up an unusual heresy that remained haughtily ignored by the high priests of the Temple at Jerusalem.

Psamtik II was succeeded by his son Apries (ap'rih-eez) in 589 B.C. (He is referred to as Pharaoh-Hophra in the Bible.) It was Apries who was on the throne when Jerusalem fell and was destroyed. He welcomed into the land a number of refugee Jews who formed the nucleus for a population of Egyptian Jews which, over the next seven centuries, was to form a most important element in Egyptian life — and, for that matter, in Jewish life as well.

Nebuchadrezzar's siege of Tyre lasted almost all the reign of Apries. Apries tried to help Tyre, but his attempts did little good. Nevertheless, Egypt could freely turn its attention to other matters, relying on the Tyrians to keep the Chaldean wolf from the Egyptian door.

Apries continued and extended the policy of the earlier kings of the dynasty with respect to the use of Greek mercenaries. For the first time in Egyptian history, an attempt was made to establish something like a navy; Apries made use of ships manned by the sea-skilled Greeks and with them, he took over the island of Cyprus, some 250 miles north of the delta. This was not merely vainglory. A strong position on that island backed by an efficient navy could outflank Nebuchadrezzar even if Tyre fell, and keep Egypt safe.

Apries may also have felt it necessary to secure his rear in preparation for any final showdown that might come with the Chaldeans. The Greek colony of Cyrene had been expanding at the expense of the Libyan tribes, and the latter called upon the pharaoh for protection. Apries could not have the tribes to his west restless and vengeful and ready to pounce upon him when his army was concentrated in the East against the Chaldeans. He therefore decided to send an army against Cyrene and teach it manners.

Here, however, he was faced with a dilemma. The heart of his army consisted of Greek mercenaries, and it would have been foolhardy indeed to send them against a Greek city. Ideally, mercenaries fought against anyone for pay, but the ideal does not always hold up in practice. Apries feared that at some crucial moment portions of his mercenary force might suddenly swing over to the other side and join their fellow Greeks against himself.

So he left his Greeks at home and sent only Egyptian contingents to Cyrene.

But the Egyptians were not at all eager to fight against the dreaded Greeks. For many years, there had undoubtedly been considerable hostility among the Egyptians against the hated foreigners, and the native Egyptians in the army must have particularly resented the favor shown the Greeks. It must have seemed to them that foreigners were given all the high posts and paid all the honor. (The fact that they did much of the hard fighting may have escaped the notice of the objectors.)

It was easy, then, for Egyptian nationalist spokesmen to harangue the army at Cyrene, telling it that Apries was simply trying to get rid of his Egyptians by pitting them against the Cyrenian Greeks to be slaughtered and that thereafter he would get along with Greeks only.

The army revolted, and Apries sent one of his officials, Ahmose, a native Egyptian who was popular with the soldiers, to quiet the men down. Ahmose, however, was entirely too popular with the soldiers, for they started an outcry that he become their new pharaoh.

Ahmose thought it over, decided that it wasn't so bad being pharaoh, and put himself at the head of the rebels. They marched enthusiastically back toward the delta, and in their excitement actually managed to defeat a contingent of Greek mercenaries (much less numerous than the Egyptian army, to be sure) led against them by the unfortunate Apries.

Apries was eventually executed, and in 570 B.C., Ahmose II was recognized as Pharaoh of Egypt. He married a daughter of Psamtik II (either a sister or half sister of the deposed Apries), thus legitimizing his rule and causing him to be included by Manetho in the Twenty-sixth Dynasty.

He is much better known by the Greek version of his name, which is Amasis (uh-may′sis).

9

PERSIAN EGYPT

THE PERSIANS

Although Amasis owed his throne to an anti-Greek reaction, he could not deny the facts of life. He had to make use of Greek mercenaries, and he did. He had to make use of Greek traders, and he encouraged the growth of Naucratis from little more than a trading camp into a full-fledged city. He needed the security of Greek alliances, and he concluded those.

In particular, he formed an alliance with the Greek island of Samos, in the Aegean Sea just off the coast of Asia Minor. The island was small, but late in Amasis's reign it developed the largest navy in the eastern Mediterranean. Amasis, who still controlled Cyprus, could well use that fleet on his side. In fact, he even married a Greek woman from the city of Cyrene.

All this wooing of Greeks was done with an eye toward the menace from the east — yet in the early part of Amasis's reign that menace seemed to be fading. Weary old Nebuchadrezzar finally died in 561 B.C., and his successors were weak, pacific, or both. For a quarter century, Chaldea was no trouble at all to Egypt — was, in fact, a comfortable neighbor.

There is nothing safer than a decaying neighbor, and a nation with its self-interest at heart tries to preserve the integrity of such a neighbor. Necho had tried to shore up dying Assyria, and now Amasis tried to perform the same service for dying Chaldea.

For Chaldea was dying, and no mistake, scarcely more than half a century after it had come to might and power. At the time of Assyria's fall, the two conquerors, Chaldea and Media, had divided the loot. Chaldea had taken the rich valley of the Tigris-Euphrates and everything to the west that it could grab. Media had been content with the much larger, but less developed and far poorer, stretch of territory to the north and east of Chaldea. For seventy-five years, Media maintained a largely peaceful and nonexpansionist rule.

In southern Media, however, there was a province just southeast of Babylonia that came to be known to the Greeks as Persis and to ourselves as Persia. The Persians were closely akin to the Medes in language and culture.

About 560 B.C., a Persian chieftain of unbounded ambition and ability rose to prominence. His name was Cyrus.

Cyrus clearly had his eye on the Median throne, and in this he had the help of Nabonidus (nab"oh-nigh'dus), king of Chaldea, who was undoubtedly willing to encourage civil strife in his large northern neighbor. Cyrus marched against the Median capital in 550 B.C., took it in a single campaign, and seated himself on the throne of the Median kingdom, which now became known as the Persian Empire.

Too late, Nabonidus realized that in helping Cyrus he had done precisely the wrong thing. What he wanted (and what nations usually want in such circumstances) was a long-drawn-out civil war that would weaken all sides and keep the nation powerless for generations. Cyrus's quick victory had replaced a quiet, stagnant monarch with a vigorous, martial one. Now

Nabonidus began to help any nation who offered to withstand Cyrus, but it was too late.

In 547 B.C., Cyrus defeated the Lydians of western Asia Minor, and all of that peninsula was added to his dominions, including the Greek cities that dotted its shoreline.

In 540 B.C., Cyrus turned on Chaldea itself. His victorious course continued, and within a year he had taken Babylon and put an end to the Chaldean Empire's short existence. Cyrus died in 530 B.C., while fighting to extend his empire far into central Asia. He is sometimes called Cyrus the Great, and the name is deserved because he was not merely a conqueror but also a humane man who treated those he conquered with tolerance.

When Cyrus died, the Persian Empire included all the great centers of civilization in western Asia and large tracts of nomadic areas as well. He had set up the greatest empire the Mediterranean world had yet seen.

In Egypt, Amasis had watched this development with horror. The memory of Assyria and Chaldea shrank to insignificance in the face of this huge new colossus. Amasis had done his best to hamper its growth by supporting each of Cyrus's opponents in turn, but he had failed in every case. Now Egypt stood alone and unprotected in the Persian path, and Persia (like Assyria and Chaldea before her) was not likely to be forgiving toward the nation which had intrigued constantly against her.

But Amasis's good fortune, which had led him to the throne first, and then to a forty-four-year reign over a prosperous Egypt, held to the very end. Persia was readying itself for the blow, and Egypt was already cringing before it, when Amasis died in 525 B.C., just too soon to see the blow delivered. His son, who succeeded as Psamtik III, was going to have to face it instead.

Cyrus's son, Cambyses (kam-bigh'seez), succeeded to the Persian throne. He was a seasoned ruler, having governed

Babylonia while his father was absent on his campaigns. Now he took up the logical next step in the Persian expansion — the showdown with Egypt.

The Egyptian army stood at a fortress on the Mediterranean shore just east of the Nile delta. They called it Per-Amen ("house of Amen"), but it is better known to us by its later Greek name, Pelusium (peh-lyoo'shee-um), which means "mud city." It was near there that the Assyrian army of Sennacherib had been withstood firmly enough to cause it to turn back, but that had been little more than a skirmish with an army that was heavily engaged elsewhere.

Pelusium was now to have its first real baptism of fire, and it was disastrous for Egypt. Cambyses simply swept the Egyptian army to one side, sent it tumbling away in headlong rout, and that was just about all the fighting there was. He marched into a quaking Memphis, and once more Egypt was under foreign domination.

We know little of Cambyses' stay in Egypt except what Herodotus tells us, and Herodotus (visiting Egypt about a century later) got his information from a nationalistic Egyptian priesthood that was bitterly anti-Persian. His picture of Cambyses is therefore a grossly exaggerated one of a cruel and half-mad tyrant who took pleasure in deliberately desecrating things holy to the Egyptians and mocking customs revered by them.

For instance, while Cambyses was in Egypt, the Egyptians discovered a bull who fulfilled the rather exacting requirements that qualified it as Apis (ay'pis), an earthly manifestation of the god Osiris. The bull is, of course, a common fertility symbol, and the finding of Apis signified good harvests and happy times. Apis was traditionally greeted with great rejoicings and given divine honors.

Cambyses (so Herodotus says) just after returning from a disastrous expedition found the Egyptians rejoicing, and imagining them to be celebrating his defeat, fell into a fury. Told that the rejoicing was in honor of Apis, Cambyses, contemptuous of such a god, drew his sword and wounded Apis.

To us, this seems like a minor atrocity (if we think of the kind of atrocities that have been committed in our own times), but to the Egyptians this was a far more horrifying deed than that of merely conquering their country. However, the chances are that this never happened and that Cambyses ruled Egypt about as reasonably as a conquered nation might expect.

Cambyses had no intention of pausing with Egypt alone. He accepted the submission of the Libyans west of the Nile and that of the Greek city of Cyrene, which had withstood the assault of Apries a half century before. He had his eye next on Nubia to the south (and perhaps even on the Phœnician colony of Carthage far to the west). He marched south into Nubia, taking and sacking Thebes on the way (as Asshurbanipal had done a century and a half before). He managed to bring the northern portion of Nubia under Persian control before returning to recoup his forces and gather additional supplies. (The hostile sources which Herodotus used transformed this into a disastrous defeat that was the occasion for the atrocity against Apis.)

Undoubtedly, Cambyses would have continued his victorious career, but a dynastic squabble broke out at home. An impostor, claiming to be an older son of Cyrus, announced himself king. Cambyses marched back hastily to deal with this, but died on the way. (Herodotus' unfavorable account hints he may have committed suicide after having been driven mad by the gods, who had been offended by his sacrilege.)

The kings of Persia are counted as Egypt's Twenty-seventh Dynasty, and this time the dynasty was really foreign. It was not like the Libyan and Nubian dynasties, who were Egyptian in everything but descent; or like the Hyksos, who became Egyptian. Nor was it like the Assyrians, who were only briefly and glancingly present.

No! The Twenty-seventh Dynasty was truly foreign, and it ruled with a strong hand.

THE ATHENIANS

To be sure, Persian rule was beneficent in some ways. Thus, after the few months of confusion that followed Cambyses' death, a member of the royal family, Darius I (duh-righ'us), seized control. He ruled for thirty-five years (521 to 486 B.C.) and was beyond question the ablest of the Persian kings, so that he is sometimes called Darius the Great.

He reorganized his huge empire to a high pitch of efficiency, and ruled Egypt well. He managed to complete the canal from the Nile to the Red Sea, that Necho had left unfinished, and Egyptian trade flourished. In fact, Egypt under Darius kept all its old ways, was as prosperous as it had ever been under Amasis, and paid a tribute to the Persians that was not unduly oppressive. What was there to complain about?

Nevertheless, the Egyptians had three thousand years of history behind them, and they chafed under foreign rule, if for no other reason than that it was foreign. They waited their chance. Sooner or later, Persia would be preoccupied at some far corner of its wide dominion and then would come the time —

Darius helped by being unable to resist engaging in some bits of foreign conquest, in order to match the deeds of his predecessors. In 515 B.C., he crossed over into Europe, conquering and annexing sections north of Greece, right up to the Danube River.

The independent cities of Greece were greatly alarmed and, in self-defense, prepared to aid any movement that might em-

barrass or weaken Persia. In 499 B.C., when some of the Greek
cities in Asia Minor, which had been under Persian rule for
half a century, revolted, the independent Greek city-state of
Athens sent ships to help them. The revolt was put down by
an indignant Darius, who determined to punish Athens for interfering, without provocation, in internal Persian affairs.

In 490 B.C., he sent a relatively small Persian expeditionary
force to Athens, and there, to the surprise of the world, it was
defeated by an even smaller army of Athenians at the Battle
of Marathon. Darius, more furious than ever, began to plan a
much larger expedition to follow.

The Egyptians had been watching the course of events carefully. The Greek cities of Asia Minor had dared revolt against
the Persian colossus. They had been crushed, to be sure, but
then the Athenians had resisted the Persians, too, and had
been victorious. Surely Persia's energies would be entirely
consumed in avenging this insult; and Darius was too old and
sick to spread himself in more than one direction anyway.
This was Egypt's chance.

Egypt therefore revolted in the aftermath of the Battle of
Marathon, and at first all went well. In 486 B.C., Darius died,
and there was every reason to hope that in the confusion of the
opening years of a new king's reign, Egypt's independence
might be won.

Coming to the Persian throne was Darius's son Xerxes
(zurk'seez), who found himself faced with Athens and with
Egypt. He had to make a choice. He had inherited his father's
grandiose schemes for revenge against Athens, but Athens was
one small city while Egypt was a large, wealthy, and populous
province. Surely, it only made sense to take care of Egypt first.

Plans to invade Greece were suspended therefore, and the
full might of the Persian army turned on unfortunate Egypt.
Egypt was defeated and brought back to submission, but the
task took three years, and this meant a three-year delay in

Xerxes' plans for invading Greece. That three-year delay was well used by the Athenians, who enlarged and improved their fleet tremendously. It was that fleet which enabled the Greeks to defeat the Persians at Salamis (sal'uh-mis) in 480 B.C. and break the back of the invasion.

The modern world, which traces much of its culture back to ancient Greece, finds the victory of tiny Greece over giant Persia to be one of those wonderful David-and-Goliath stories of which one can never weary. The surprise and relief at the salvation of Greece has carried on from generation to generation for twenty-five centuries, and yet, without lessening the Greek achievement, it is only fair to point out that without Egypt's unsuccessful revolt, the Greek victory might never have come.

Egypt, which on several occasions had encouraged her small neighbors to sacrifice themselves to Egyptian self-interest, had now (against her will and without the intention, of course) sacrificed herself for the sake of Greece. Never in her history, perhaps, had she served mankind better.

Nor was Egypt pacified merely because she had been smothered into quiet. Her people, egged on by the priests, were always ready for revolt. The crucial time was the end of a Persian reign, for then there was the chance of a disputed succession and a civil war that would leave the Persians no time to attend to distant rebellions. Better still, the new king might turn out to be a weakling without interest in long, weary expeditions designed to bring a distant province back into the fold.

And so, when Xerxes died in 464 B.C., that was the signal for another revolt. The leading spirits this time were the nomadic tribes in the Libyan desert, who remained relatively free even though nominally under Persian control. One of their chieftains, Inaros, led his forces into the delta, where many Egyptians joined him gladly. The Persian viceroy, brother of the dead Xerxes, was killed after a sharp battle, and Egypt seemed independent again.

Egypt's position seemed all the more secure since Persia was in trouble. Athens, ever since the days of Salamis, had kept up a steady war with Persia, one in which she nibbled constantly about the edges of the empire. This Athenian activity did not really endanger Persia's core, but it kept Persia too busy to exert her full strength against Egypt.

What's more, at the first signs of an Egyptian revolt, Athenian ships came to the aid of the rebels and landed an Athenian expeditionary force.

The new Persian king, however, was (unfortunately for Egypt) not a weakling. He was Artaxerxes I (ahr"tuh-zurk'seez), a son of Xerxes. He sent a large force into Egypt and it drove the rebels back, pinning them down on an island in the delta. Here, the rebels were unassailable as long as the Athenian ships were with them, but Artaxerxes managed to divert the branch of the Nile on which the island was located, leaving the ships beached and helpless. They were destroyed. A second contingent of Athenian ships was more than half destroyed even before they could reach the scene of the battle.

The rebellion was put down by 455 B.C. Most of the Greek force was wiped out, and Inaros was taken and executed.

The whole affair was an Athenian disaster of great magnitude, but one that is not much mentioned in the histories, partly because it happened in the midst of the great Athenian "Golden Age" (in some ways the greatest such age the world has ever seen), and the somber colors of the Egyptian defeat are lost in the glory of what was going on in a city that was building the Parthenon, writing the world's greatest tragedies, carving her greatest statues, and creating her greatest philosophies.

Nevertheless, the Athenian defeat disrupted her foreign policy, disheartened her friends, encouraged her enemies, and helped pave the way for the disaster that was to engulf her a half century later. If the first Egyptian revolt against the Persians had saved Athens, the second had helped ruin her.

THE LAST OF THE NATIVES

Again Egypt waited. Two more Persian kings came and went, and in 404 B.C., the second of these, Darius II, died. This time there was a hotly disputed succession. Darius's younger son led an army made up largely of Greek mercenaries against his older brother. The older brother won, and ruled as Artaxerxes II, but while this was happening, Egypt had time to rebel effectively and to establish a precarious independence once more.

For sixty years that independence was maintained, largely with Greek help. As it turned out, Greek mercenaries were particularly plentiful in this period because two Greek city-states, Athens and Sparta, had fought a tremendous war from 431 to 404 B.C., and Sparta, had finally won, establishing a brief supremacy over Greece. The end of the war had put out of employment many soldiers who could find nothing much to do in a Greece worn out and ravaged by the long war. They therefore hired themselves out willingly to Egypt or to Persia.

Three short-lived native dynasties ruled over Egypt in this last period of independence. They were the Twenty-eighth, Twenty-ninth and Thirtieth dynasties. All waited for the one crucial moment, when Persia felt strong enough to return in force to Egypt. By 379 B.C., when the Thirtieth Dynasty came to power, a Persian invasion seemed imminent.

The first king of the Thirtieth Dynasty was Nectanebo I (nek-tan'ee-boh), and he promptly proceeded to bolster his position by obtaining the best he could find in the way of Greek mercenaries. He hired Chabrias (kay'bree-as), an Athenian general who had a heartening record of victories behind him. Chabrias accepted the position without the permis-

sion of Athens (which did not want, at this time, to offend
Persia). He reorganized the Egyptian army, drilled it in the
latest tactics, and converted the delta into a strong armed camp
even while the Persians were gathering at the borders.

Artaxerxes II hesitated to attack while Chabrias faced him.
He therefore successfully placed pressure on Athens to recall
the general. Chabrias was forced to leave the Egyptians, but
his work had been well done. When the Persians attacked, they
were met by such firm resistance that they had to retire and
leave Egypt free. Nectanebo I died in 360 B.C., ruler of an independent and quite prosperous nation to the end.

He was succeeded by Teos (tee'os), who still had to face the
problem of Persia. By that time, though, the situation in
Greece had taken a surprising turn. Sparta had been defeated
by the Greek city of Thebes and, after centuries of military
prowess, was suddenly reduced to helplessness. One of her two
kings at the time was Agesilaus (uh-jes''ih-lay'us), and he
was one of the best generals in Greece at the time, even though
he could not save Sparta. So desperate was Sparta's situation,
so dire her needs, that Agesilaus, who, in his younger years,
had dominated Greece and had even led an expeditionary
force into Asia Minor to fight victoriously against Persia itself,
was forced to sell his talents in an effort to gain money with
which to continue to fight for the defense of fallen Sparta.

The proud Spartan king had to be a mercenary for hire. He
sold himself to Teos and landed in Egypt with a contingent
of his Spartans. Teos, however, could only stare in disappoint-
ment at this old man (Agesilaus was over eighty years old by
then), wizened, small, and lame. Teos refused to allow the old
hero full control of the Egyptian forces, but forced him to
head the mercenaries only. Meanwhile, Chabrias had returned and was put at the head of the Egyptian fleet.

Teos felt strong enough now to take the offensive against
Persia. Persia was steadily declining. Several times Greek
forces had marched at will through the country, and Arta-

xerxes II, coming to the end of a long reign of nearly half a century, had grown old and irresolute. The giant, it seemed, was tottering.

Egyptian forces, therefore, struck into Syria. There were too many cooks, however, and dissension broke out among Athenians, Spartans, and Egyptians, aborting the entire project. What's more, one of Teos's relatives claimed the throne, and when Teos ordered Agesilaus to put him down, the old Spartan testily refused. He had come to fight Egypt's enemies and not Egypt's people, he said.

Teos was forced to flee to the Persians, and the new claimant ascended the throne of Egypt as Nectanebo II. Agesilaus had had enough and decided to return to Sparta, but he died at Cyrene on the way back.

In 358 B.C., Artaxerxes II died at last and was succeeded by a son, Artaxerxes III, under whom Persia showed surprising vigor.

Artaxerxes III organized his first attack against Egypt in 351 B.C. but was repelled by the Egyptians with their fine Greek-mercenary cutting edge. For three centuries now, the Egyptians had been using the Greeks against their enemies, but this was the last time they were to do so successfully. (When next the Greeks returned, it was to be as masters, not as servants.)

The Persian monarch had to delay his next attempt because of revolts in Syria and continuing troubles with Greek raiders. With difficulty, he cleared out dissidents and imposed peace. In 340 B.C., he marched against Egypt once again, this time with himself at the head of the army.

It was largely a fight of Greek against Greek, for there were mercenaries on both sides. After a long-drawn-out and hard fight, the Persian Greeks won out over the Egyptian Greeks at Pelusium. Nearly two centuries before, the Persians under Cambyses had taken all of Egypt after a single victory at Pelusium, and now the Persians under Artaxerxes III did the same. Once the hard crust of Pelusium was penetrated, there was nothing behind it that could effectively stop the Persians.

Nectanebo II fled to Napata and the safety of Nubia. He had the melancholy distinction of being the last native ruler of all Egypt, ending a line that had begun with Menes nearly three thousand years before.

Manetho, writing a half century later, ended his listing of dynasties with Nectanebo II. We, however, shall continue.

THE MACEDONIANS

Artaxerxes III reestablished Persian rule with great cruelty, but Persia had not long to live. Great and surprising events were taking place in Greece.

For centuries the Greek cities had fought each other, and by 350 B.C., the fight was clearly a standoff. No one city could possibly dominate the rest. Athens, Sparta, and Thebes had tried, in that order, and each had failed miserably.

Some Greeks were beginning to feel that the various cities were ruining themselves and that only an outside war — a great, united "holy war" — against the common enemy, Persia, could save them.

But then, who was to lead the crusade? The winner of the tug-of-war among the cities, of course — but there was no winner, and it looked as though there would never be a winner.

And there wasn't; not among the city-states.

North of Greece, however, was the land of Macedon (mas'-eh-don). It had absorbed the Greek language and culture, but was looked down upon by the Greeks as semibarbarous.

To be sure, it had made no great mark in earlier Greek history. During the great period when the Greek cities fought against Persia and defeated its armies, Macedon had remained under the Persian yoke and had even fought on the Persian side.

In 356 B.C., however, when Egypt was in its last gasp of independence, a most unusual man placed himself on the Macedonian throne. This man, Philip II, reorganized the Macedonian army and introduced the "phalanx," a close-set rank and file of heavily armed men who had learned, by continual drill, to handle long spears to perfection so that the entire group resembled a marching porcupine.

Little by little, through the use of bribes, of lies, and of military action when all else failed, Philip gained control of northern Greece. In 338 B.C., in a climactic battle at Chaeronea (ker"oh-nee'uh) near the Greek city of Thebes, he defeated the combined armies of Thebes and Athens and was dominant over all of Greece.

Now the great holy war against Persia could be fought, for the leader had been found. Philip II was voted into that position by the subdued Greek cities. But in 336 B.C., just as the invasion was about to begin, and when the first contingents were crossing over into Asia Minor, Philip, as a result of domestic squabbles, was assassinated.

For a moment, the whole project trembled. Then, stepping into the breach, came Philip's son, the twenty-year-old Alexander III. The tribes and cities whom Philip had dominated naturally considered a twenty-year-old successor as a sufficient signal for revolt, but no greater mistake could have been made because one can make a good case for supposing that Alexander III was, in some ways, the most unusual man who ever lived. For one thing, he never lost a battle even under the most arduous and disheartening conditions, and for another, he never seemed to take more than a moment to come to a decision (and a correct decision, if we judge by results). He eventually masterminded a collection of some of the greatest generals who were ever gathered into a single army and had no difficulty in dominating them all. (Only Napoleon could be compared to him in this last respect.)

At the start of his reign, Alexander marched quickly against the revolting tribes, beat them down with one blow apiece, dashed south into Greece, and took care of the cities with another blow. In 334 B.C., he left Greece for Asia.

Meanwhile Artaxerxes III of Persia had died in 338 B.C., and after some unsettled times a good-natured weakling found his way to the throne in 336 B.C., ruling as Darius III. No one could successfully have faced Alexander (soon to be known as Alexander the Great — and of all the monarchs known as "Great," surely there can be least argument about Alexander), but Darius III couldn't even begin to do so.

The Persian advance guard, completely overconfident, was defeated almost at once at the Granicus River (gruh-nigh′kis) in northwestern Asia Minor.

Alexander marched down the coast of Asia Minor, then struck into the interior, defeating the main Persian army (far superior in numbers to his own soldiers, but not in the quality of tactics or generalship) at Issus (is′us), a town near the northeastern corner of the Mediterranean Sea.

He then moved down the Syrian coast, pausing only to reduce Tyre after a nine-month siege (perhaps the roughest fight of his career — but compare this to the thirteen years it took Nebuchadrezzar).

In 332 B.C., Alexander stood at Pelusium, but Egypt did not fight him at that spot as it had fought (however ineffectually) against Sennacherib, Cambyses, and Artaxerxes III. It had been only nine years since Persia had beaten down Nectanebo II and bathed Egypt in blood, and the memory was fresh. Alexander was greeted in a transport of joy as a liberator. Indeed Egyptians are supposed to have approached Alexander while he was yet at Issus and implored him to rescue their country.

Alexander was careful to do nothing to spoil this first favorable impression. He obeyed Egyptian customs, made the necessary sacrifices to Egyptian gods in Egyptian ways. He was intent on being considered not a conqueror of Egypt, but an Egyptian pharaoh.

To help accomplish that purpose, he journeyed to the Siwa (see'wuh) oasis in Libya, about three hundred miles west of the Nile, where a venerated temple to Amen stood. There he went through the rites necessary to his establishment as pharaoh, and even accepted a position as a divine son of Amen, according to Egyptian custom.

This is often interpreted as proof that Alexander was becoming megalomaniac with victory and aspiring to godhood, but since the Egyptians would not accept a pharaoh who wasn't a god, Alexander had no reasonable choice in this matter. Still, it did set a precedent, and later monarchs, right down to the time six and a half centuries later when the Mediterranean world turned Christian, often insisted on being treated as divinities, although this was something that was not at all in accord with earlier Greek tradition.

The Greeks knew Amen as Ammon and since he was the greatest of the Egyptian gods, by a tradition that dated from the Eleventh Dynasty, seventeen centuries before, they equated him with their own chief god, Zeus. The temple at Siwa was therefore felt to be dedicated to "Zeus-Ammon" (or "Jupiter-Ammon" in the later Roman fashion).

There is a peculiar connection between this temple and modern chemistry. Fuel is, naturally, very scarce in the desert, and the priests at Siwa made use of camel dung. The soot that settled out of the burning fuel on the walls and ceiling of the temple contained white saltlike crystals which were then called, in Latin, *sal ammoniac* ("salt of Ammon"). A gas can be obtained from these crystals and that gas came to be called *ammonia*.

In this way, the great god of Thebes, whom Ikhnaton had

unsuccessfully defied, and whom Ramses II had considered second only to himself, survives today in the name of a pungent gas, known to the housewife chiefly as a constituent of cleaning mixtures!

Alexander could not, of course, continue to remain in Egypt as pharaoh, for he had the rest of Persia to conquer, and years of campaigning ahead. He picked native Egyptians to serve as governors in his absence, but did not entrust them with financial power. (It takes money to finance rebellions.) The control of finances he put into the hands of a Greek from Naucratis, one Cleomenes (klee-om′ih-neez). This man, with the power to tax, was the real ruler of the country, though, to save Egyptian face, he lacked the title.

Before Alexander left, he surveyed a spot at the mouth of the westernmost branch of the Nile, where a small town existed. He marked out the foundations of a suburb to be built west of the town. The old city and the new suburb, taken together, were to be called Alexandria in his own honor. Cleomenes saw to it that the city was built after Alexander left Egypt in 331 B.C., never to return. It was designed by the architect Dinocrates (dy-nok′ruh-teez) of Rhodes who laid it out in straight streets, crossing at neat right angles.

Alexander ordered the building of many cities, almost all of which were named Alexandria, but by far the most important of all was the Egyptian Alexandria. It took over the commercial functions of Naucratis, which declined in consequence. Since the old commercial city of Tyre had been destroyed, as a result of Alexander's siege, Alexandria became the trade center of the eastern Mediterranean and quickly grew into a metropolis that served as capital of Egypt. The old capitals of Memphis and Thebes declined steadily after that.

10

PTOLEMAIC EGYPT

THE FIRST PTOLEMY

Egypt prospered under Cleomenes and retired temporarily into the backwater of events while Alexander went charging across the length and breadth of the Persian Empire, winning two great battles, innumerable smaller ones, and finally establishing himself as monarch of all of it. (Darius III, the last Persian king, was assassinated by his own men in 330 B.C.)

Alexander returned to Babylon in 324 B.C. from his expeditions in far-off corners and may have been making plans for new conquests in new directions when he died in 323 B.C.

He was still a young man at his death, thirty-three years old, and he left behind no secure succession. He had a termagant mother, a Persian wife, a mentally deficient half brother, and a posthumous baby son. Not one of them counted.

There is a legend that Alexander, as he was dying, was asked to whom he bequeathed his empire. With his dying breath he is supposed to have said, "To the strongest."

He may not really have said it, but his generals acted as if he had. Each snatched a part and then tried to use that part as a base from which to grab all the rest. The most important generals, from the standpoint of this book, were Ptolemy (tol'eh-mee), Seleucus (see-lyoo'kus), and Antigonus (an-tig'oh-nus). The last was ably assisted by his son Demetrius (dee-mee'tree-us).

Ptolemy (or, in Greek form, Ptolemaios) was the son of a Macedonian nobleman, although there were rumors that he was an illegitimate son of Philip and therefore a half brother of Alexander. (This rumor may have been deliberately spread by Ptolemy himself to enhance his own image. Bastardy was a small price to pay for a family connection with the great Alexander.)

As soon as Alexander was dead, Ptolemy seized the governorship of Egypt for himself and quickly had Cleomenes executed (a poor reward for an excellent administrator). Ptolemy's choice of territory was a prudent one. Egypt was a rich land, whose agricultural produce, thanks to the regular Nile flood, and the skilled industry of her people, gave her rulers wealth beyond compare.

Ptolemy was clever enough also to have Alexander's body seized and buried in Memphis — a clever psychological stroke, considering that the whole world was in awe of Alexander's lightning-filled life and considered him a kind of demigod.

Ptolemy was the first of the generals to see that total victory and rule over the entire empire was impossible. He may well have considered it undesirable. He would be comfortable as ruler of rich Egypt; why expose himself to the problems and troubles of trying to deal with all the rest of the empire? All that he wanted besides the Nile Valley were its immediate approaches on the west and east, to serve as defenses against possible invaders, and a navy that could control the sea to the north.

The west was easy. Ptolemy had only to obtain the submission of Cyrene and the Libyan oases, which had been under the rule of Persia and of Alexander, and which made no trouble at all about passing under the rule of Ptolemy.

The east was almost as easy. In 320 B.C., Ptolemy led an army into Syria and shrewdly attacked Jerusalem on the Sabbath day. The ultrapious Jews of the period refused to fight on the Sabbath, even in self-defense, and Jerusalem, which had withstood Sennacherib and Nebuchadrezzar with admirable tenacity, fell to Ptolemy without lifting a hand.

It was in the north where he ran into trouble. He built his navy and sent an expedition into Greece itself and into various Greek islands in an effort to seek allies and assert his domination. There he was opposed by Antigonus and Demetrius, and in 306 B.C., the ships of father and son inflicted a spectacular defeat upon Ptolemy's fleet.

Antigonus, who was seventy-five years old at the time and eager to obtain supremacy before he died, at once adopted the title of king of Asia in anticipation of final victory. Ptolemy, although smarting under the sting of defeat, could not allow this psychological move to go uncountered. He proclaimed himself king as well; then managed to beat off a weak attempt on the part of Antigonus and Demetrius to invade Egypt, thus lending force to his new title.

Ptolemy, as king of Egypt, founded a line that lasted for three centuries, longer than any of the native dynasties that had ruled in Egypt over a stretch of three thousand years. Ptolemy's line might be called the Macedonian Dynasty or the Lagids, after Ptolemy's father, or reputed father, Lagos — or the Thirty-first Dynasty if it is to be given a number.

Most commonly, the dynasty is referred to as "the

Ptolemies" since every king of the line, without exception, bore that name. One can speak of Egypt of this period as Ptolemaic Egypt.

Nor were Antigonus and Ptolemy the only generals to become kings at this time. Seleucus, who was based in Babylonia, also adopted the title of king. The line of his successors are known as the Seleucids, and the empire they ruled in western Asia is the Seleucid Empire.

Ptolemy I, as we may now call him, did not retire from the north as the result of a single defeat. He rebuilt his fleet and waited his chance. In 305 B.C., Demetrius laid siege to the island of Rhodes, which had maintained its alliance with Egypt despite Ptolemy's defeat. The Rhodians put up a stout defense, and Ptolemy's ships sailed to help that defense. Demetrius had to give up and sail away, and the grateful islanders gave Ptolemy the title of Soter ("savior").

It was customary, in the centuries after Alexander, for kings to adopt, or be given, some flattering nickname by which they could be distinguished from each other and be known to history. (Usually the worse or weaker the king, the more pretentious and flattering the nickname.) This was true of the Seleucid kings and a number of other dynasties in the eastern Mediterranean, but I shall use them only in connection with the Egyptian kings. Thus the first Ptolemy can be called Ptolemy I Soter.

Since, of all the generals, Antigonus was the most ambitious and the least desirous of compromise or of anything short of the supreme power, Ptolemy, Seleucus, and some others combined against him. In forming this combination, Ptolemy and Seleucus agreed informally to divide Syria between themselves, Ptolemy to retain the southern half.

As the campaigns against Antigonus progressed, the cautious Ptolemy began to fear defeat and to withdraw his forces. When the final battle was fought, however — in 301 B.C., at Ipsus (ip'sus) in central Asia Minor — it was Antigonus who was defeated and slain, while his son Demetrius was driven into temporarily helpless exile.

Seleucus was now riding high. He was able to establish his control over virtually all the Asian portion of Alexander's empire. He laid claim to southern Syria in addition, maintaining that Ptolemy had forfeited control by his pusillanimous behavior prior to Ipsus. Ptolemy was, however, in possession and refused to give it up. Southern Syria, and Judea in particular, remained under the domination of Egypt for over a century. This was Egypt's first venture in Asian imperialism (except for Necho's three-year stay) since the time of Ramses III eight centuries before.

Nevertheless, Syria remained a matter of dispute between the Ptolemies and the Seleucids for a century and a half and occasioned a series of wars that, in the end, destroyed both realms.

Ptolemy I was blessed with long life, to the advantage of Egypt, which he ruled justly and mildly — so well, in fact, that he was popular with his subjects to the end, although he was a foreigner. He was the first Egyptian monarch to coin money in Egypt and under him, Egypt's economy flourished. The second half of his reign was spent in peace, but he remained always aware that Seleucus, equally long-lived, was no friend.

By 285 B.C., Ptolemy I was eighty-two years old and no longer capable, in his own estimation, of discharging the duties of office. He therefore decided to abdicate, but before he could do so, he had to decide the matter of the succession. He wanted the next king to be as prudent as himself, and as capable of warding off Seleucus and *his* successors.

Ptolemy I had had a number of sons, of whom two (by different mothers) were, at this stage, important. Both bore the name Ptolemy. The older was Ptolemy Ceraunus (see-roh'-nus), or "Ptolemy the Thunderbolt," and the younger was

Ptolemy Philadelphus, a name given to him late in life for reasons that will be gone into later.

The older was indeed a thunderbolt, quite apt to go off half-cocked and to damage others and himself in doing so. The younger was as wise and moderate as his father. Without hesitation, Ptolemy exiled Ceraunus, associated his younger son with himself in the government, and then abdicated in 285 B.C. in favor of that younger son. He lived on to 283 B.C. and died peacefully at the end of a long and successful life.

Ptolemy Ceraunus eventually found himself in the court of Seleucus, who gladly welcomed him. Seleucus saw in the younger man a possible claimant for the Egyptian throne and one, therefore, who might serve as a handy tool in case of need. Seleucus was not at all like Ptolemy. His great age did not put him in mind of abdication at all. He still followed the lure of power and continued the endless wars with the vigor and persistence of a much younger man.

He won one last battle in 281 B.C. and defeated and killed another of Alexander's aged generals in that fight. With Ptolemy I also dead, Seleucus was now the last of all of Alexander's generals to remain alive, a fact that gave him the keenest possible delight. (He was about seventy-seven years old when he achieved this pinnacle of longevity.)

The delight did not last long. As fruits of his last victory, he traveled on to Macedon where he intended to take possession of the home territory of the great Alexander. But once Seleucus arrived, Ptolemy Ceraunus took action. He had lost a chance at a throne in Egypt, but he was determined to rule somewhere. There seemed to be no use in waiting for the apparently immortal Seleucus to die of his own accord, so Ceraunus, in 280 B.C., settled matters by knifing him down.

The last of Alexander's generals was dead, and now the two sons of Ptolemy Soter were each kings. The younger was king of Egypt; the older, king of Macedon. But the older, who had won his throne by assassination, was not to enjoy it long. Macedon was invaded by barbarous tribes from the north the next year, and in the horrible confusion and devastation that followed, Ptolemy Ceraunus lost his life.

ALEXANDRIA

Ptolemy I ruled from the new city of Alexandria as his capital, as did all the Ptolemies that succeeded him. Alexandria was, indeed, virtually all of Egypt that counted, as far as foreigners were concerned. To Egyptians, it was scarcely part of Egypt at all. The Ptolemies respected Egyptian customs and paid lip service to all Egyptian gods, and there was never a truly serious revolt against them as there had been against the Hyksos, the Assyrians, and the Persians. Nevertheless, to Egyptians, Alexandria seemed a little corner of non-Egypt. It was ruled by Greek customs, and it was filled with Greeks and Jews (the latter migrating there freely from a Judea that was part of the Egyptian realm at that time).

Perhaps it was even a good thing from the Egyptian point of view. By isolating the Greeks in the capital city, the rest of the nation was all the more Egyptian.

One can say, as a rough rule of thumb, then, that Alexandria under the Ptolemies was one-third Greek, one-third Jewish, and one-third Egyptian. Considering its wealth, its sophistication, its cosmopolitanism, and its lack of ancient history, Alexandria was the New York of its day.

Ptolemy I, and his son Ptolemy II, were not content merely to make Alexandria large, populous, and wealthy. Both la-

bored to make it a center of learning, and in this they succeeded. (The first two Ptolemies were so at one in this respect
that it is hard to say exactly what one accomplished and what
the other.)

Ptolemy I was himself a writer, and prepared a biography
of Alexander the Great in straightforward and unassuming
prose. It is one of the great losses to scholarship that this biography — based on firsthand knowledge — does not survive.
However, a Greek historian, Arrian (ar'ee-an), writing four
and a half centuries later, wrote a biography of Alexander
which he based very largely on Ptolemy's work. Arrian's biography does survive, and through it we have, indirectly,
Ptolemy's.

Ptolemy I had inherited the library of the great Greek
philosopher Aristotle, and he made every effort to enlarge that
collection. He imported an Athenian scholar to supervise the
organization of a large library which eventually became the best
and most renowned in all the ancient world; a library, in fact,
that could not be matched, let alone exceeded, for seventeen
more centuries — until the invention of printing made books
commonplace.

Attached to the library was a temple to the Muses
(*Mouseion* in Greek and *Museum* in Latin) in which scholars
might work in peace and security, free of taxes and supported
by the state. Athens, which till then had been the center of
Greek learning, lost ground to Alexandria in every field but
philosophy. Scholars went where the money was (as they do
today when the "brain drain" of European scholars to the
United States is much in the news). At its height, the Museum
was host to some 14,000 students, it is said, so the establishment
was a large university even by modern standards.

It was in Alexandria that Euclid prepared his geometry,
that Eratosthenes measured the circumference of the earth
without ever leaving Egypt, that Herophilus and Erasistratus
made enormous strides in anatomy, and that Ctesibius refined

and elaborated the cleverest clock of ancient times, one that worked by dripping water.*

Alexandrian learning was chiefly Greek in its inspiration, but Egyptian technology contributed to it, too. If Egypt was weaker on theory than Greece was, it was stronger in practice. Centuries of experience in embalming had yielded much information in both chemistry and medicine.

Greek scholars did not hesitated to adopt Egyptian knowledge. To the Egyptians, Thoth, the ibis-headed god, was the repository of all wisdom, and the Greeks associated their own Hermes with him. They spoke of Hermes Trismegistus ("Hermes the thrice-greatest") and under his divine aegis devised the science we now call alchemy.

The first important worker in Greek-Egyptian "khemeia" that we know by name was Bolos of Mendes, a town in the Nile delta. He wrote about 200 B.C. and used the name Democritus as a pseudonym so that he is often referred to as Bolos-Democritus.

Bolos devoted himself to the belief, which may have been prevalent at the time, that the different metals could be converted one into the other, if only the proper methods were discovered. The conversion of lead into gold ("transmutation") remained an elusive goal of scholars for two thouand years thereafter.

While the Ptolemies remained Greek in language and culture, they were careful to patronize Egyptian culture as well. It was Ptolemy II, for instance, who sponsored Manetho's history of the Egyptians and who accompanied a voyage of exploration up the fabled Nile.

The Ptolemies also respected the Egyptian religion. Indeed, they attempted to encourage a variety that would fuse the Egyptian way with the Greek and produce something that would be particularly associated with themselves. Thus, Osiris,

---

* For more on this subject, see my book *The Greeks* (Houghton Mifflin, 1965).

together with his earthly manifestation, the bull, Apis, became Serapis (see-ray'pis) to the Greeks. He was associated with Zeus, and Ptolemy I built a magnificent temple in his honor in Alexandria. This was the Serapeion or, in Latin, the Serapeum (ser"uh-pee'um).

Ptolemy II carried his observance of Egyptian custom to the point of reviving the pharaonic custom of brother-sister marriages. For his second wife, he married his full sister, Arsinoe (ahr-sin'oh-ee), who had previously been married to her half brother Ptolemy Ceraunus. Because of this marriage — a very successful and loving one — Arsinoe came to be known as Philadelphus ("brother-loving"), and this nickname was eventually applied to Ptolemy II as well (after his death.) Both Ptolemy and Arsinoe were fairly mature at the time and had no children.

Even the Jews received a share of this Ptolemaic patronage. Indeed, the Jews seem to have been the object of a kind of amused curiosity on the part of the earlier Ptolemies. They were recognized as a people of ancient history with a rather odd, but interesting, set of sacred books. Ptolemy I seems to have known enough about Jewish customs to attack Jerusalem on the Sabbath, knowing it would be unprotected then. The Ptolemies allowed the Jews to keep their peculiar customs and to have a certain amount of self-rule within Alexandria — even though this was not entirely popular with the Greeks.

The environment in Alexandria was made so congenial for the immigrant Jews, in fact, that Greek soon became their language to the exclusion of the Aramaic spoken in Judea, or the Hebrew in which their sacred scriptures were inscribed. The scriptures were lost to them as long as that situation was allowed to remain. Under the patronage of Ptolemy II, therefore, scholars were imported from Judea to assist in the translation of those scriptures into Greek.

The Greek translation of the Bible is referred to as the Septuagint (sep'tyoo-uh-jint), from a Greek word for "seventy," because of the tradition that it had been translated by seventy scholars.

When the Bible eventually appeared in Latin, it was from the Septuagint that that version was first obtained. Thus, in early Christian days, it was the Septuagint that was used, whether in Greek or Latin, so that this version, made possible by the Ptolemies, had an important role indeed in Christian history.

Nor did Ptolemy II forget his Macedonian heritage. He transferred the body of the great Alexander from Memphis to Alexandria and built a special monument over it.

Thanks to the enlightened labors of Ptolemy I and Ptolemy II, Alexandria became not only the commercial center of the Greek world, but its intellectual center as well. It was to remain this for some nine centuries.

THE PTOLEMIES AT THE PEAK

Ptolemy II was interested in continuing and extending Egyptian prosperity. Under him, the canal system, upon which Egypt's agriculture depended, was kept at a high pitch of efficiency. He refurbished the canal linking the Nile and the Red Sea; he explored the upper Nile, placed garrisons and founded cities on the Red Sea and, across it, on the Arabian coast, to safeguard trade in that direction.

He also reversed the earlier pharaonic policy with respect to Lake Moeris. Instead of trying to keep its water level high, he had it partially drained and then arranged to have the fertile soil thus exposed irrigated by an extensive canal network linked to the Nile. Population rose in the area, and cities multiplied. The region continued to flourish as the richest province in a rich land for some four centuries afterward.

For the protection of Mediterranean shipping, Ptolemy II had a lighthouse built in Alexandria's harbor on the island of Pharos at a cost of 800 talents (at least two million dollars in modern money), the greatest of the ancient world. It was considered by the admiring Greeks to be one of the "Seven Wonders of the World." It had a square base 100 feet on each side, and at its top (variously reported to be 200 to 600 feet high) a fire was kept perpetually lit. A large statue of Poseidon, god of the sea, stood at the apex. A wood fire perpetually burning was supposed to be visible at distances of twenty miles. The details of its structure cannot be checked any longer except from some surviving Ptolemaic coins, for fifteen centuries after the lighthouse was built, an earthquake completely demolished it.

The rivalry between the Ptolemies and the Seleucids continued, however. Seleucus I had been succeeded by his son, Antiochus I (an-tigh′oh-kus), and son faced son with enmity undiminished. From 276 to 272 B.C., they fought the "First Syrian War," and Egypt was generally the victor so that Ptolemy II extended his rule over Phoenicia and sections of Asia Minor. A Second Syrian War was fought from 260 to 255 B.C. with Antiochus II, the third Seleucid king. This was less fortunate for Egypt, and some of the earlier gains were lost.

Perhaps the most important step taken by Ptolemy II in the realm of foreign policy was one to which little attention was probably paid at the time. In Italy, a city named Rome had been slowly taking over much of the peninsula. By the time that Ptolemy II came to the throne, Rome was in control of all of central Italy and was threatening the Greek cities in the south.

The Greeks called to their aid Pyrrhus (pir′us), a Macedonian general who was a distant relative of Alexander the Great. Pyrrhus, a capable fighter and a lover of war, responded eagerly and used his phalanx and some war elephants that he brought with him (a trick Alexander had learned while fighting in India) to beat the Romans twice. The Romans, however, persevered doggedly and in 275 B.C. finally defeated Pyrrhus and drove him out of Italy. By 270 B.C. they had taken all the Greek cities in southern Italy.

Ptolemy II did not let Greek sympathies mislead him here. It seemed to him that the Romans were a coming nation and that it would be far better to be with them than against them. He formed an alliance with them, an alliance that he clung to when Rome got into a long war with Carthage over Sicily. Indeed, the alliance became a traditional one for Egypt, and one from which the Ptolemies never departed.

Ptolemy II died in 246 B.C., and his eldest son, Ptolemy III, succeeded to the crown. Again, Egypt found at its head a vigorous, enlightened ruler. He regained Cyrene, which, for a few years, had managed to make itself independent of Egypt.

There continued, however, the eternal quarrel with the Seleucids, exacerbated this time by family problems.

At the conclusion of the First Syrian War, Ptolemy II had given his daughter Berenice (ber″uh-nigh′see), the sister of the young prince who would eventually become Ptolemy III, in marriage to the young prince who became Antiochus II.

Antiochus II died in the same year as Ptolemy II did, so that Ptolemy III, on coming to the throne, expected to see his sister's infant son become the fourth Seleucid king. However, Antiochus II had had a previous wife who was still alive. She had Berenice and her son killed, and the son by this first wife ruled as Seleucus II.

This was war-cause enough for Ptolemy III. To avenge his sister, he marched into the Seleucid dominions in the Third Syrian War. He reached Babylonia and temporarily occupied Babylon itself. No Egyptian monarch in all the land's long history had ever ventured so far from the Nile, and that march represents the height and peak of Ptolemaic power. For the first time since the days of Ramses II, a thousand years before, Egypt was the strongest power in the world.

However, Ptolemy III realized that his advance was a bit on the unrealistic side. He did not think he could actually control indefinitely the ground he had temporarily occupied. Voluntarily, he fell back, relinquishing the core of the Seleucid kingdom to the Seleucids and retaining only those portions near Egypt which he thought he might with profit attempt to control.

He brought back with him some of the statues and religious items that had been carried off by Cambyses three centuries before and restored them to their proper places. The grateful Egyptians bestowed upon him the name of Euergetes (yoo-ur'-jih-teez) — meaning "well-doer" or "benefactor" — and it is as Ptolemy III Euergetes that he is best known in history.

There is a story to the effect that in the course of Ptolemy's campaign in the Seleucid dominions, his queen, a Cyrenian princess also named Berenice, prayed for his safe return and, to insure it, had her long hair cut off and dedicated to the gods in a temple to Aphrodite. The hair was stolen, and to console her a Greek astronomer told her it had been taken by the gods to heaven and pointed out some faint stars which, he insisted, represented her hair. Those stars are still said to represent the constellation of "Coma Berenices" or "Berenice's Hair."

Ptolemy's warlike vigor extended in another direction as well, for he advanced to the south, penetrating into Nubia, as the pharaohs had once done, in times that were already ancient by then.

Ptolemy III did not neglect the arts of peace, either. He continued the support of the Museum with all the enthusiasm of his father and grandfather. By his reign, the library held perhaps 400,000 volumes and he ordered all incoming travellers to turn over their books for copying. Indeed, all the Ptolemies, even the worst of them, were avid patrons of the arts.

Ptolemy III continued the policy of favoring the Jews. He admitted them to full Alexandrian citizenship on an equal basis with the Greeks — at a time when native Egyptians were still denied the privilege. In fact, on his return home from his campaign against the Seleucids, Ptolemy III, in the course of a studied program of giving thanks to all the gods of the peoples over whom he ruled, sacrificed at the Temple at Jerusalem in proper manner.

By the time Ptolemy III died in 221 B.C., Egypt had enjoyed 111 years of wise and beneficent rule from the moment Alexander the Great had appeared at Pelusium. It was a record scarcely to be equaled at any time under the long list of native pharaohs. In succession, Alexander, Cleomenes, and three Ptolemies had safeguarded Egypt's security, prosperity, and internal peace.

But now the great days were passing once more.

THE PTOLEMIES IN DECLINE

Ptolemy IV, the oldest son of the great Euergetes, succeeded, and he quickly named himself Philopater (fih-lop′uh-tor), or "loving his father." Since the first act of his reign was to have his mother (the Berenice whose hair is memorialized in the skies) and sister executed, there is a cynical feeling that he adopted the name as a mask for a complete lack of family love.

However, perhaps not. In the absence of the kind of full documentation we now have of historical events, we must sometimes rely on gossip, and the gossip that is most likely to survive is that which is most interesting — which means, most shocking.

The new Ptolemy does appear to have been a weak, luxury-loving monarch who left the government to his ministers and favorites. This was particularly unfortunate for Egypt because the Seleucid Empire had just come under the rule of a vigorous and ambitious monarch. Antiochus III was the younger son of Seleucus II who ascended the Seleucid throne in 223 B.C.

Determined to pay back the defeats suffered by his father at the hands of Ptolemy III, Antiochus III attacked Egypt in the Fourth Syrian War almost as soon as the great Ptolemy was safely dead. Antiochus III won initially, but in 217 B.C. he met the main Egyptian army, with Ptolemy IV himself at its head, at Raphia (ruh-figh'uh) on the Egyptian border. Both sides had elephants. Antiochus had Asian elephants while Ptolemy had the larger but less tractable African elephants. It is the only battle in which the two species faced each other. The Asian species proved victors here, but the Asian army was defeated nevertheless. The Egyptian army managed to win a smashing victory, and for a time it seemed that the luck of the Ptolemies was holding.

Under the pressure of the Seleucid advance, however, the Egyptian government had allowed the arming of the Egyptian natives themselves. This turned out to be an unfortunate move for the government. The Ptolemaic rule was no longer what it had been, and armed Egyptians began to indulge in occasional revolts, though none proved serious.

Ptolemy IV and his ministers managed to keep the lid on. While Ptolemy IV lived, Egypt remained under control, and Antiochus III busied himself elsewhere.

Ptolemy IV had one unusual hobby. He loved to order the construction of immense ships — ships far too large to be useful because they were so cumbersome and unmaneuverable. His largest ship was 420 feet long and 57 feet wide. It had forty banks of oars, with a city of men pulling at four thousand oars. It must have looked like a gigantic super-centipede. It was only for show, of course; it would have met instant disaster in any battle.

The reign of Ptolemy IV was also witness to a melancholy incident that marked the decline of Greece.

Ever since the time of Philip II of Macedon, the Greek cities had been dominated by that northern kingdom. The attempts of individual cities to free themselves failed. When they tried to combine into "leagues," those leagues fought each other, with the loser invariably turning to Macedon.

In 236 B.C., when Ptolemy III was on Egypt's throne, a reforming king, Cleomenes III, came to power in Sparta and dreamed of restoring that city to what it had been in the days, a century and a half before, when it was the leading power in Greece. The Achaean League (a combination of cities north of Sparta) fought against him, however, and when they were defeated by Cleomenes, they called in Macedon, abandoning, by this act, the last chance of Greek independence. The Macedonians crushed Cleomenes and his Spartans in 222 B.C. The king and some men managed to escape to Egypt as refugees.

Ptolemy III greeted them kindly, possibly because he saw them as useful tools in case of war with Macedon. When Ptolemy IV came to the throne, however, he saw in Cleomenes only an incumbrance and placed him under virtual house arrest in Alexandria.

Cleomenes, chafing in what was obviously imprisonment, seized a time, in 220 B.C., when Ptolemy IV was absent from Alexandria. He broke out and tried to harangue the Alexandrian Greeks to rise against Ptolemy and establish a free government in the old-fashioned Greek style. But the crowds only gaped at this queer fellow mouthing gibberish at them, for they no longer knew what liberty meant. Cleomenes, born out of his time, and realizing that at last, killed himself.

Ptolemy IV died in 203 B.C., and for the first time the Ptolemies lacked an adult heir. The prince who succeeded was a five-year-old boy, Ptolemy V, who was called Ptolemy Epiphanes (ee-pif'uh-neez), or "Ptolemy the God Made Manifest," though the poor child was anything but that. Egyptian government was paralyzed as officials struggled for power, and the natives seized the opportunity to revolt.

And as if that were not enough, Antiochus III suddenly realized his chance had come. He had spent his time since the battle of Raphia conducting campaigns in the eastern reaches of what had once been the Persian Empire, areas that had been gained by Alexander and inherited by Seleucus I. Recently, they had gained their independence, but now Antiochus III had forced them back into line, and his empire, on paper at least, was immense. He took to calling himself Antiochus the Great.

When Ptolemy IV died and a five-year-old boy became the new pharaoh, Antiochus at once made a deal with Philip V, who then ruled over Macedon. They were to unite in war against Egypt, win easily, and cut up the corpse. Philip fell in greedily with this scheme, and the Fifth Syrian War began in 201 B.C.

One factor, however, the two kings left out of account — the western nation of Rome.

In the time of Ptolemy II, half a century before, Rome had begun a tremendous war against Carthage, which had continued with some pauses ever since. Indeed, at one point, in 216 B.C., when the Carthaginian general Hannibal (one of the very few military leaders who might have given even Alexander a run for his money) had invaded Italy and hammered Rome to the ground under the force of three mighty victories it looked as though Rome might lose.

She recovered, however, in the most magnificent comeback of her entire history, and by 201 B.C., just as Antiochus and Philip were combining against Egypt, Carthage was finally defeated, and Rome was supreme in the western Mediterranean.

The government of Egypt, facing utter ruin at the hands of its united enemies, and mindful of the old treaty with Rome, to which it had always adhered faithfully, called to Rome for help.

Rome was only too willing. After all, in the dark days of Hannibal's victories, Ptolemy IV of Egypt had shipped grain to Rome whereas Philip V of Macedon had made a treaty of alliance with the Carthaginian. Rome had no intention of requiting Philip's enmity with sweet forbearance. She engaged in war with Macedon at once, and Philip V had scarcely begun his part in the slicing up of Egypt when he found himself having to turn about to face Rome.

Antiochus III went right ahead anyway. He could handle Egypt alone while Macedon neutralized Rome. With only himself in Egypt, there would be that much more for his share. Nor was he concerned about Rome. He himself was Antiochus the Great, conqueror of vast territories. Why worry about some western barbarians?

He continued, therefore, with the war, and indeed, by 195 B.C., he had defeated the armies of Egypt. Antiochus promptly annexed all of Syria, including Judea, which thus, after experiencing a century and a quarter of mild Ptolemaic rule, found itself under what turned out to be a much harsher Seleucid domination.

But there remained the Romans. They had defeated Macedon, though not without some difficulty, and Philip V had retired into a grim and sullen isolation. The small Macedonian-ruled nations of western Asia Minor, who had always feared the Seleucid power to the east (especially under the ambitious Antiochus III), hastened to place themselves under Roman protection. All urged Rome to do something about Antiochus, who had been encroaching into the erstwhile Egyptian holdings in Asia Minor.

The Romans ordered Antiochus III out of Asia Minor, but

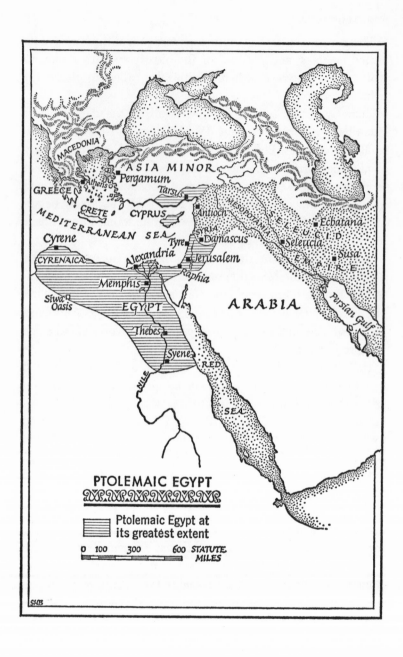

MACEDONIA

ASIA MINOR

GREECE
Athens
Pergamum
Tarsus

CRETE
CYPRUS
Antioch
MESOPOTAMIA
S E L E U - C I D
Ecbatana

MEDITERRANEAN SEA
SYRIA
Damascus
Seleucia
E M P I R E
Susa

Cyrene
Tyre

CYRENAICA
Alexandria
Jerusalem

Memphis
Raphia
ARABIA
Persian Gulf

Siwa
Oasis
EGYPT

Thebes

NILE
Syene

RED

SEA

PTOLEMAIC EGYPT

Ptolemaic Egypt at
its greatest extent

0   100   300   600 STATUTE
                          MILES

SHB

Antiochus III paid no attention. Hannibal, the Carthaginian general, was in exile in his court, and he urged Antiochus to give him an army with which to invade Italy once more. Antiochus, however, felt that Rome could be taken care of with no trouble. He moved an army into Greece and wasted his time in carousing.

The Romans marched into Greece and clouted Antiochus hard. Waking to reality, the Seleucid monarch tumbled back to Asia Minor, where the Romans stolidly followed and struck him even harder. Antiochus III had learned the facts of life. He made a most disadvantageous peace and got out of Asia Minor.

However, he held on to Syria, which Egypt did not regain. Rome had saved the essential Egypt, the Nile Valley; she didn't feel called upon to insure Egypt's imperial possessions. Everything Egypt had ever owned in Asia Minor was divided up among various of the nations on that peninsula — all of whom were essentially Roman puppets now. The only territory Ptolemaic Egypt retained outside the Nile Valley was Cyrenaica to the west and the island of Cyprus to the north.

With that done, Rome left the eastern kingdoms to their own devices. They could fight among themselves all they wanted as long as no one of them grew too strong by completely crushing its opponents.

By now Ptolemy V was old enough to rule. His majority was celebrated suitably, and a routine proclamation in honor of his coming of age was incised in Greek and two forms of Egyptian on a piece of black basalt. It was this inscription that was recovered just two thousand years later and, as the Rosetta Stone, served as the key to ancient Egyptian history. For that alone, Ptolemy V had not lived in vain.

With foreign dangers wiped out, thanks to Rome, the young Ptolemy could pay attention to internal order. He succeeded in quieting some troublesome revolts. After Antiochus III died in 187 B.C., Ptolemy V even began to dream of winning back Syria, but he himself died in 181 B.C., when he was only about thirty. Possibly he was poisoned.

He left behind two young sons. The elder, Ptolemy VI, was known as Philometer (fil"oh-mee'ter), or "lover of his mother." While his "beloved" mother lived, she controlled Egypt and kept the land at peace. When she died in 173 B.C., Ptolemy VI, still too young to be much of a force, was under the influence of fire-eating ministers who dreamed of reconquering Syria. Once again the old game of fighting the Seleucids began.

But Ptolemy VI was no warrior. (Actually, he was the mildest and most humane of all the Ptolemies.) Opposing this nonwarrior was a new king at the head of the Seleucid Empire, Antiochus IV, a younger son of the so-called Antiochus the Great. Antiochus IV was actually more capable than his overrated father, but he was plagued with a tendency toward rashness and temper.

At the first sign of Egyptian belligerence, Antiochus IV dashed toward the frontier, defeated the Egyptians at Pelusium, penetrated to the very walls of Alexandria, and actually captured Ptolemy VI. Perhaps he would have taken Alexandria, but Rome, from afar, indicated that that would be going too far.

Since Ptolemy VI could not serve as monarch while in captivity, the Egyptians, in 168 B.C., made his younger brother king as Ptolemy VII. Antiochus at once liberated Ptolemy VI, giving him his support, and hoping for a good, juicy civil war. The two Ptolemies, however, trumped Antiochus's ace by agreeing to rule jointly.

Antiochus, annoyed, marched into Egypt once again, ready to take Alexandria and settle the whole matter. But he was stopped again. This time a Roman ambassador stalked toward him under the walls of Alexandria and ordered him out of Egypt. Antiochus IV had no choice but to retire his entire army before this unarmed man who spoke in the powerful name of Rome. He scurried home.

He turned in humiliation against someone he felt he *could* defeat, and sacked Jerusalem. He desecrated the Jewish Temple and, as a result, forced Jewish nationalists into a long-drawn-out revolt under the leadership of a family known as the Maccabees.

By 163 B.C., Antiochus IV was dead in the course of a futile campaign in the east, and thereafter the Seleucid Empire began to decline even more drastically and precipitously than Ptolemaic Egypt had. A series of dynastic squabbles kept the land constantly in turmoil, and the continuing Jewish rebellion was a running sore.

At one point, even the pacific Ptolemy VI was lured into interfering in internal Seleucid affairs in the hope of winning back all his father had lost. He tried to convert what was left of the Seleucid Empire (the eastern provinces had broken away again, this time permanently) by first supporting and then attacking a Seleucid usurper named Alexander Balas. While in Syria, however, he fell from his horse and, in 146 B.C., died of the injuries he sustained.

That left Ptolemy VII ruling alone. He has been consistently vilified by ancient historians. Although, officially, his name was Euergetes, like that of his great-grandfather, he is universally known as Physcon (fiz'kon), or "potbelly," because he was supposed to have grown so fat through overindulgence. All kinds of wickedness and cruelties are laid to his charge, but it is not certain to what extent this has been exaggerated.

Inscriptions show him to have been a patron of learning and to have done much to restore Egyptian temples and to encourage native prosperity. It may well be that he was disliked by the Greeks just because he was overindulgent, in their opinion, to the natives. It was the Greeks, not the Egyptians, who wrote the histories, and Ptolemy VII may well have suffered in their report as a result.

The Egyptian realm began to break up after the death of Ptolemy VII in 116 B.C. He willed Cyrene to one son and Cyprus to another, while Egypt itself remained under a third son who reigned as Ptolemy VIII Soter II.

The last was ousted by his younger brother, Ptolemy IX Alexander, but the people of Alexandria ousted Ptolemy IX and brought back Ptolemy VIII.

This sort of in-and-out business really didn't matter any more, however, for Egypt and all the rest of the east was sinking into insignificance. Only one power counted now, and that was Rome.

Indeed, only one event of importance need be mentioned of this period. Some time after Ptolemy VIII was restored to the throne in 88 B.C., the city of Thebes rebelled. Exasperated, Ptolemy led an expedition against the city, laid siege to it for three years, and finally sacked it so thoroughly that it never recovered but sank into final ruin.

This was the end, after two thousand years of glory, of the capital of the Middle Kingdom and of the New Kingdom, of the city that under Ramses II was the greatest in the world.

But Memphis, a thousand years older still, yet remained as a center of native Egypt and a reminder of long-gone greatness.

11

CLEOPATRA

JULIUS CAESAR

Despite the feebleness and fecklessness of the Ptolemies who followed Physcon, Egypt experienced a half century of peace, broken only by rioting in Alexandria over which particular Ptolemaic nobody would have the right to wear the gorgeous robes, sit through the stately ritual, and experience the wasteful amusements that went with being king of Egypt.

The Ptolemies had the leisure to snatch at the powerless throne because the occasion for war had vanished. The Romans were in total charge and were sweeping up all the powers in the east.

Macedon had become a Roman province in 146 B.C., and Greece itself was a protectorate of the great city to the west. The western portion of Asia Minor became a Roman province in 129 B.C., and much of the rest of the peninsula, while nominally independent, had been reduced to puppet kingdoms.

When Pontus, a kingdom in eastern Asia Minor, fought Rome and won some victories, Rome exerted her full strength and finally cleared out the east altogether. In charge of this once-for-all settlement was a young Roman general named Gnaeus Pompeius, better known in English as Pompey (pom'pee). The last remnant of the Seleucid Empire, under Antiochus XIII, was confined to Syria, and in 64 B.C., Pompey, by his mere word of command, absorbed it into the Roman realm as the province of Syria. That was the end of the century and a half of warfare between Ptolemies and Seleucids and the six great wars fought by Ptolemies II, III, IV, V, VI, and VII. All down the drain! Both sets of Macedonians lost, and parvenu Rome had won. And when Syria was absorbed, so was Judea.

Outlying sections of the Ptolemaic dominions also went under. The son of Ptolemy VII, Physcon, who inherited Cyrene, willed it to the Romans when he died in 96 B.C., and it became a Roman province in 75 B.C. The island of Cyprus fell to all-engulfing Rome in 58 B.C.

By 58 B.C., all that was left of the vast Macedonian holdings that were gained by the victories of Alexander the Great two and a half centuries before was an Egypt consisting of the Nile Valley only. And it, too, was a Roman puppet, for no Ptolemy could be king without Roman permission.

A case in point is that of Ptolemy XI (or possibly XII or XIII; for there are disputes as to the manner in which the last few shadowy Ptolemies ought to be counted). His official name was Ptolemy Dionysus, but he was popularly known as Ptolemy Auletes (oh-lee'teez), or "Ptolemy the Flute-Player," since flute-playing seemed to be his major accomplishment. He was an illegitimate son of Ptolemy VIII (who had sacked Thebes), and since there were no legitimate heirs, he aspired to the throne.

He was proclaimed king in 80 B.C., but to be quite secure in that title (considering his illegitimacy), he needed the approval of the Roman Senate. This required a discreet bribe, and an enormous one, and it took years to manage to negotiate one that was large enough and quiet enough. To raise the bribe, he raised taxes, and the financial exactions that resulted finally provoked the Alexandrian mob to drive him out in 58 B.C.

His response was to travel to Rome where the general, Pompey, was now in control. Auletes promised another immense bribe to the Romans if they would put him back on the throne. (He was prepared to squeeze the Egyptian peasant to the last penny if he had to, or even rifle the temple treasuries, which was a much more risky procedure than merely starving millions.)

The Roman leaders were never immune to money, and in 55 B.C., Auletes was reinstated, to the absolute disgust and fury of the helpless Egyptians. He was maintained in his position only by the presence of a large Roman bodyguard.

In 51 B.C., however, he did the world a favor and died, leaving Egypt to his young son, Ptolemy XII. In his will Auletes placed his son under the protection of the Roman Senate, and they in turn assigned the job to Pompey himself.

Ptolemy XII was only ten years old, but he ruled jointly with his older sister, who was seventeen. This joint brother-sister rule was not uncommon practice among the Ptolemies, for it was a custom that stretched back to Ptolemy II and his sister-wife-queen Arsinoe, two centuries before.

The young king's sister possessed a name that was common among Ptolemaic queens. She was, in fact, the seventh of that name and is properly known, therefore, as Cleopatra VII. She is, however, *the* Cleopatra, and the Roman numeral is virtually never used in connection with her name. (It is important to remember that Cleopatra was not an Egyptian in descent and that she had no "Egyptian blood" at all in her, so that any attempt to make her a "dusky temptress" is foolish.

All her ancestors were either Greeks or Macedonians.)

The Ptolemy women tended to be capable, even when the men were not, and this Cleopatra was the most capable of the lot. It was natural that the intriguing courtiers should prefer the little brother to the big sister, since the big sister was not at all easily dominated. In particular, Pothinus (poh-thy'nus), a eunuch who at that time controlled the throne, was a bitter enemy of the girl.

In 48 B.C., Cleopatra took the usual way out for the Egypt of those days. She left Alexandria in search of an army, collected one in Syria, and prepared to return and settle matters by means of a neat little civil war. The two armies, hers and her brother's, faced each other at Pelusium, but before actual battle could break out, something happened that changed everything.

Rome was having a civil war of its own in those days. Pompey was in a desperate struggle with another, and even greater, general, Julius Caesar (see'zer). The armies of the two Romans had met in Greece, and Caesar had been victorious. There was nothing left for Pompey to do but flee, and the natural refuge (as in the case of Cleomenes the Spartan two centuries before) was Egypt. Egypt was near at hand and nominally independent. It was weak but rich, and would supply Pompey with the money needed to attract a new army. Also, it owed him a favor, for he had helped put Ptolemy Auletes on the throne, and he was the actual guardian of Auletes' son, the present boy-king of the realm.

But the Egyptian court was in agony as Pompey's ship neared their shore. The last thing they wanted was to take sides in a Roman civil war at just the moment when their own was about to break out. If they helped Pompey, Caesar might in turn back Cleopatra and destroy the Pothinus faction. If they refused to help Pompey, he might win in the end without them, and then come back for revenge.

Pothinus thought of a way out. A boat was sent to Pompey's

ship. Pompey was greeted with great gladness and asked to come to shore quickly so that he might be acclaimed by the men of Alexandria. Then, when Pompey stepped ashore (and while his wife and son watched from the ship), he was calmly knifed to death.

It seemed just the thing to do. Pompey was dead now and could never take revenge. Caesar would have to be grateful, and he would now help Pothinus against the threat of Cleopatra's army. Two birds with one stone.

Sure enough, Caesar, with a small contingent of four thousand men landed in Alexandria a few days later, determined to take Pompey prisoner and keep him from serving as a nucleus about which a new army might build. It was also in Caesar's mind to collect some needed money — generals always need money — from the ever-rich Alexandrian court.

Pothinus at once brought out the head of Pompey and asked for help against Cleopatra. It is possible that Caesar, on receiving enough money, would have given that help. After all, what did he care which Ptolemy ruled Egypt?

But no one counted on Cleopatra. She had an advantage that Pothinus did not have, for she was a young and fascinating woman. No one knows how beautiful she may have been by modern standards, or whether she was beautiful at all, for no portraits of her survive. There is no question, however, that, beautiful or not, she had the knack of attracting and holding men — and she knew it.

It was only necessary, then, for Cleopatra to get past her brother's army, somehow, and come into the presence of Caesar. After that, she was certain that she would be in control. She set sail from Syria, therefore, landed in Alexandria, and (according to legend) had a large carpet delivered to Caesar. Pothinus's forces saw no reason to stop the delivery, for they did not know that wrapped in the carpet was Cleopatra herself.

Cleopatra's stratagem worked perfectly. The amazed Caesar stared at the young lady who was revealed when the carpet was unrolled. She convinced him of the rightness of her cause, and he ordered the original arrangement to be restored, with Cleopatra and her young brother serving as joint monarchs.

This did not at all suit Pothinus. Pothinus knew that Egypt couldn't possibly win a war against Rome, but it might win a war against Caesar's small force. Once Caesar was dead, there would be plenty of chance for Caesar's opposition in Rome to seize control, and then they would have only praise and gratitude for Pothinus. Such, at least, must have been Pothinus's reasoning.

He therefore stirred up a rebellion against Caesar, and for three months the Roman was besieged on the island of Pharos (the one with the lighthouse). Caesar maintained himself only by personal bravery and by the skill with which he handled his few troops. (In the course of this small "Alexandrian War," the famous library of Alexandria was badly damaged.)

But Pothinus was not helped, personally, by the trouble he had fomented. As soon as the Egyptians attacked, the decisive Caesar had Pothinus seized and executed.

Finally, reinforcements reached Caesar, and the Egyptians were defeated. In the Egyptian flight that followed, the young Ptolemy XII tried to escape on a barge on the Nile River. The barge was too heavily loaded, and it sank. That was the end of him.

Caesar could now settle affairs in Egypt. He and Cleopatra, according to the universally accepted story, were lovers now, and he was determined to keep her on the throne. However, a queen had to have some sort of male associate, and for that purpose Caesar made use of another, still younger, brother of Cleopatra. He was a ten-year-old boy who reigned as Ptolemy XIII.

Caesar could not remain in Egypt forever. There was a war going on against the Romans in Asia Minor that had to be settled. There were armies still faithful to Pompey in western

Africa and in Spain, and they had to be taken care of. Most of all, there was a government in Rome that had to be reformed and reorganized. He therefore sailed away from Egypt in 47 B.C. and, eventually, returned to Rome.

Caesar brought something back to Rome with him. In Egypt, he had observed the workings of the calendar based on the sun (see page 10), which was clearly much more convenient and efficient than the moon-based calendars in use in Rome and Greece.

He sought the help of an Alexandrian astronomer, Sosigenes (soh-sij'uh-neez), and prepared a similar calendar for Rome. The year was given twelve months, some thirty days long and some thirty-one. This was not quite as orderly as the uniform thirty-day month of the Egyptians with their five-day additional unit at the end, but an improvement was added that the Egyptians themselves had never accepted. Since the length of the year was 365¼ days, not 365 days, every fourth year was given an extra "Leap Day." This "Julian Calendar" (named for the great Julius) was changed in minor fashion sixteen centuries later, but, in essence, is still in use today. Our calendar, then, can be traced back directly to Egypt and to Caesar's short stay in that country.

Not long after Caesar's departure, Cleopatra had a son. He was named Ptolemy Caesar, and was called Caesarion ("little Caesar") by the Alexandrians.

MARK ANTONY

Caesar's life was brief after he returned to Rome. A conspiracy against him was organized, and in 44 B.C., he was assassinated. As soon as Caesar was dead, Cleopatra had her young brother, Ptolemy XIII, executed. He was getting inconveniently old, anyway — fourteen — and was beginning to demand some say in the government. Cleopatra now reigned jointly with her son, Ptolemy Caesar (less than three years old at the time), who is known as Ptolemy XIV.

In Rome, a period of disorder was settled finally when two men rose to supremacy. One was Marcus Antonius, better known in English as Mark Antony, who had been a trusted lieutenant of Caesar. The other was Octavian Caesar, grand-nephew and adopted son of Julius Caesar.

Essentially enemies, the two men agreed to a compromise peace with each other, one in which they blocked off spheres of influence within the Roman realm. Octavian took the west, including the city of Rome; Mark Antony took the east.

The nature of the division showed the nature of the men. Mark Antony was attractive, jovial, a drinker and carouser, very popular with his men. He showed streaks of ability, too, but he was shallow, incapable of planning with cold rationality, and always swayed by the passion of the moment. The eastern half of the Roman world was the richer and more civilized half. In it, Mark Antony could expect comfort, luxury, and fun.

Octavian, on the other hand, was shrewd, deep, and subtle. He spared no effort to attain his objective and had the patience to wait through the hard times. The western half of the Roman realm was rather cold and bare, but it held Rome, and that was the nucleus of true power. It was true power that Octavian was after.

Octavian was greatly underestimated by Mark Antony, down to the very end, and historians generally favor the romantic Mark Antony over the cold and humorless Octavian, but they are wrong to do so. Looking back at that period of history from the vantage point of two thousand years, it is easy to see that Octavian was actually the ablest man in Roman history, not even excluding Julius Caesar himself — even if he lacked his great-uncle's military genius.

The party that had assassinated Caesar was defeated in a battle in Macedon in 42 B.C., and Mark Antony then sailed off to take up his position in the east. He made Tarsus, a city on the southern coast of Asia Minor, his headquarters.

Antony's great need, of course, was money, and that was always to be had in Egypt. He therefore, in royal manner, summoned Cleopatra to meet him in Tarsus and there give an accounting of Egyptian policy after Caesar's assassination. Egypt had, of course, held off and tried to maintain a cautious neutrality since it wasn't certain till the end which side would win. That wasn't so criminal an action, really, but it could be made to appear so by someone looking for an excuse to bleed the nation.

But Cleopatra still had the same ace of trumps she had used seven years before with Caesar. She came to Tarsus with ships decked out to the utmost that wealth could buy or luxury imagine — and its most precious piece of cargo was herself, still only twenty-eight. Mark Antony, like Julius Caesar, found himself completely fascinated with the Macedonian enchantress.

Where Caesar, however, never allowed love to obscure his policy, Mark Antony was never able to wrench policy away from his love.

The story of the Roman general and the Egyptian queen has gone down in history as one of the great love stories of all time, all the more so because it had a tragic end, and because the two lovers appear to have thrown away everything for love. William Shakespeare helped immortalize them in his magnificent play *Antony and Cleopatra,* and when the English poet John Dryden published his version of the story, the title he used seems to have condensed the romantic popular view of the matter into a couple of phrases: *All for Love; or, The World Well Lost.*

Actually, while there is no doubt that the two were in love, it was not entirely a matter of sheer romance. Cleopatra had the money that Mark Antony needed. She financed him for a dozen years in his battle for supreme power. And Mark Antony had the armies that Cleopatra needed. Cleopatra managed to make use of Mark Antony quite cold-bloodedly in her struggle to serve her own ambitions as queen of Egypt, which was what she was — first, last, and always.

Antony spent the winter of 41–40 B.C. in Alexandria with Cleopatra, devoting himself entirely to pleasure, and afterward, Cleopatra bore him twins. Mark Antony acknowledged them, and they were named Alexander Helios and Cleopatra Selene ("Alexander, the Sun" and "Cleopatra, the Moon").

The two lovers separated for a while, but Antony eventually rejoined Cleopatra and even married her, despite the fact that in Rome he was married to Octavian's sister. He calmly sent his Roman wife a notice of divorce.

Octavian, in Rome, made good use of Antony's shortsighted folly, pointing out what a wastrel and playboy Antony was. The Roman populace noted that well, and noted also that Octavian remained in Rome, working hard for its greatness; that he led a frugal life and married a respectable Roman woman. Undoubtedly most Romans would far rather have been Mark Antony in Cleopatra's arms than Octavian hard at work in his study; but since they couldn't be the first, they preferred the second.

Mark Antony paid little attention to Octavian's slow manipulation of public opinion, feeling, probably, that Octavian was a very poor general (true!) while he himself was a very good general (but not quite as good as he thought himself). Therefore, he went his own way, uncaring, and made error upon error.

Cleopatra was intent on winning back the wider dominions that had belonged to her predecessors, and Mark Antony humored her. He gave her back Cyrene and Cyprus (which he had no right to do) and even assigned to her those sections of coastal territory in Syria and Asia Minor that had once belonged to Ptolemy III at the peak of Ptolemaic power. He also, according to legend, transferred to her the library in Pergamum (a city in western Asia Minor, whose book collection was second only to that in Alexandria) in order to make up for the damage done in the little war against Caesar.

This was all perfect propaganda material for Octavian. He found it quite easy to make it look as though Antony were intending to turn over whole provinces to his beloved queen. The rumor was, in fact, that in his will he bestowed the entire east on Cleopatra, to be inherited by their children. It drove Romans mad to think that a Macedonian queen could win, by her charms, what no Macedonian king had ever been able to win from Rome by force of arms.

Octavian used the popular Roman fear and hatred of Cleopatra to persuade the Senate to declare war against Egypt, a war that was really against Mark Antony.

Mark Antony tried to rouse himself. Still certain that he could easily defeat Octavian, he collected ships, moved into Greece, and set up headquarters in the western regions of that country, preparing to invade Italy at the first opportunity and take over the city of Rome.

But if Octavian was himself no general at all, he had some good generals among his loyal supporters. One of these was Marcus Vipsanius Agrippa (uh-grip′uh). Octavian's fleet, under Agrippa, appeared also in the waters west of Greece.

After endless maneuverings and preparations, Cleopatra urged Antony to force a naval battle. Antony's ships were twice as numerous as Octavian's and were larger besides. If Antony won the naval battle, his army — also more numerous than Octavian's — would be sure to sweep all before them. Final victory would be Antony's.

The battle took place on September 2, 31 B.C., off Actium (ak′shee-um), a promontory on the coast of western Greece. At first, Octavian's ships could make little impression on An-

tony's large vessels, and the battle seemed to be a useless one
between maneuverability and power. Finally, though, Agrippa
nudged Antony into stretching his line so that Agrippa's ships
could dart through the openings that resulted, making straight
for Cleopatra's fleet of sixty ships that lay behind the line.

According to the story, Cleopatra, in a panic, ordered her
ships to retreat and row off. When Antony was made aware
that Cleopatra and her ships were leaving the scene of battle,
he proceeded to the most foolish act of a career which included
a large number of such acts. He got into a small vessel, abandoned his loyal ships and men (who might still have won victory), and sailed after the cowardly queen. His deserted fleet
did its best, but without its commander the heart was out of it,
and before evening Octavian was in possession of complete
victory.

THE LAST OF THE PTOLEMIES

Antony and Cleopatra could do nothing more now than
cower in Alexandria and wait for Octavian to spare the time
to go to Egypt after them. In July, 30 B.C., Octavian did so,
arriving at Pelusium. Antony tried to resist, but it was no use.
On August 1, Octavian entered Alexandria, and Mark Antony
committed suicide.

That left Cleopatra. She still had her beauty and charm,
and she hoped to use it on Octavian as she had used it on Caesar and Antony. She was thirty-nine now, but perhaps that
was not too old.

Octavian was six years younger than she, but that was not
the trouble. The real trouble was that Octavian had a definite
objective in mind — that of reforming Rome, reorganizing its

government, and establishing it so firmly that it would last for centuries. (All of this he accomplished.)

In pursuit of that objective, he would allow himself no detours and certainly not the fatal one of Cleopatra. His interview with the fascinating queen made it quite plain that he was one man who was completely immune to her. He spoke softly to her, but she knew that that was only to keep her quiet until he could seize her and carry her back to Rome to walk in chains behind his triumphant chariot.

There was left but one way of escape from that ultimate humiliation — suicide. She pretended complete submission and made her plans. The farsighted Octavian foresaw the possibility and had all cutting utensils and other instruments of death removed from Cleopatra's apartment. Nevertheless when the Roman's messengers arrived to direct her to accompany them, they found her dead.

Somehow, she had managed to commit suicide and cheat Octavian of the final victorious climax. How she did it, no one knows, but the tradition arose that she had made use of a poisonous snake (an asp) that had been smuggled to her in a basket of figs, and this is perhaps the most dramatic and best-known incident of her entire glamorous career.

Egypt was made a Roman province and became virtually the personal property of Octavian, who proceeded to establish what we now call the Roman Empire. He made himself the first emperor under the name of Augustus.

Thus came to an end the line of Ptolemies that ruled over Egypt for just three centuries from the time when Ptolemy I Soter first came to Egypt after the death of Alexander the Great.

And yet Cleopatra was not quite the end of the line of Ptolemy Soter. To be sure, Octavian cold-bloodedly ordered her young sons, Caesarion and Alexander Helios, executed lest they serve as nuclei around which revolts would form, but there still remained Cleopatra Selene, the daughter of Antony and Cleopatra.

Octavian didn't feel it necessary to execute a ten-year-old girl, but he decided to marry her off in some far corner of the world, where she would never be a danger. His eye fell upon Juba (yoo'buh), the son of a king of Numidia (a nation that occupied the area of modern-day Algeria). Juba's father, also named Juba, had fought against Julius Caesar, was defeated, and killed himself. His young son was taken to Rome, where he obtained an excellent education and became a scholar. He was completely unworldly and unmilitary — nothing but a dry-as-dust academician.

Juba was the man Octavian's sharp eye judged to be suitable as a living grave for the daughter of Cleopatra. Cleopatra Selene was married to him, and he was reinstated as Juba II in his father's kingdom of Numidia. A few years later, Augustus (as Octavian was now known) decided it would be desirable to annex Numidia as a Roman province, and Juba and his wife were moved westward to Mauretania (equivalent to modern-day Morocco) where their rule as Roman puppets continued peaceably.

They had a son, moreover, whom, out of pride of ancestry, they called Ptolemy, and who is known to history as Ptolemy of Mauretania. This grandson of Cleopatra came to the throne about A.D. 18,* four years after the death of Augustus, and reigned peacefully for twenty-two years.

In 41, Rome came under the rule of its third emperor, Caligula (kuh-lig'yoo-luh), the great-grandson, on his mother's side, of Augustus. He had begun his rule well, but suffered a severe sickness which seemed to have affected his mind and driven him mad. His extravagance grew extreme, and he was

---

* The initials A.D. stand for Anno Domini ("in the year of the Lord") and are applied to years falling after the birth of Jesus. Henceforward in this book, such years will be given without initials. Those that come before the birth of Jesus will still be marked as B.C. ("before Christ").

in dire need of money. As it happened, Ptolemy of Mauretania had a rich treasury which he had carefully husbanded. Caligula called him to Rome on some pretext and had him executed. Mauretania was made a Roman province, and the Mauretanian treasury flowed into Caligula's hands. Thus ended the last Ptolemaic monarch, the grandson of Cleopatra, seventy years after Cleopatra's suicide.

Yet, oddly enough, a particularly famous Ptolemy was still to come. A century after the death of Ptolemy of Mauretania, a great astronomer was working in Egypt. He wrote under the name of Claudius Ptolemaeus and, in English, he is known as Ptolemy.

Virtually nothing is known of him, not when he was born, or when he died, or where he worked, or even whether he was Greek or Egyptian. All we have of him is his astronomical books, and since those are completely in the Greek tradition, it is fair to assume that he was Greek by descent.

He was not any relation to the royal Ptolemies at all, of course. In fact, he may have obtained his name from his place of birth, which, according to the scraps of information we have from later Greek writers, may have been an Egyptian city, Ptolemais Hermii, which was one of those populated in Roman times chiefly by Greeks.

Ptolemy, the astronomer, summarized in his books the work of preceding Greek astronomers and prepared, in thorough form, the theory of the structure of the universe which places the earth at the center and all the rest of the universe — the sun, moon, planets, and stars — in orbits about it.

This is the "Ptolemaic system," and the phrase is known to many today who know nothing of the royal Ptolemies — except perhaps for Cleopatra.

12

ROMAN EGYPT

THE ROMANS

Egypt's passage from Ptolemaic kingdom to Roman province was not as great a wrench as might be imagined. To be sure, the ruler of Egypt now resided in Rome rather than in Alexandria, but to the Egyptian peasant, this was not a very great matter. Rome was no more foreign to him than Alexandria had been, and the Roman emperor no more distant than a pharaoh or a Ptolemy.

To be sure, Augustus and the emperors who followed considered Egypt their personal property to be looted at will, but Egypt was used to that. It had once been the personal property of the pharaohs and later of the Ptolemies, so things were as they had been. If the Romans exacted a stiff toll in the way of taxes, they did so no more than the later Ptolemies had done, and under the Romans (at least at first) governmental efficiency made those taxes easier to pay.

From the standpoint of material prosperity, Egypt benefited greatly. Under the later Ptolemies, the kingdom had decayed, but now the vigorous Roman administration put matters to rights. The intricate canal system upon which the entire agricultural economy depended was completely refurbished. The Romans also built roads, dug cisterns, and reestablished the Red Sea trade. The population of Egypt may then have risen to about seven million, well above the level at the height of the nation's imperial past.

Nor was intellectual progress allowed to languish. The library and Museum of Alexandria continued under government sponsorship under terms no less generous than before. That the priest placed at the head of the institution was appointed by a Roman emperor rather than by a Macedonian Ptolemy made no difference. Alexandria remained the largest city in the Greek world, was exceeded only by Rome itself in size and by no city in wealth and culture.

Besides, Rome as a matter of policy permitted the Egyptians complete religious liberty, and the Roman viceroys who governed the province on the spot gave satisfactory lip service to the native beliefs. That was more satisfying to the Egyptian peasant than anything else could have been. Never did their religion flourish as under the early Romans, never were so many temples built and enriched. Egyptian culture continued without a break, the Greeks continued to confine themselves to Alexandria and a very few other towns, while the presence of the Romans was represented chiefly by the ever-outstretched hand of the tax collector.

Most of all, Egypt under the Romans enjoyed for centuries a profound peace. All the Mediterranean world participated in the felicity of the "pax Romana," or "Roman peace," but nowhere was it deeper or more enduring or more nearly unbroken than in Egypt. There were, of course, occasional famine and plague, now and then skirmishes between opposing armies in disputes over the imperial succession, but in the long view these might be considered minor.

Augustus himself inaugurated the Roman peace as a matter of settled policy. He was interested in expanding the northern reaches of the empire at the expense of barbarous tribes south of the Danube and west of the Elbe, but this was merely a search for easily defended boundaries behind which the empire might rest comfortably. For those civilized portions of the empire which already had reasonable boundaries, there must be no war.

Thus, shortly after the Roman occupation of Egypt, it seemed to the Roman viceroy Gaius Petronius (peh-troh'-nee-us) that it might be a good idea to take on the habits of Pharaonic imperialism . He, too, might invade Nubia, and, in 25 B.C., he did. What's more, he won victories. However, Augustus recalled him. There was nothing Rome needed in Nubia as badly as it needed all the peace it could get. Still, the expedition encouraged trade as did another expedition across the Red Sea into Southwestern Arabia. Under a warlike emperor, that, too, might have led to warfare and an attempt at annexation, but Augustus vetoed any such attempt firmly.

For nearly half a century thereafter, scarcely a whisper of the outside world reached Egypt. The land might have been sleeping in the sun.

In 69, there was a momentary fright. Nero, Rome's fifth emperor, had committed suicide after various army contingents had risen in rebellion against him. No one else of Augustus's line was alive to take the throne, and from different ends of the empire, Roman generals lunged toward Rome, each eager for the gorgeous prize.

Men must have held their breaths. It might have meant a long civil war, with the provinces ravaged by contending armies. It might even have meant the breakup of empire and a return to the anarchy that followed the breakup of Alexander's empire.

Fortunately, the matter was settled almost at once. Vespasian (ves-pay'zhun), a Roman general who happened to be suppressing a rebellion in the east, placed his army in Egypt, thus gaining control of Rome's grain supply. (Throughout the early centuries of empire, Egypt was Rome's breadbasket.) That ensured him the throne after only a few brief skirmishes.

Egypt was fortunate. No harm had been done, and Vespasian's army had passed through the land without doing any damage to speak of.

The second century opened with a line of particularly enlightened emperors on the imperial throne. One of them, Hadrian (hay'dree-an), spent much of his reign as a kind of royal traveler, visiting the various provinces of his empire. He visited Egypt in 130, certainly the most distinguished tourist the ancient land had seen since the landings of Pompey, Julius Caesar, Mark Antony, and Octavian a century and a half before (and *they* had come on business).

Hadrian traveled up and down the Nile and was most flatteringly appreciative of everything. He visited the pyramids and the ruins of Thebes. At Thebes he paused to wonder at the singing Memnon (see page 84). There wasn't much time left to do so. Some decades after Hadrian's visit, the statue's need for repairs could no longer be delayed. Masonry was added, and whatever was done ruined the device that produced the sound. The singing Memnon never sang again.

A sad note to Hadrian's visit is that a young man who was the Emperor's constant and beloved companion, Antinous (an-tin'oh-yoos), drowned in the Nile. (Some suggest he committed suicide.) Hadrian went into extravagant mourning for the youngster and even founded a city (Antinoöpolis), named in his honor, at the site of the drowning. The story struck the romantic imagination of artists, and many paintings and sculptures of the dead favorite were produced.

THE JEWS

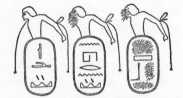

The most violent development within Egypt during the first two centuries of the Roman Empire concerned the fate of its Jews.

The Jews had experienced great prosperity under the Ptolemies, had been granted freedom of worship, and were treated as equals to the Greeks. Never until modern times were the Jews so well treated while a minority in a foreign country (with the possible exception of Moslem Spain in medieval times). And, in return, they contributed to the prosperity and culture of Egypt.

One of the major Alexandrian philosophers, for instance, was Philo Judaeus (figh'loh), or "Philo the Jew." He was born in 30 B.C., the year of Cleopatra's suicide, or possibly a few years later. He was not only thoroughly educated in Jewish culture but in Greek as well, and was therefore equipped to interpret Judaism for the Greek audience of the classical world. His line of thought was so close to that of Plato that he is sometimes called the Jewish Plato.

Unfortunately, the situation was darkening for the Jews in Philo's lifetime. Numbers of them could not reconcile themselves to the loss of their independence and waited constantly for the arrival of a divinely inspired king, or "anointed one." (This last phrase is "Messiah" in Hebrew, "Khristos" in Greek, "Christus" in Latin, and "Christ" in English.) The Messiah would lead them to victory over their enemies and establish an ideal kingdom with himself at its head, with its capital at

Jerusalem, and its sway over all the world. This denouement had been predicted over and over in the Jewish scriptures, and it prevented many Jews from settling down in the world as it was. Indeed, a number of Jews proclaimed themselves as Messiahs now and then, and there were never lacking others to accept this claim and to raise disturbances against the Roman authorities in Judea.

The Alexandrian Jews were less prone to Messianic dreams than their compatriots in Judea, but there was considerable hard feeling between themselves and the Greeks. Their respective ways of life were radically different, and each was particularly hard to live with. The Jews were firm in their contention that only the Jewish God was a true god, and they despised other religions in what must have seemed a most irritating fashion to non-Jews. And the Greeks were firm in their contention that only Greek culture was real culture, and despised other cultures in what must have seemed a most irritating fashion to non-Greeks.

The Greeks, moreover, resented the special privileges the Jews received. The Jews were not required to share in idolatrous sacrifices, pay divine homage to the emperor, or serve in the armed forces where all this was required of the Greeks and Egyptians.

The Roman rulers in Judea were equally irritated at Jewish stubbornness in the matter of religion and in their refusal to accord even the most trifling lip service to the imperial cult. At one point, the mad emperor, Caligula, was determined to have a statue of himself erected in the Temple at Jerusalem, and the Jews prepared to engage in a desperate revolt if that order was carried through.

Philo Judaeus himself (an old man now) headed a delegation to Rome to try to prevent this sacrilege and failed. It was only Caligula's death by assassination and the countermanding of the order by his successor that saved the situation.

But that only postponed the inevitable. In 66 the re-

pressed fury of the Jews at independence denied and taxes exacted broke out in a violent explosion. Roman legions were
rushed into Judea, and for three years a war of unexampled
ferocity raged. The Jews held out with inhuman tenacity,
decimating the Roman troops at great expense to themselves.

The war shook the Roman government to bits, for Nero, who
was emperor at the start of the rebellion, was assassinated,
partly because the ill news from the Jewish front was laid to
his charge. It was the general of the Roman forces in Judea —
Vespasian — who eventually became emperor in Nero's place.
In 70, Judea was finally pacified. Jerusalem was taken and
sacked by Vespasian's son, Titus; the Temple was destroyed
and Judaism was brought down to its lowest state since the time
of Nebuchadrezzar.

The Jews outside Judea did not take part in the revolt and
in most places were treated by the Romans with reasonable jus-
tice. (This is rather remarkable when we think of our own
panicky measures against Americans of Japanese descent in the
months following the attack on Pearl Harbor.)

In Egypt, however, the hard feelings on both sides broke out
beyond control. Riots began and grew bloody. Neither Jews
nor Greeks were free from blame for instigating them, and wild
atrocities were committed on both sides. But, as is almost invariably the case throughout the tragic history of the Jews, it
was the Jews who were in the minority and the Jews, conse-
quently, who suffered the more. The Jewish temple in Alexandria was destroyed, thousands of Jews were killed, and Alexandrian Jewry never recovered.

After these events, the Jews maintained a bitter enmity
against the Roman government and against the Greeks in
Egypt. There was still a strong Jewish colony in Cyrene, and
they thought they saw their chance in 115. The Roman emperor, Trajan (tray'jan), was at that time engaged in warfare far to the east, and, in a last fit of Roman expansion,
brought the Roman legions to the Persian Gulf.

Perhaps false rumors of his death seeped back to Egypt (the Emperor was sixty years old), or perhaps word of a new Messiah had come, but, in any case, the Jews in Cyrene rose in fanatical and suicidal revolt. They massacred those Greeks they could reach and were massacred in turn when the surprised Romans could send troops against them. For two years, the disorders continued, and by 117, the Jews of Egypt were virtually exterminated.

Again, though, the revolt affected Roman history. News of the disorders in Egypt helped decide Trajan to turn back. (His age and the risky length of his communication lines were other factors.) The tide of Roman conquest never reached so far again, and from that day on the fortunes of Rome began to ebb.

Succeeding Trajan was Hadrian, whom I have already mentioned as a kind of imperial tourist. Before visiting Egypt, as I have described, he passed through desolate Judea and was troubled by the veneration paid to the ruins of Jerusalem by the remaining Jews. It seemed to him this could be the occasion of another revolt. He therefore ordered that Jerusalem be rebuilt as a Roman city, to be named Aelia (ee'lee-uh) after his own family name, and that a temple to Jupiter be built on the site of the destroyed Jewish Temple. Jews were absolutely forbidden to enter the new city.

But Hadrian's action merely inspired the rebellion he was trying to prevent. The Jews rose in revolt again, following one more self-proclaimed Messiah. Driven to distraction by the profanation of the holy site of their Temple, they fought for three years, from 132 to 135. It ended with Judea wiped as clean of Jews as Egypt had been.

From then on, the future of Judaism lay with the important Jewish colonies in Babylonia, which had been there since the time of Nebuchadrezzar, and in European colonies which had not taken part in the revolts and which were allowed to live on under the rather suspicious eyes of the Romans.

THE CHRISTIANS

The spread of Greek culture to the peoples of the older civilizations of Africa and Asia after the time of Alexander the
Great was by no means a one-way transmission. The Greeks
came in contact with the foreign cultures and were themselves
attracted to certain aspects thereof despite themselves.

Foreign religions were particularly interesting, for these
were often more colorful, more intensely ritualistic, and more
emotional than the official cults of the Greeks and Romans.
(The Greeks had popular "mystery religions" which dealt
with the agricultural cycle, but these amounted almost to secret societies rather than widespread religions.) The religions
of the Orient began to seep westward.

Once Rome had established its broad dominions across all
the Mediterranean and placed the stamp of peace upon the
world, the intermixture of cultures continued even more rapidly and easily, and what had once been local religions
stretched their influence from end to end of the empire.

In the first couple of centuries, Egypt was the source of one
of the most lively of these spreading religions. The Greek-
tinged Egyptian cult of Serapis (see page 156) spread first to
Greece and then to Rome. Augustus and Tiberius, the first two
emperors, disapproved of it, for they had the futile dream of
restoring the primitive virtues of Rome, but it spread anyway.
By the time of Trajan and Hadrian there was no corner of the
empire that did not have its devotees to this form of religion,
one that stemmed from the time of the pyramid builders and
their predecessors three thousand years before.

Even more attractive was the cult of Isis, the chief goddess
of the Egyptians, pictured as the beautiful "Queen of Heaven."

Her influence began to penetrate Rome as early as the dark days of Hannibal, when Romans felt that defeat was sure without some sort of divine help and were willing to grasp at any straw. Temples to Isis were eventually built, and her rites celebrated, even in the far-off island of Britain, two thousand miles from the Nile.

But if Egypt gave a religion to the world, she also received one from outside — from Judea.

In the last century of Judea's existence, when many proclaimed themselves to be the Messiah for whom the Jewish people waited so hungrily, one arose whose name was Joshua. He was born in the reign of Augustus, no later than 4 B.C., and was accepted as Messiah by his disciples. He was Joshua the Messiah, in other words, or, in the Greek form of the phrase, Jesus Christ. In 29, in the reign of Tiberius, he was executed by crucifixion as a political rebel aspiring to the kingship of the Jews.

The belief in the messiahship of Jesus did not end with his crucifixion, for the story soon spread that he had been resurrected from the dead. To the various sects of Jews that flourished in this period of their history, there was therefore added one more — the followers of the teachings of Jesus Christ, or, as they soon came to be called, the Christians.

In the first few years of this sect's existence, one might not have thought that they would have much of a future except within Judaism, and Judaism itself was not nearly as successful an invader of Greek and Roman thought as were, for instance, the Egyptian rites.

To be sure, there was an attraction about the stern monotheism of the Jews and their elevated moral code that attracted many who were weary of the superstition and sensualism of most of the religions of the day. Therefore, a number of non-Jews (some quite highly placed in the social structure of the empire) adopted Judaism.

Such conversions were not numerous, however, because the

Jews themselves did not choose to make it easy. They would not compromise with the Gentile way of life but insisted on the adoption, in full, of a most complicated set of laws. What's more, they insisted on the Temple at Jerusalem as the one true place of worship and refused to allow converts to participate in the rites of emperor-worship.

The converts to Judaism were thus made subject to an alien nationalism and were cut off from their own society. After the Jewish Rebellion of 66–70, conversion to Judaism began to seem treasonable to many Romans, and they virtually stopped.

Christianity, however, operated under far fewer disadvantages in this respect, thanks, chiefly, to the work of one man. This was Saul (or Paul, as he was later known), a Jew of Tarsus (the city in which Antony first met Cleopatra). He was strongly anti-Christian at first, but was converted and became the most famous and effective of all Christian missionaries.

He addressed himself to the Gentile world and preached a form of Christianity in which Jewish law and Jewish nationalism were abandoned. In its place, he preached a universalism in which all men could be Christian without distinction of nationality or social status. He offered monotheism and lofty morality, without the complicated restrictions of the Mosaic laws, and Gentiles began to flock to Christianity in surprising numbers — in Egypt as well as elsewhere.

Nevertheless, Christians were still forbidden to participate in emperor-worship rituals and were, like Jews generally, liable to suspicion of treason. In 64, during the reign of Nero, Christians in Rome were savagely persecuted in reprisal for a great fire which destroyed the city and which they were accused (falsely, of course) of having set. According to tradition, Paul was executed in Rome not long after this persecution.

Paul's work led to a split within Christianity between those who clung to the Jewish tradition and those who rejected it. The turning point came with the Jewish Rebellion. Those Jews who followed Christian teachings were strongly pacifistic. To them, the Messiah (in the person of Jesus) had already come, and they waited his return. A struggle for the political independence of Judea in the name of anyone but Jesus was therefore meaningless to them. They retired to the hills and took no part in the war. The surviving Jews considered Christians to be traitors, and the conversion of Jews to Christianity virtually halted.

From 70 on, therefore, Christianity became almost entirely Gentile and clearly distinct from Judaism. As it penetrated the Gentile world, it was itself affected, of course, picking up and assimilating Greek philosophies and pagan festivals — all of which made it still more clearly distinct from Judaism.

As late as 95, the Roman emperor Domitian (doh-mish'an), a younger son of Vespasian, enacted measures against Jews and Christians alike, apparently thinking of them as essentially the same. That was probably the last time no distinction was made.

There was a natural rivalry between Judaism and Christianity. Christians regarded Jews with strong disapproval because of their rejection of Jesus as the Messiah and because of the role played by Jewish officials in the Crucifixion (forgetting, sometimes, that Jesus' disciples had also been Jewish). The Jews, on the other hand, regarded Christianity as a heresy, and were embittered by their own disasters and the steadily increasing strength of their rivals.

And yet the bitterness between the two religions might not have grown as intense as it did had it not been for the influence of Egypt. Christianity made its initial strides in an Egypt which had gone through the bitter episodes of the riots in Alexandria and the rebellion in Cyrene. Anti-Jewish feeling in Egypt was stronger than anywhere else in the empire, and that may have contributed to the growth of Gnosticism in the early Church.

Gnosticism was a pre-Christian philosophy that stressed the evil of matter and the world. To the Gnostics, the great abstract God, who was truly real, good, and the omnipotent ruler of all, was a personified Wisdom (or, in Greek, *gnosis,* hence "Gnosticism").

Wisdom was utterly divorced from the universe — unreachable, unknowable. The universe was created by an inferior god, a "demiurge" (from a Greek word meaning "worker for the people" — a practical ruler, an earthly sort of being rather than a divine god above and beyond matter). Because the ability of the demiurge was limited, the world turned out to be evil, as was all in it, including matter itself. The human body was evil, and the human spirit had to turn away from it, and from matter and the world, in an attempt to strive backward to spirit and Wisdom.

Some Gnostics found themselves attracted to Christianity and vice versa. The outstanding leader of this line of thought was Marcion (mahr'shee-on), a native of Asia Minor, and supposedly the son of a Christian bishop.

Writing during the reigns of Trajan and Hadrian, Marcion held that it was the God of the Old Testament who was the demiurge — the evil and inferior being who had created the universe. Jesus, on the other hand, was the representative of the true God, of Wisdom. Since Jesus did not partake of the creation of the demiurge, he was pure spirit, and his human shape and experiences were merely a deliberate illusion taken on to accomplish his purposes.

The Gnostic version of Christianity was quite popular in Egypt for a time, since it fitted in well with the anti-Jewish feeling in the land. It made of the Jewish God a demon, and made of the Jewish scriptures something that was demon-inspired.

Gnostic Christianity, however, did not endure long, for the mainstream of Christianity was firmly set against it. Most of the Christian leaders accepted the God of the Jews and the Old Testament as the God spoken of by Jesus in the New Testament. The Old Testament was accepted as inspired scripture and as the necessary preface to the New Testament.

Nevertheless, though Gnosticism passed away, it left behind some dark strains. There remained in Christianity some feeling concerning the evil of the world and of man, and with it an anti-Jewish feeling that was stronger than before.

What's more, the Egyptians themselves never abandoned a kind of Gnostic view with regard to Jesus. They consistently interpreted the nature of Jesus in such a way as to minimize its human aspect. This not only contributed to a continuing debilitating internal struggle among the Christian leaders but was an important factor, as we shall see, in the eventual destruction of Egyptian Christianity.

Another, more joyful, influence of Egyptian ways of thought on Christianity involved the lovely Isis, Queen of Heaven. She was surely one of the most popular goddesses, not only in Egypt but in the Roman Empire, and it was fairly easy to transfer delight in beauty and gentle sympathy from Isis to the Virgin Mary. The important role played by the Virgin in Christian thought lent to the religion a warmly feminine touch that was absent in Judaism, and certainly the existence of the Isis cult made it easier to add that aspect to Christianity.

This was the easier still because Isis was often shown with the infant Horus on her lap (see page 26). In this aspect Horus, without the hawk head, was known to the Egyptians as Harpechruti ("Horus, the Child"). He had his finger on his lips as a sign of infancy — an approach to sucking his thumb, so to speak. The Greeks mistook the sign as one that asked for quiet, and in their pantheon he became Harpocrates (hahr-pok'ruh-teez), god of silence.

The popularity of Isis and Harpocrates, mother and child, was transferred to Christianity, too, and helped make popular the idea of the Virgin and Christ Child that has captured the imagination of millions upon millions in the Christian centuries.

THE ROMANS IN DECLINE

The days of Trajan and Hadrian and their successors, Antoninus Pius and Marcus Aurelius, marked the high plateau of the Roman Empire — eighty years of relative peace and security.

But that came to an end. Marcus Aurelius's worthless son Commodus (kom'oh-dus) came to the throne in 180 and was assassinated in 192. With that, the empire was thrown into another period in which generals fought for the succession, as in the days after Nero's death — a period which lasted longer this time and cost the empire far more.

The most popular of the competing generals was Pescennius Niger (nigh'jer), who was stationed at Syria. He quickly seized Egypt, Rome's breadbasket, as Vespasian had once done, a century and a quarter before. Niger, however, was no Vespasian. Instead of driving hard for Rome, he remained where he was, comfortable in his popularity and apparently sure that the crown would come his way automatically as Rome felt the pinch of food shortages.

In Rome, however, was the hard-bitten leader of the legions on the Danube, Septimius Severus (se-vee'rus). That general, having secured his status in the capital, lunged eastward, caught Niger in Asia Minor and defeated him. It was Septimius Severus who reigned as Roman emperor.

His elder son, Caracalla (kar"uh-kal'uh), succeeded to the throne in 211 and in the next year, 212, issued a famous edict whereby all the free inhabitants of the empire were made Roman citizens. Native Egyptians who had never been welcomed previously into the inner circle of Greek and Roman superiority suddenly found themselves Roman citizens on a plane of equality with the proudest men of Alexandria and Rome. Egyptians were raised to the rank of Senators and welcomed into the Roman Senate (which, however, no longer had any political power at all and was nothing more than a social club, really).

But times were growing hard for Rome. A serious plague had depopulated the empire in the time of Marcus Aurelius and economic decay was far advanced. The money required to run the government was progressively hard to squeeze out of the increasingly impoverished nation, and Caracalla's action might have been inspired by more than idealism. There was an inheritance tax applicable only to citizens, and by Caracalla's edict it became applicable to all free men, and much additional revenue was produced.

Caracalla was the first emperor, after Hadrian, to visit Egypt. The occasions were entirely different, however. Hadrian, nearly a century before, had been an interested tourist, wandering about over an empire at peace. Caracalla lived in a harsher time, when enemies to the north and east were attempting to tear at the Roman frontiers. He was in Egypt on his way to the eastern fighting zones and, no doubt, was in a most unpleasant mood.

Under the pressure of the tight money squeeze (made worse by the wars), Caracalla ended the state support of the scholars attached to the Museum at Alexandria.

Perhaps this was not entirely without justification from Caracalla's point of view. The Museum had been fading for over a century and had contributed little of value to the world after the year 100. The last scientist in Egypt of any importance had been Ptolemy the astronomer (see page 185), and his contribution had consisted chiefly of summarizing the work of earlier astronomers. Perhaps Caracalla felt the Museum was moribund and did not merit the sums expended upon it, sums that a declining empire could ill afford. Still, cutting off the support certainly made it unlikely that the Museum would ever manage to effect a restoration of vitality.

Caracalla's action undoubtedly offended scholars everywhere, and the historians of the time are most hostile to him and accuse him of all possible crimes and savagery. He is supposed to have ordered Alexandria to be sacked and thousands of its citizens killed in reprisal for some trifling offense. Undoubtedly, the tale is exaggerated.

But if science declined in Alexandria, learning itself did not. A new kind of learned man arose, the Christian theologian, and Alexandria, following this line, *still* led the world in thought.

In the first century after Paul, Christianity spread chiefly among the lower classes and among women; that is, among the poor and uneducated. The educated and well-to-do classes remained resistant. To those who had been trained in the subtlety and intellectual rarefaction of the great Greek philosophers, the Jewish scriptures seemed barbarous, the teachings of Jesus naïve, and the preachings of most Christians laughably ignorant. It was the task of the Alexandrian theologians to combat this point of view.

Actively engaged in this combat was Clement, a priest born in Athens about 150, who taught in Alexandria. He was trained in Greek philosophy as well as in Christian doctrine, and he was able to interpret the latter in terms of the former in such a way as to make Christianity respectable (even if not always convincing) to the cleverest Greek. What's more, he reinterpreted Christian doctrine so as to make it less of a social revolutionary doctrine, and devised arguments to show that rich men, also, could find their way to salvation. In addition, he was a potent force against the dying notions of Gnosticism.

Clement was, of course, a Greek, who happened to teach in

Egypt. Following him, though, and possibly a pupil of his, was one who, apparently, was actually an Egyptian. This was Origen (or'ih-jen).

He was born in Alexandria about 185 and may have been of pagan parents, for his name is Greek for "son of Horus." Like Clement, he mingled much of Greek philosophy with his Christianity, and was able to take up the cudgels against pagan philosophers on equal footing.

He entered the lists against a Greek writer named Celsus, a Platonist pagan philosopher who had written a cool and un-impassioned book against Christianity. It was the first pagan book to be forced to treat Christianity seriously — a result, perhaps, of Clement's labors. Origen's retort in a book entitled *Against Celsus* was the most complete and thorough defense of Christianity published in ancient times.

Celsus' book no longer survives but about nine-tenths of it is quoted in Origen's book, which does survive. It is only thanks to Origen that the views of his adversary are still known.

Thus Egypt contributed in very important fashion to the in-tellectualization of Christianity and to the task of making it acceptable to men of classical learning. In the early centuries of Christianity, indeed, Alexandria was the most important Christian center in the world.

But times continued to grow worse. In 222, Alexander Se-verus, a grandnephew of Septimius Severus, became emperor. He was a kindly but weak ruler, dominated by his mother. He was assassinated in 235.

What followed was a veritable orgy of emperors. General after general claimed the title and was then quickly killed by competing claimants or by barbarian invaders. Despite the stolid bravery of the legions, so much energy was consumed in internal fighting that the German barbarians in the north flooded into the empire, and fragments here and there set up independent governments.*

* See *The Roman Empire*, Houghton-Mifflin, 1967.

This was the chance for Persia.

That land had experienced a rebirth since Alexander the Great had laid her low six centuries before. After the time of Antiochus III, the eastern provinces of the Seleucid Empire had achieved a permanent independence and made up a kingdom known to the Romans as Parthia (a word that is really a form of "Persia").

For over three centuries, Rome had faced Parthia in a see-saw battle that in the long run gained nothing but blood and ruin for both sides. Then, in 228, while Alexander Severus was on the throne, a new dynasty succeeded to the rule of the Parthian territories, a dynasty that traced its birth from a Persian chieftain named Sassan. The dynasty is spoken of, therefore, as the Sassanids (sas'uh-nidz).

In the time of Roman anarchy that followed the death of Alexander Severus, the Persians seized their opportunity and pushed strongly westward. In 260, they met the Roman armies at Edessa (ee-des'uh), just east of the upper Euphrates. The Romans were led by their emperor, Valerian (vuh-lee'ree-an).

Exactly what happened we don't know, but apparently the Romans, inexpertly led, were maneuvered into a trap, were forced to accept defeat, and Valerian himself was taken prisoner. It was the first time in Roman history that an emperor was captured by an enemy, and the clang of doom was deafening. The Persian army marched exuberantly into Asia Minor.

And then a surprising thing happened. In Syria, about 130 miles from the sea and near the eastern border of the empire, was the desert town of Palmyra (pal-migh'ruh). It served as a trading center which grew fat and prosperous during the peaceful times when Roman power was at its peak.

At the time of Valerian's defeat, Palmyra was under the rule of Odenathus (od"eh-nay'thus), a chieftain of Arab descent. He did not choose to exchange the loose and beneficial sway of Rome for the closer and possibly harsher Persian sway. He therefore attacked Persia.

He made no attempt to meet Persia's armies (which were far to his west) but stabbed, instead, eastward and southward toward Ctesiphon (tes'ih-fon), the lightly guarded Persian capital. The chagrined Persians had to retreat, and their chance to smash Rome was gone.

The grateful Romans loaded Odenathus with titles and made him virtually an independent king. But royalty was an insecure profession in those days, and in 267 Odenathus was assassinated.

Into the empty place sprang his wife Zenobia (zeh-noh'-bee-uh), a woman as ambitious and forceful as Cleopatra. She claimed all her husband's titles for her son and made ready to seize the emperorship of Rome itself. In 270, her armies took over Asia Minor, and that winter she marched into Egypt.

The surprised Egyptians found a hostile army on the Sinai doorstep, something they had not seen since Augustus had appeared there three centuries before. They made no resistance.

Once in control of the easternmost third of the empire, Zenobia proclaimed herself and her son co-emperors of Rome.

But by now another emperor was in power in Rome itself. He was Aurelian (aw-ree'lee-an), one of the more capable holders of the throne during the period of anarchy. Hastily and forcefully, he led his army into Asia Minor. At once, Zenobia's troops fell back on their home base, evacuating Egypt. By 273, Aurelian had completely mopped up the Palmyrene army, had taken Palmyra, and ended the threat. Zenobia was less fortunate than Cleopatra. She was captured and taken back to Rome to grace Aurelian's triumph.

Aurelian was not quite through once Zenobia was made captive. A rich Egyptian named Firmus took advantage of the confusion to declare himself emperor. On the way back from Palmyra, Aurelian knifed into Egypt, took Alexandria, and had Firmus crucified.

Egypt, recovering from the fright of the double invasion,

first by Zenobia and then by Aurelian, found herself essentially unharmed and went back to the even tenor of her ways.

But something was gone. In the brief fracas between Firmus and Aurelian, the buildings of the Museum at Alexandria had been destroyed. The greatest achievement of the Ptolemies — something that had endured nearly six centuries and outlasted the dynasty itself by three — was gone.

And yet not all gone, either. The countless papyrus rolls of the library itself still existed, and with them, there remained the accumulated knowledge and learning of a thousand years of Greek culture.

13

CHRISTIAN EGYPT

PERSECUTION

The growth of Christianity in the early centuries of the empire was not entirely smooth, not entirely without opposition. There were competing religions: the official imperial cult, the Greek mystery religions, the Egyptian rites of Serapis and Isis. All existed and continued to exist.

Stronger than any of these was Mithraism, a religion of Persian origin that was, in essence, a form of sun worship. Traces of it began to appear in Rome in the time of Augustus and Tiberius. A century later, when Trajan and Hadrian ruled, it had become prominent indeed, perhaps the most popular of the new religions. Anyone surveying the Roman Empire about 200 might well have decided that if any single religion was going to become dominant in the realm, it would be Mithraism and not Christianity.

But Mithraism had a fatal flaw. It allowed only men to participate in its rites. Women, excluded from it, often turned

Christian, and it was they who brought up the children and influenced those children in the choice of a religion.

There was competition, too, from strengthened versions of the old Greek philosophies, and here an important role was played by Plotinus (ploh-tigh'nus), a man of Egyptian birth. He was born in 205 at Lycopolis, a city only about fifty miles south of where Ikhnaton's ill-fated city of Akhetaton had once stood. He studied in Alexandria and evolved a system of philosophy based upon the teachings of the Athenian philosopher Plato, but one which was extended much further in the direction of the new religions. It was, in fact, a kind of fusion of the rational Greek and the mystical East, a fusion that came to be called Neo-Platonism. This was the most popular and important of the pagan philosophies in the next couple of centuries.

Of all the religions and philosophies of the empire, Christianity was the most exclusive (if we ignore Judaism, which was by now quite unimportant). All the rest lacked any real desire to impose themselves by force on the others but were content to compete good-humoredly in the open marketplace of ideas. Opposed to all of them, however, was Christianity, which refused any compromise and saw itself as the one true religion, facing a pack of demon-inspired falsehoods.

It was very irritating to non-Christians that the Christians' hostility never prevented them from appropriating what was useful from other religions. Thus, Mithraism celebrated December 25 as the birth of the sun, a most popular and joyous festival. The Christians adopted it as the birthday of the Son, and it became Christmas. Christianity also adopted into its own philosophy much that was Neo-Platonic in nature.

Furthermore, Christians in the time of the early empire were strongly pacifistic. They refused to fight for the cause of pagan emperors (especially since, as soldiers, they would be required to participate in emperor worship). They maintained instead that if only the empire would turn Christian, war would disappear, and an ideal society would fill the land.

All of this made the Christians increasingly unpopular with men of all other beliefs (which we can lump together as "pagan").

There had been early periods of persecution of Christians, notably under Nero and Domitian. These had been relatively short-lived, however, and had not done much harm. Now in the period of anarchy that followed the assassination of Alexander Severus, when the empire was in so much trouble, the search for a scapegoat was intensified and who would serve the role better than a group of unpopular extremists who went about spreading radical pacifistic notions?

About 250, the emperor Decius (dee'shus) therefore instituted the first thoroughgoing, empire-wide persecution of Christianity, and for nearly a decade, Christians went through a serious crisis. Two things saved them.

First, Christianity was so fanatically set on the sole truth of its beliefs that many Christians were quite willing to die for them, sure of earning eternal happiness in heaven in return for a martyr's death on earth. The firm constancy of so many Christians in the face of torture and death was a most impressive thing, and many who witnessed it must have been convinced of the value of a belief that could win such loyalty. The persecutions undoubtedly made more Christians than they killed.

Second, the persecutions were never kept up sufficiently long and in sufficiently thorough a manner to wipe out the Christians. Always, the persecuting emperor was eventually followed by one of gentler mind, and always harsh treatment in one province might be counterbalanced by relative leniency in another.

Thus, in 259, Gallienus (gal-ee-ee'nus) became emperor. He was a disciple of Plotinus, who was then teaching in Rome, and Neo-Platonism preached toleration. Plotinus felt that truth could not be imposed by force and that falsehood must wither under the force of reasoned argument. The pressure on Christianity was therefore relieved.

The decade of persecution left its mark, though. Many bishops were killed, and in Alexandria, Origen was treated with such violence that, although not killed outright, his health was fatally impaired. He retired to Tyre, where he died in 254.

Furthermore, after every period of relaxation, another period of persecution would come, and over a period of nearly a century, Christians could never feel really safe. In Egypt, one response was made to this period of persecution that introduced an important thread into the Christian way of life.

It was the response of withdrawal.

There was precedence for this. Judaism had always had a streak of asceticism, and the austerities that some felt were necessary in the true worship of God were best conducted away from the temptations of the world. There were Jews who had retired into isolation so they might lead a frugal and self-denying life dedicated to the worship of God. They might do so in solitary fashion, as Elijah did in the ninth century B.C., or in groups and communities, as was true of the Essenes in Roman times.

During periods of persecution, there would be these examples before Christian eyes. In fact, Elijah's retreat was in part to save himself from the persecutions of Jezebel, queen of Israel, and the Essenes found safety in isolation when Maccabees, Herods, and Romans made life difficult for the stricter Jewish sects.

Why should not Christians retire, too, then? The world was wicked; it was better abandoned. To live in the world was to be constantly exposed to the tortures of pagan persecutors and to the temptation to abandon Christianity to save one's life. In the wilderness, one would be left alone to save one's soul.

In Egypt, particularly, the climate was such as to make solitary retirement more attractive than elsewhere. The desert was nearby, solitary and peaceful, and there one would find no frigid winter, no howling rainstorms or blizzards. Life could be simple and untroubled.

The first important such recluse was an Egyptian named Anthony. He was born about 250, and when he was twenty years old he decided to practice asceticism. By 285, he came to the conclusion that this was only practical away from the continuing temptations of society, and he retired to the desert.

The fame of his piety and holiness spread, and many decided to imitate him. Each year additional numbers fled away from the pagan world and toward the Christian God till the Egyptian desert was virtually peppered with solitary hermits practicing austerities. None achieved the fame of Anthony, however, and legends multiplied concerning the temptations to which he was subjected by the devil and over which he rose triumphant. He was reputed to have reached the great age of one hundred and five before dying.

Anthony was the first Christian monk, from a Greek word meaning "alone," or "hermit," from a Greek word meaning "desert." The word "monk" continued to be applied to those who retired from the world, even when they did so in communities and were no longer "alone."

Anthony may thus be considered to have helped found the institution of "monasticism," which was to play so important a role in later Christian history — and thus one more aspect of Christianity had its origin in Egypt.

THE ARIANS

The Roman Empire received a new lease of life when a rough and capable soldier, Diocletian (digh″oh-klee′shun), became emperor in 284. He overhauled the machinery of em-

pire and abolished the last traces of the old republican system
to which Augustus and his successors had paid lip service. In
its place, he established an absolute monarchy.

What's more, he accepted a co-emperor, and both he and
that partner appointed two "Caesars" as assistants. There were
four men, therefore, sharing the administrative and military
duties of the empire. Diocletian, intent on facing the Persian
menace, kept the Asian provinces and Egypt under his own
direct control and established his capital at Nicomedia (nik"-
oh-mee'dee-uh), a city in northwestern Asia Minor.

The bad customs of the period of anarchy persisted, however. Generals still felt they could have themselves declared
emperor by their troops whenever the mood struck them. A
general in Egypt, named Achilleus (uh-kil'yoos), had himself
declared emperor in 295. That was in Diocletian's own territory, and he himself led an army into Egypt. Alexandria was
placed under siege for eight months before it was finally taken
and Achilleus executed.

In 303, Diocletian initiated the last, and, in some respects,
most severe of the general persecutions of Christians. This
was carried on by Diocletian's successor in the east, Galerius
(guh-lee'ree-us), and, to a lesser extent, by his successor, Licinius (ligh-sin'ee-us).

The rulers in the western half of the empire were generally
more sympathetic to Christianity. In 306, Constantine I came
to power over sections of the west. That power gradually increased until, by 312, he was in complete control of the entire
western half of the empire. Constantine was a shrewd poli-
tician who saw that if he could gain the support of the Christians (now making up a strong minority of the population —
and by far the most active and vocal portion), he would be
well on his way to supreme power. He therefore forced Licinius, then in control of the eastern half of the empire, to join
him in an "Edict of Toleration" whereby equal rights were proclaimed for all religions.

Licinius observed that edict rather poorly, but by 324, he was finally defeated by Constantine I, who, as he had planned, had the full and enthusiastic support of the Christians of the realm. It was yet to be half a century before the Christian victory was complete, but the period of outright persecution had passed. (Thirteen years later, on his deathbed, Constantine I had himself baptized so that he became the first Christian emperor.)

But if the period of persecution by pagans had passed, there remained the danger of internal quarrels. There had always been differences of opinion among Christians. Even Paul's epistles written at the very beginning of the spread of Christianity had to deal with such differences. During the period when Christianity as a whole had been in constant danger of persecution, however, such differences could lead to angry words, but nothing more. But once the Roman emperors became Christian, they could take one side against another, and the side out of favor might then face the power of the state. Thus, if Christians generally were no longer persecuted by pagans, some Christians, nevertheless, continued to be persecuted by other Christians.

Alexandria, as the chief center of Christian thought, played an important part in these internal disputes. This was true, for instance, in the time of Constantine I, when a bitter wrangle arose over the question of the nature of Jesus.

The question was whether Jesus had a divine aspect or not. One viewpoint, which might be called *unitarian,* was that Jesus was not divine at all. This held that there was but one God, the God of the Old Testament. Jesus was a created being, as was everything in the universe *but* God. Jesus might be the greatest and best of men, the holiest of the prophets, the most divinely inspired teacher, but he was nevertheless not God.

The other viewpoint was that God had three aspects, all of which were equal in every way, and that all three aspects had always existed. These were the Father, an aspect which manifested itself in the Creation particularly; the Son, an aspect which manifested itself in the bodily form of Jesus; and the Holy Spirit (or Holy Ghost) which manifested itself at various times by way of ordinary men, inspiring them to actions of which they would have been incapable without divine help. The three aspects of God are referred to as the Trinity (from a Latin word meaning "threesome"), and belief in these three equal aspects can be called *trinitarianism.*

The chief advocate of the unitarian view was an Alexandrian priest named Arius. So firm was his advocacy of this view that it is usually known as Arianism after him, while those who uphold the view are Arians.

Despite the advocacy of this view by an Alexandrian, the most important stronghold of Arianism in the time of Constantine I was in Asia Minor. Egypt was still touched by memories of Gnosticism in which Jesus was spirit, not matter (see page 197). How then could he be entirely human? He *had* to be divine as well as human.

Most of the Alexandrian priesthood were therefore trinitarians, and Alexander, the bishop of Alexandria, was constantly being pushed to take strong action against the disturbing priest. By 323, Alexander had called together a gathering of bishops (a "synod") who officially condemned the Arian view, but Arius would not accept the decision.

It was just at this time that Constantine was making himself supreme over the entire empire, and there was a movement to appeal the matter to him. (The bishops might denounce, but it was the emperor who had the army that could put iron teeth into the denunciation.) Constantine was anxious to rule in the matter. He knew nothing about the theological points at dispute and didn't care, but he understood perfectly well the political dangers. He depended on the Christians of the empire to support him in return for his own pro-Christian attitude. But if the Christians were going to war among themselves, their support would not be much good. In fact, rivals to his throne might always bid for the support of one faction by promising to suppress the other.

In 325, Constantine I therefore called a huge gathering of bishops to the city of Nicaea (nigh-see′uh), about thirty-five miles south of his capital at Nicomedia, and ordered them to settle the matter once and for all. This was the first "ecumenical council" — the first, that is, that was "worldwide" — for it was attended by bishops from all over the empire, rather than merely from a province or two.

The dispute *was* settled, at least on paper. The Council voted the adoption of a formula ("the Nicene Creed") to which all Christians were to adhere, and this accepted the trinitarian viewpoint. Arius and several of the most inveterate Arians were sent into exile.

The trinitarian view was, in theory, accepted by the entire Church, the Universal Church, or, to use the Greek term for "universal," the Catholic Church. Those who upheld the trinitarian view are therefore usually termed Catholics, and Arianism is generally pictured as a heresy (a minority view that is not officially accepted by the Church).

By 325, then, Alexandria seemed to have reached a new peak of importance. Rome itself had to take a back seat. The half-century period of anarchy preceding Diocletian's accession to the throne had led to a serious decline in the wealth and prestige of the city of Rome. In 271, Aurelian had to have walls built around Rome — a tacit admission that the city was no longer certain of safety from enemies.

Then, when Diocletian established his capital at Nicomedia, Rome lost further in prestige, for it was no longer the home of the emperor. Nor did Nicomedia gain in proportion. Despite the presence of the emperor, it remained a minor provincial town.

That left Alexandria without a peer. It was the great city of the empire, the center from which influence radiated, the leader of Christian theology, the force behind the trinitarian victory at Nicaea. Never had Alexandria and Egypt so seemed to dominate the world since the days of Ptolemy III six centuries before.

CONSTANTINOPLE

And then Constantine I did something that dealt a staggering blow to Alexandria's position. He decided to establish a new capital. The site he chose was on the European side of the Bosporus, the narrow strait that separates Europe from Asia Minor, and on which the Greek city Byzantium had been standing for nearly a thousand years.

Constantine spent four years building his new capital, taking every pain to see that it was large, lavish, and luxurious; rifling the cities of the empire for artistic masterpieces to shift to the new capital; encouraging the bureaucracy and aristocracy of Rome to come to the "new Rome." In 330, the new city was dedicated and named Constantinople ("Constantine's city"). Alexandria suddenly found itself second again, for the new city gained rapidly in wealth, splendor, and population, and soon became what it was to remain for nearly a thousand years — the greatest city of the Christian world.

Alexandria's position became harder to bear than it had been in the past. To be second to Rome, a distant, non-Greek city, renowned for war rather than science, for muscle rather than mind, was one thing. To be second to Constantinople — also Greek-speaking — was quite another.

Much of the religious dispute that followed was made the more bitter because of the rivalry between the cities of Constantinople and Alexandria. This held particularly for the Arian controversy, which had not, after all, been settled at Nicaea.

The Arians had been defeated at Nicaea, but they had not been wiped out. A number of bishops in Asia Minor continued to preach Arian doctrine. Outstanding among these was Eusebius (yoo-see'bee-us), who was bishop of Nicomedia, where Constantine's court sat prior to the establishment of Constantinople as the capital.

Eusebius had the ear of the court, and his influence over Constantine and others of the royal family increased steadily. Constantine soon came to regret the manner in which he had given the bishops free reign at Nicaea. He clearly saw that the bishops' decision did not, of itself, settle matters and sway Christendom generally. Indeed, the majority of Christians in Asia Minor, the province nearest himself, remained Arian, and Constantine did not wish to put himself in opposition to this majority.

In 335, he therefore called together a synod of bishops (*not* an ecumenical council) at Tyre and had them reverse the decision at Nicaea. Arius was reinstated in his post (but died before that decision could be implemented), and Arianism suddenly gained in power.

But then, neither did Catholicism die out because of a decision by a set of bishops. There remained Alexandria.

A decade before, attending the Council of Nicaea as the private secretary of Bishop Alexander of Alexandria, had been a young priest, Athanasius (ath"uh-nay'shus). In 328, he succeeded Alexander as bishop and quickly became the most vocal and forceful of all the advocates of the trinitarian doctrine of Catholicism. As a result of the decision of the synod of Tyre, Athanasius was sent into exile, but that did not stop his voice, and even at long distance, it spoke with the weight and influence of Alexandria and Egypt behind it.

When Constantine I died, in 337, his three sons succeeded to the rule over various portions of the empire. Constantius II (kon-stan'shee-us), the middle son, ruled in the east. He was a convinced and thoroughgoing Arian and, in 339, he made the arch-Arian Eusebius bishop of Constantinople. Naturally, Eusebius, and his successors in that post, felt that as bishop of the capital city of Christendom, they had every right to consider themselves as the head of the Church. (This same view was held, for the same reasons, by the bishop of Rome, and the argument between the two finally led to a split among Christians that has endured to the present day.)

Eusebius and Athanasius were separated, therefore, not only by a doctrinal dispute but by a real struggle for power. While Constantius II reigned, Athanasius remained in exile for the most part. By 353, when Constantius' brothers were dead and other pretenders to the crown defeated and killed, Constantius II ruled alone over the entire empire, and it looked as though Arianism might win out completely.

But Constantius could not live forever. He died in 361 and was succeeded by his cousin Julian, who (despite his Christian education as a child) declared himself a pagan. He at once established complete religious freedom in the empire, partly out of idealism, and partly because he felt that the best way to ruin Christianity was to allow the various sects to tear each other apart at will.

Matters did not turn out as Julian had hoped. He reigned less than two years, dying in battle against the Persians in 363. Then, too, the various Christian sects, shocked at this sudden revival of paganism, muted their own quarrels and tended to unite against the common enemy.

Julian's short reign did, however, serve to break the stranglehold of the Arians. Under Julian's edict, the Catholic bishops could return from exile and resume their posts. Even Athanasius had another period of return to Alexandria (though not for long). Once the Catholics had been reinstated, it was difficult to remove them, for succeeding emperors were never as strongly Arian as Constantius II had been.

By the time Athanasius died, in 373, the Catholic doctrine was clearly headed for victory. That victory came in 379, when Theodosius I became emperor. He was as convinced a Catholic as Constantius II had been an Arian. In 381, he called a second ecumenical council, this one at Constantinople.

Arianism was again outlawed, and this time the full vigor of the state stood behind the decision. Arians and all other heretics were forbidden to assemble, and their churches were seized. There was to be no longer any freedom of worship for any Christians but those who adhered to the official position of the Catholic Church.

Alexandria had won again, this time over Constantinople itself, at least within the boundaries of the empire. (Arianism continued to exist for nearly three centuries among some of the German tribes who were soon to flood into the Roman dominions.)

Theodosius I was as hard upon the pagan remnants within the empire as he was upon Christian heretics. In 382, Theodosius' co-emperor in the west, Gratian (gray'shan), had removed the pagan altar of victory in the Senate, had put a halt to the institution of the Vestal Virgins who had tended their sacred flame for over a thousand years, and had given up the pagan high-priestly title of Pontifex Maximus. And, in 394, Theodosius himself put an end to the Olympian Games which had endured as one of the great religious festivals of the pagan Greeks for nearly twelve centuries. Then, in 396, invading barbarians (who happened to be Arian Christians) destroyed the temple to Ceres near Athens and put an end to the Eleusinian Mysteries, Greece's most revered mystery religion.

Yet somehow, some sorry remnants of paganism lingered. In

Athens, pagan Greek philosophers still taught to dwindling audiences at the Academy, the school founded by Plato himself shortly after the close of Athens' Golden Age.

Nor did the age-old religions of Egypt escape. Little by little, the Egyptian population had made the switch from Osiris to Jesus, from Isis to Mary, from the numerous gods to the numerous saints. The old temples fell into neglect or were converted to churches. The note of doom sounded most clearly in 391, when the Serapion itself was destroyed in Alexandria under imperial order, after six centuries of existence.

Alexandria was to suffer even worse. The last important pagan philosopher teaching in Alexandria was Hypatia (high-pay'shee-uh). She was considered a danger by Cyril, who became bishop of Alexandria in 412, partly because her popularity was attracting too many students to her lectures on pagan philosophy, and partly because she was a friend of one of the secular officials of Egypt, an official with whom Cyril was at odds.

It was supposedly at Cyril's instigation that a mob of monks brutally killed Hypatia in 415 and then went on to destroy much of the Alexandrian library as well. The manner in which certain factions within the Church despised and denigrated worldly learning was an ominous foretaste of the darkness that was soon to follow and out of which mankind was so painfully to have to climb.

Yet even in Cyril's time, one last bit of the ancient religion persisted.

Far to the south, near the First Cataract, on the island of Philae (figh'lee), a temple to Isis had been built by Nectanebo II, the last native king of Egypt, seven centuries before. It had been rebuilt by Ptolemy II Philadelphus and again repaired in the time of Cleopatra.

There, while the world turned Christian, the fading smile of the Queen of Heaven could still be seen, and the age-old rites were still performed in secret far from the center of Christian power.

THE MONOPHYSITES

But Alexandria continued to be the great rival of Constantinople, and religious strife between them continued.

In 398, for instance, John Chrysostom (kris'us-tam) was appointed bishop of Constantinople. His second name, which means "golden-mouth" in Greek, was given him shortly after his death, in memory of his eloquence.

This eloquence was used unsparingly in the denunciation of luxury and immorality, and he spared no one, not even the empress. Annoyed, the empress laid plans for Chrysostom's exile, and here she found her natural ally in Theophilus (thee-of'ih-lus), who was then bishop of Alexandria, and the predecessor of Cyril. Together, though with some difficulty, they achieved their purpose, and Chrysostom died in exile. Alexandria won again.

That, however, was a matter of personalities. More dangerous disputes of a doctrinal nature involved the two cities.

In 428, Nestorius, a priest of Syrian extraction, became bishop of Constantinople under the emperor Theodosius II. Under this emperor, Arians and other heretics of the past were subjected to nothing less than the death penalty — but what about new heresies?

Nestorius himself sparked a new dispute over the nature of Jesus. It was granted that Jesus had a divine aspect, now that Arianism had been totally defeated, but there was still a human aspect to his character, and the question arose as to what the relationship might be between those two aspects.

Nestorius appears to have taught the doctrine that the two were rather separate and that Mary was the mother only of the human aspect, not of the divine aspect. She might be called Mother of Christ but not Mother of God. In this view, which came to be called Nestorianism, Jesus seemed almost to be a human being in whom an aspect of God had settled, using the human being as a tool.

This was at least a partial step back toward Arianism, and once again it was Alexandria that led the fight against this view. Cyril of Alexandria was an unrelenting enemy. Theodosius II called a third ecumenical council in 431, which met at Ephesus (ef'uh-sus), a city on the Asia Minor coast. It was a wild council with different groups of bishops seizing control at different times. In the main, though, Cyril dominated its proceedings, and the views of Nestorius were denounced and outlawed. Nestorius himself was removed from his post and sent into exile in upper Egypt.

For the third time, at three successive ecumenical councils, Alexandria had won.

Nevertheless, Nestorianism continued to exist in Asia Minor and in Syria, and eventually, when official force against it grew too great to endure, its believers went into exile eastward into Persia. They were eventually instrumental in spreading Greek culture as far east as China.

But now a priest at Constantinople, named Eutyches (yoo'-tih-keez), swung to the opposite view. He maintained that Jesus had only one nature that was wholly divine, having completely absorbed the human. This is taken as the founding of the "Monophysite" (Greek for "one nature") view, one which received a sympathetic hearing in Egypt, although it was spurned in Constantinople.

Cyril of Alexandria died in 444, and his successor was strongly Monophysite in his beliefs. The dispute had grown as serious and dangerous as the Arian question had been a century before, and Theodosius II did not know how to handle it.

Theodosius II died in 450, however, and his successor, Marcian (mahr'shan), was strongly in favor of the two-nature doctrine. He called the fourth ecumenical council in 451 at Chalcedon (kal'seh-don), a suburb of Constantinople, just across the strait in Asia.

There, at last, Alexandria lost. The two-nature doctrine, upheld by both Constantinople and Rome, became part of the Catholic dogma, and the one-nature view of Monophysitism was declared a heresy. Eutyches was sent into exile.

Alexandria did not take its defeat with good grace, however. Stubbornly, it adhered to Monophysitism, all the more so because Constantinople was opposed to it.

The religious disunity of the empire (which persisted despite ecumenical council after ecumenical council) was made all the more dangerous by the military disasters that struck the empire after the death of Theodosius I.

After his death, his two young sons succeeded, one in the east and one in the west, and the empire was never thereafter completely reunited. There were two halves in actual practice, usually referred to as the East Roman Empire and the West Roman Empire. Rulers such as Theodosius II and Marcian, who presided over the third and fourth ecumenical councils, respectively, served as East Roman emperors. Egypt was, of course, part of the East Roman Empire.

It was the West Roman Empire that bore the brunt of the disaster. In the century that followed the death of Theodosius I, the Huns and various German tribes marched and countermarched over the European provinces of the empire. One German tribe, the Vandals, even crossed the narrow strait south of Spain, entered Africa, and established a kingdom centered about Carthage. Some of the provinces of the East Roman Empire were also temporarily invaded. Egypt, however, remained untouched, just about the only province to remain entirely at peace during this catastrophic century.

In 476, the West Roman Empire came to an end, in the sense that the last ruler recognized as emperor was deposed.

The East Roman Empire remained intact, however, and for a while it even seemed that she might win back all that was lost. A strong and capable emperor, Justinian, came to the throne in 527, and he sent his armies westward to win back the barbarian-occupied provinces there.

Those armies did succeed in destroying the Vandal kingdom in North Africa and in reuniting that region with the East Roman Empire. Italy also was recaptured, and part of Spain. For a moment, it almost looked as though the barbarian tide would, as in Aurelian's time, two and a half centuries before, be turned back.

And yet conquests in the west merely sharpened Justinian's problems with respect to religion. Justinian was an ardent Catholic, and under him the final vestiges of paganism disappeared. In 529, he closed the Academy at Athens, after its nearly nine centuries of existence, and the sorrowing philosophers went into Persian exile. It was in this century also that the temple of Isis at Phylae was finally shut down and the old Egyptian religion died, nearly four thousand years after the time of Menes. Justinian dealt harshly, too, with Jews and with the heresies of the past.

But what about the Monophysites? Monophysitism had been growing ever stronger in Egypt and in Syria, and Justinian was torn. His wife, Theodora, was strongly Monophysite in sympathy, but he himself was not. Furthermore, his new conquests in the west were unshakably anti-Monophysite, and they demanded stern measures against the heresy.

Justinian wanted to do nothing to alienate the western provinces, rewon so recently and with such difficulty, but he did not want to weaken his hold on the important and wealthy provinces of Egypt and Syria, either.

In 553, he summoned a fifth ecumenical council, which met at Constantinople, and there he attempted to placate the Monophysites somewhat and work out a reunion. Imperial force was used to persuade the bishops of Alexandria and of Rome to agree to the decisions of the council, but that did no good. The main body of Christians in the west and the main body of Christians in Egypt and Syria were alike opposed to any compromise.

Indeed, Justinian's effort served merely to promote Monophysitism as a national movement in Egypt and Syria. In Egypt, for instance, where the Greeks of Alexandria and elsewhere moved toward the Constantinopolitan position under imperial pressure, the Egyptians themselves clung ever more fiercely to Monophysitism. They even began to use their own language (with characters borrowed from the Greek) in their devotions, spurning the Greek of Constantinople and Alexandria.

The native language has come to be called Coptic (a distortion of "Egyptic"), and so Egypt's Monophysite Church is sometimes referred to as the Coptic Church.

In a way, the Coptic Church was evidence of Egyptian resurgence. Through all the long centuries of foreign domination, Egypt had stubbornly clung to her identity by keeping her own culture and religion. She had remained Egyptian while Assyrian, Persian, Greek, and Roman influences had flooded over her.

Only with the coming of Christianity did Egypt give in and take over a new way of life imposed from without. And even here, she struggled to put her own stamp upon Christianity, did so in many ways, and then finally found a variety she could make her own. The Coptic Church became Egypt's nationalistic counterattack to the Catholic Christianity of the Greek East and the Latin West.

14

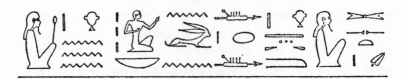

THE FINAL SCENES

THE PERSIANS

The Imperial expansion, under Justinian, was short-lived. Soon after Justinian's death in 565, new barbarian invasions smashed into Italy, and by 570 most of the peninsula was lost again.

And, what's more, there were sources of worry other than the barbarians in the west; the East Roman Empire had enemies to the east as well. All the years that the emperors (not only Justinian, but those who preceded him and succeeded him) had been keeping their eyes fixed on the west and on the hope of reestablishing the Roman dominions there; they had been forced to fight a holding action against Persia to their rear.

Even while Justinian was conquering the west, he had to fight two wars with Persia and, in the end, had to buy peace. Matters reached a climax, finally, during the reign of the Persian king Khosrau II (khos-row´), known to the Greeks as Chosroes II (koz´roh-eez).

Chosroes II seized his chance when the East Roman Empire was being harassed and weakened by the inroads of a nomadic people called the Avars. Based on the Danube, they had been raiding the Balkan provinces ever since the death of Justinian.

The Persian king was therefore able to make unprecedented advances, marching right across Asia Minor. By 608, Chosroes II had reached Chalcedon, just across the straits from Constantinople itself.

His armies also marched into Syria, where the Monophysites saw in him not an enemy invader but a liberator and rescuer from Constantinopolitan orthodoxy. Conquest was easy under these conditions. Chosroes II took Antioch in 611 and Damascus in 613.

In 614, the empire suffered a peculiarly disheartening blow when the Persian army marched into Jerusalem itself and carried off the "True Cross" (that is, the one on which, according to legend, Jesus had been crucified).

And in 619, the Persians entered Egypt and, thanks to the Monophysite controversy, took it as easily as Alexander the Great had taken it a thousand years before. Then Alexander had been viewed as a liberator from the Persian yoke, and now the Persian king, by an ironic turnabout, was viewed as a liberator from the Greek yoke.

In fact, by that victory, Chosroes II seemed finally to have undone the work of Alexander. A thousand years after the great Persian defeat there came the climax of the struggles of generations of Persian leaders with first the Seleucid kings and then the Roman emperors. Finally, they had taken back all that was lost: the Iranian highlands, Mesopotamia, Syria, Asia Minor, even Egypt.

A new emperor, Heraclius (her"uh-kly'us), rose to meet the crisis, but he seemed to be ruling an empire that had shrunk down almost to the vanishing point. Not only was the entire east lost to the Persians, but by 616, the German tribes in Spain had retaken all the empire's holdings there. Meanwhile, the Avars were pressing down from the Danube, appearing on the land approaches of Constantinople in 619, even while the Persian hosts glowered from across the straits.

Heraclius needed ten years to reorganize and strengthen his army. He bought peace with the Avars and, amid a burst of tremendous religious enthusiasm, hurled his army into Asia Minor. In 622 and 623, he cleared that peninsula of the Persians, and then he began a long and arduous push into the Persian heartland. He let nothing deter him from that, not even the news that the Avars had broken the peace and, by 626, were actually attempting to storm Constantinople. Heraclius decided to let the capital take its chances, rather than to release the grip he was tightening on the chief enemy.

Constantinople survived, its walls withstanding the Avar assault. Then, toward the end of 627, on the site of ancient Nineveh, Heraclius defeated the main Persian army in a hard-fought battle. With that, the Persians finally had enough. Chosroes II was desposed and killed, and his successor made a hasty peace. All the Persian conquests were restored, including Egypt. The True Cross was given back, too, and in 630 Heraclius returned it to Jerusalem in person. The Avar tide in the Balkans began to recede, as well, and for a few years it seemed that all was restored as it had been in Justinian's time (except for the loss of Italy and Spain).

But Heraclius realized that there was one fatal flaw in the empire, and that was the persistent diversity of religious belief. Syria and Egypt had fallen so easily because they were at religious odds with the capital, and Heraclius knew that it would happen again and again, as often as a foreign army approached those lands, if some reconciliation was not carried through.

He attempted, therefore, to find a compromise. Constantinople held that Jesus had two natures, the divine and the human, while Egypt and Syria held out for only one. Well, then, why not have everyone agree that although Jesus had two natures, he had only one will — in other words, the two natures could not possibly be in conflict. This two-natures-always-acting-as-one idea is called Monothelitism ("one will"), and surely it seemed that everyone ought to agree on this happy compromise.

Perhaps they might have, if the religious dispute had been purely religious. The trouble was that the nationalist elements in Syria and Egypt were not interested in conciliation. It is possible that if Constantinople had accepted Monophysitism completely, Syria and Egypt would soon have found some other reason for dispute. Disaffection remained and was not to be plastered over with either words or deeds.

THE ARABS

Besides, the whole problem of the Monophysite controversy and religious disaffection was about to become purely academic — even while Heraclius was still on the throne. A great turning point was approaching.

The four centuries of war between the empire and Persia — and, in particular, the last twenty years of desperate conflict — had drained both sides of almost every scrap of energy. They had fought each other to a standstill and lay gasping, each in a separate corner — and now a new fighter, fresh and fanatical, entered the field.

The new factor came, to everyone's utter surprise, from an unexpected corner — the Arabian peninsula.

Arabia, largely desert, had developed interesting civilizations on its fertile fringes, and these had occasionally impinged upon the more settled portions of the world. The Egyptian kings had traded with southwestern Arabia, where the land of Punt lay; and there, too, had been located the Biblical lands of Sheba and Ophir.

At no time were the Arabs anything more than nuisances at most, and whenever the empires to the northwest or the northeast chose to exert their full strength, the Arabs were crushed.

But now, as it happened, the Arabic tribes found themselves under new and dynamic leadership at just a time when both kingdoms to the north were hanging on the ropes and had no "full strength" worth speaking of.

It came about as a result of an Arabic religious revival. The primitive Arabic polytheism had been giving way before the more sophisticated beliefs of Jews and Christians. The advance of monotheism, however, was slow, for national reasons, since both Judaism and Christianity seemed foreign and alien. Some native version of these faiths was badly needed.

At Mecca (mek'uh), a holy city for the Arabic tribes, and just across the Red Sea from Egypt, there was born about 570 a boy named Mohammed (moh-ham'ed). He passed his youth in obscurity, but when he was about forty, he began to preach a kind of monotheism based on the tenets of Judaism and Christianity, but with modifications to suit Arabic tastes and temperament. His discourses were, eventually, collected into a book called the Koran (from an Arabic word meaning "to read").

The new religion he was preaching is called Islam ("submission" — to the will of God, that is), although it is very frequently called Mohammedanism in the prophet's honor. Those who accepted Islam are Moslems ("those who surrendered" — again to God).

Mohammed found, as Jesus had found in his time, that it was difficult to gain the sympathetic attention of his own countrymen. In 622, Mohammed was forced to flee Mecca (the "hegira," an Arabic word meaning "flight") with a handful of supporters. He found refuge in the city of Medina (meh-dee'-nuh) 350 miles to the north.

Then, while the world's attention was riveted on the herculean efforts of Heraclius to invade and defeat Persia, a similar fight, even more momentous, was going on — completely unnoticed — in Arabia. Slowly, little by little, Mohammed organized his followers in Medina and beat them into a dedicated fighting force, filled with the fervor of a new faith.

By 630, he had fought his way back into Mecca, which had ejected him eight years before. In that year, the world watched Heraclius return in triumph to Jerusalem; and only a few obscure tribes were aware of Mohammed's triumphant return to Mecca.

Mohammed's progress was now rapid. By the time of his death in 632, all or almost all the Arabic tribes were united under the banner of Islam. They were ready to spread the faith with fanatic self-confidence in the name of Allah (a word related to the Biblical "El," meaning "God"). With Allah on their side, they could not lose, for even if they were killed, death in battle against the infidel meant immediate translation into an eternal paradise.

Succeeding Mohammed was Abu-Bakr (uh-boo''bak'er), the aged father-in-law of Mohammed and one of the earliest of his disciples. He was the first caliph (from an Arabic word meaning "successor"). Under him, Arabic armies spilled northeastward into the Persian realm, as well as northwestward against Syria, for the unsophisticated Arabs seemed to see no miscalculation in taking on Persia and the East Roman Empire at the same time.

Certainly, it might have meant the end for them if they had launched their attack twenty years earlier, before the disastrous Roman-Persian war, or twenty years later after both realms had had a chance to recover. But, as it happened, Allah seemed to guide them to strike at just the right time.

Heraclius underestimated the Arab danger. Weary with the incredible exertions of the Persian War, sated with the glory of his victory, he longed only for peace and rest in his final years and was determined not to take the field himself. He sent his brother instead, with inadequate forces. The Arabs defeated them and marched into Damascus in 634. According to legend, Abu-Bakr died that same day, and was succeeded by Omar, another old companion of Mohammed.

The initial defeat of the East Roman Empire had stirred Constantinople, and now a powerful imperial army was marching southward into Syria to settle matters. The Arabs fell back, abandoning Damascus for the time.

However, the imperial army was strong only in appearance. It consisted largely of mercenaries who were not sure of their pay, and the Monophysite population of Syria was apathetic or worse. They didn't know much about these Arabs and their newfangled Islam, whatever that was, but they knew for certain that they hated Constantinople and its religious policies.

On August 20, 636, then, was fought one of the decisive battles of world history. It was fought on the banks of the Yarmuk River (yahr-mook'), a river that flows westward through the Transjordan into the Jordan River just south of the Sea of Galilee. The battle was a hard one, the Arabs retreating again and again before the weight of the imperial army.

On their horses and camels, however, the tireless Arabs always veered and returned, and when the imperial army had finally exhausted itself, they were slaughtered almost to a man.

The Arabic victory was a final one. The East Roman Empire remained almost exclusively on the defensive for the remaining eight centuries of its life.

As for the Arabs, they could expand freely into provinces that greeted them with sympathy at best and apathy at worst.

In 638, the Arabs took Jerusalem after a four-month siege. Only eight years before, Heraclius had brought back the True Cross, and all Christendom had rejoiced, and now the city was gone again — and this time permanently.

The rest of Syria was also taken; as was Mesopotamia, from the faltering hands of the Persian monarchs. In fact, Persia, which had fought so stalwartly and tenaciously against the Romans, found itself helpless before a new force that seemed almost demonic in its irresistibility. The Persians lost battle after battle, and by 641 they were no longer capable of organized resistance. The Persia which, only a short twenty years before, had seemed restored to the very peak of its power, was now no more. The Arabs were left only the task of occupying and cleaning up, of fighting an occasional skirmish and looting an occasional town.

Meanwhile, other Arabic armies in Syria turned southward, under a general, Amr ibn-al-As (am-roob'nil-ahs'). In 640, his host appeared at Pelusium, where once the armies of Sennacherib had stood, thirteen and a half centuries before.

After a month's siege Amr took the city, and as in the case of so many of Egypt's invaders, from the Hyksos onward, the first battle was also the last, and Egypt was taken with virtually no fight.

Heraclius died in 641, sinking to final rest amid the knell of utter defeat, despite all the victories of the mid-portion of his reign, and the next year, 642, Amr took Alexandria. An imperial counterattack from the sea briefly retook the city — but only briefly. Nearly a thousand years of Greek and Roman glory passed forever.

There is a legend that the library at Alexandria was finally destroyed at this time. The disposition of its contents was placed before Omar, the harsh and rigidly primitive caliph. He is reported to have said, "If these books agree with the Koran, they are unnecessary; if they disagree with the Koran, they are pernicious. In either case, destroy them."

However, as with so many legends, historians suspect there is interest, but no truth, in the tale. In the centuries of strongly antipagan Christian rule in Egypt, little could have been left of the library for Omar to destroy.

MOSLEM EGYPT

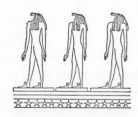

The Monophysites of Egypt might have felt that the removal of Constantinopolitan control would give them the free exercise of their religion and, indeed, the Arabs tended to be tolerant of Christianity. There was, however, the attraction of success.

Within twenty years after the Arabic conquest of Egypt, the Moslem armies were raiding southward into Nubia and westward against the remaining Roman provinces in North Africa. Carthage was taken in 698, and by 711 all the North African coast was Moslem. How could one argue against victory?

Nor could the Egyptian Christians feel any kinship with those of Europe. In 680, a sixth ecumenical council was held in Constantinople, and all possible compromise of the two-nature belief was thrown out.

The Egyptian Christians must have felt doubly isolated, first by Moslem victory and second by European intransigence. Little by little, then, Egypt changed.

Memphis, the 3500-year-old capital, sank into final ruin at last. A new Moslem capital, Al Fustat, was built near it.

The old language changed, and by 706, Arabic was made the official tongue of the country. Christianity diminished as the people found that conversion to Islam opened the road to governmental preference. Worst of all, prosperity vanished. The Arabs — sons of a desert society unused to agriculture — made no effort to keep up the canal system. It fell into decay.

Starvation and famine spread through the land, which sank into the abject poverty that continues to this present day.

The native Egyptians rose in revolt several times. A revolt in 831 was crushed so bloodily, however, that there was never another. (To be sure, Christianity never died out altogether. Even today, the Coptic Church includes 5 per cent of Egypt's population and uses the old language in its liturgy. Before the Arabs came, Egyptian missionaries had established Christianity in Nubia and in the region now called Ethiopia, and that is still the dominant religion in that nation. Both the Coptic and Ethiopian churches remain Monophysite to this day.)

With all the ancient Egypt gone — cities, language, religion, prosperity — there is a strong temptation to end the story. But the land and the people are still there, and I will briefly bring their history up to date.

The vast Moslem Empire, established in the eighth century, was too large to hang together. In the ninth century, it began to break apart into mutually quarreling fragments.

In 866, Egypt became, for a time, an independent nation again, under a feeble dynasty, the Tulunids. In 969, a more forceful line, the Fatimids, took over. The first of the Fatimids decided to abandon Al Fustat, which had served as capital for over three centuries. In 973, a new city was built three miles to the north and was named Al-Qahirah ("the victorious"). We call it Cairo, and it has now been the capital of Egypt for a thousand years.

The most notorious of the Fatimid rulers of Egypt was al-Hakim. A religious bigot, he bitterly persecuted the Christians. In 1009, he demolished the Church of the Holy Sepulchre in Jerusalem. This created great indignation in Europe and helped lay the foundation for the Crusades.

It was with the Crusades that Egypt reentered western history. For four centuries, while Europe had struggled its way through a period of darkness, Egypt had remained beyond their horizon. Beginning in 1096, however, poorly organized

Christian armies poured eastward toward Palestine, managing to win clumsy victories against the disunited Moslems. In 1099, they took Jerusalem.

By now, the Fatimid Dynasty was far gone in decay. A vizier (what we would call a prine minister) named Salah-al-Din Yusuf ibn Ayyub seized power. Westerners know him better as Saladin (sal'uh-din).

Saladin was the most capable ruler Egypt had had since the time of Ptolemy III, nine centuries before. He controlled Syria as well as Egypt and all but drove the Crusaders into the sea, retaking Jerusalem in 1187.

Under his weaker successors, however, the Crusaders recovered and even attempted to invade Egypt itself. The most ambitious European attempt was that of Louis IX of France ("St. Louis"), who landed in the Nile delta in 1248. Louis was defeated and captured in 1250, however.

For a long time, the Egyptian rulers had governed with the aid of a personal army of slaves, or "Mamelukes" (from an Arabic word meaning "slave"). In the confusion that attended Louis' invasion, their power increased.

Baybars (by-bars'), one of the Mameluke generals, commanded the Egyptian army at a time when the Mongols — a thundering horde of nomads from Central Asia — were sweeping all before them. They had taken China and Persia, and even while the Crusaders were fighting useless battles in Syria and Egypt, the Mongols had taken all of Russia. Now they were ravaging southwestern Asia.

There seemed no hope for anyone. In forty years, the Mongols had not lost a battle.

But they faced Baybars now in northern Palestine in 1260. To the surprise of the world, it was Baybars and his Mamelukes who were victorious. The Mongols were turned back, the myth of their invincibility shattered. And Baybars took over control of Egypt.

The Mamelukes continued to rule in a piratical sort of way

for several centuries, but met their match at last in the Ottoman Turks. These had slowly expanded their holdings in Asia Minor, poured into Europe and, in 1453, had taken the great city of Constantinople. They continued to expand, not only against the Christians of Europe, but against the Moslems of Asia and Africa.

In 1517, the Ottoman Sultan, Selim I ("the Grim"), crushed the Mamelukes in battle and marched into Cairo. For a while, Egypt receded into the backwaters again. The Ottoman Empair slowly decayed, however, and in 1683, following one last offensive that carried it to the walls of Vienna, it began to recede before the onslaughts of the Austrians and Russians. By 1769, Ottoman power had so far declined that Egypt was again under the control of the Mamelukes.

But now it was western Europe that contained the great powers of the Earth. In 1798, a French army invaded Egypt for the first time since Louis IX had tried it five and a half centuries before. The new French army was under Napoleon Bonaparte.

Once again the Mamelukes rallied against an invader, but, brave as they were, their sabers and old-fashioned charges were no match for the disciplined order of a western army under the greatest general of modern times. At the Battle of the Pyramids, the Mamelukes were crushed. When Napoleon was forced out of Egypt, it was because of the activity of the British fleet which cut his line of communications and not because of anything the Egyptians or Turks could do.

From 1805 to 1848, Egypt was again virtually independent under the firm rule of Mohammed Ali. In 1811, he lured the Mameluke leaders to a fortress on the pretext of inviting them to a victory feast. There, all were slaughtered, and the Mameluke power came to a final end after six centuries.

Schemes for once again connecting the Mediterranean Sea and the Red Sea by means of a canal were in the air. In 1856, the Egyptian ruler, Abbas I (grandnephew of Mohammed

Ali), granted the French promoter Ferdinand de Lesseps permission to organize the construction of a canal across the isthmus of Suez. In 1869, the Suez Canal was officially opened by the new ruler, Ismail (is-mah'eel), a grandson of Mohammed Ali.

In its honor, Ismail had commissioned the great Italian composer Giuseppe Verdi to write an opera on some Egyptian theme. The result was *Aïda*, which had its grand opening in Cairo on Christmas Eve, 1871. It was a beautiful and impressive treatment of the ancient wars between the Egyptians and the Ethiopians (Nubians).

Ismail's generally extravagant way of life, however, drove Egypt into bankruptcy, and in 1875, he was forced to sell Egyptian control of the canal to Great Britain in return for enough money to put his affairs in order. By 1882, Great Britain was in outright occupation of Egypt.

In the course of World War I, the Ottoman Empire came to a final end, and the various Arabic-speaking lands were promised their freedom. In 1922, Great Britain agreed to allow Egypt nominal independence, and her ruler, Fuad I (fooahd'), the youngest son of Ismail, declared himself king. Great Britain, however, retained military control of Egypt.

In 1936, Fuad I was succeeded by his son, Farouk I, and in 1937, Egypt joined the League of Nations.

In 1939, Britain went to war against Nazi Germany, and British troops were in Egypt to keep her on the British side by force, if necessary. Then, in 1940, Italy joined Germany. Since Italy had been in control of Libya, to the west of Egypt, since 1911, a war in North Africa began at once.

An Italian invasion of Egypt was repelled with ease, and Great Britain carried the fighting into Libya. Germany came to the relief of her ally, however, and in 1942, the German forces had succeeded in forcing their way deep into Egypt. Great Britain stood with its back to the wall at El Alamein, only sixty-five miles west of Alexandria.

In November, 1942, the British launched an offensive at El Alamein that quickly developed into their greatest victory of the war. The Germans were forced into a thousand-mile retreat, Egypt was saved, and the turning point of World War II had been reached.

After World War II, however, Egyptian demands for full independence had to be met. Little by little, Great Britain was forced out of the country, retaining control over the Suez Canal only.

Meanwhile, a new enemy had arisen to Egypt's northeast. For many centuries, Jews had been dreaming of an eventual return to their old homeland in Judea, and now the time had come at last. In 1948, over the continuing and furious opposition of the Arabic-speaking world, an independent Jewish state, Israel, was founded in Palestine. Egypt attempted to interfere by force of her arms, but her troops were quickly and humiliatingly defeated by the Israelis.

A general Egyptian anger against foreigners, and particularly against the British, kept rising. In 1952, a revolution broke out. Foreigners were killed; King Farouk was forced to abdicate, and Egypt freed herself of almost her last ties with the West.

In 1954, an Egyptian army officer, Gamal Abd-al-Nasser, seized power and established a complete dictatorship.

Egypt was planning to build a huge dam near the First Cataract at Aswan, one which would produce a large man-made lake that would bring millions of additional acres of fertile land into production. Financial help was expected from the United States. However, Egypt was attempting to improve her relations with the Soviet Union and other Communist powers as well, and the American Secretary of State, John Foster Dulles — an inept diplomat — disapproved of this. Abruptly, he announced, in 1956, that the United States would not be able to help.

An offended Egypt was virtually forced into the Soviet embrace. Nasser nationalized the Suez Canal, removing the last traces of foreign control, then proceeded to get a promise of financial help from the Soviet Union.

Great Britain, France, and Israel, left holding the bag by Dulles, united in an attempt to keep Egypt from drifting completely into the Communist camp and took the undiplomatic step of launching an open war of aggression.

Egypt could not possibly resist, but the Soviet Union demanded an immediate cessation of hostilities, and Dulles, trapped by his own follies, was forced to put the United States on the Soviet side in this. America could not afford to back aggressive warfare and permanently lose Arabic friendship.

The invading powers were forced to withdraw.

What followed, however, was not peace. Egypt persisted in considering itself at war with Israel, refused to allow her passage through the Suez Canal, and openly tried to organize a united Arab war of revenge against Israel. The Soviet Union, seeing a chance to win influence over the entire Middle East (thanks to Western fumbling in the 1950's) poured arms into Egypt and other Arab states. Israel, meanwhile, obtained arms from France and organized her population of two million for battle against the hostile sixty million Arabs in surrounding states.

Nasser continued to aspire to Arabic leadership based on his anti-Israel policy. In 1965, he was elected president for another six-year term — after running unopposed. He maintained particularly close ties with Syria, organized opposition to those Arab governments who attempted to cling to a moderate position with respect to Israel and the West. He even began a long, brutal, and unsuccessful war against his fellow-Arabs in Yemen in southwest Arabia.

Finally, in 1967, he felt himself in the proper position. He mobilized his forces on the Israeli frontier, closed the southern entrance to the Red Sea against Israeli shipping, formed an alliance with Jordan, Israel's neighbor on the east. His hope was to goad Israel into attacking, then crush the "aggressor" by sheer weight of numbers and arms.

Nassar had half his wish. He goaded Israel into attacking on June 5. For the third time Israel inflicted humiliating defeat on Egypt (and on Jordan and Syria, too). After six days, all the Sinai Peninsula was hers and Israeli forces stood on the east bank of the Suez Canal.

And so it stands now. Egypt — still abysmally poor — has a population of nearly thirty million. Cairo has a population of over three million. It is the largest city in Africa and, indeed, one of ten largest cities in the world. Egypt might yet play a great role in the world if it can solve its internal problems.

To solve its problems it must, however, come to some agreement with Israel. It cannot continue to base all its actions on a perpetually renewed war it apparently cannot win while its population sinks deeper and deeper into misery.

And yet this may be too much to expect as long as the Middle East remains a pawn in the general world rivalry between the two great powers of the Soviet Union and the United States. In the world of today can there be peace anywhere until there is peace everywhere?

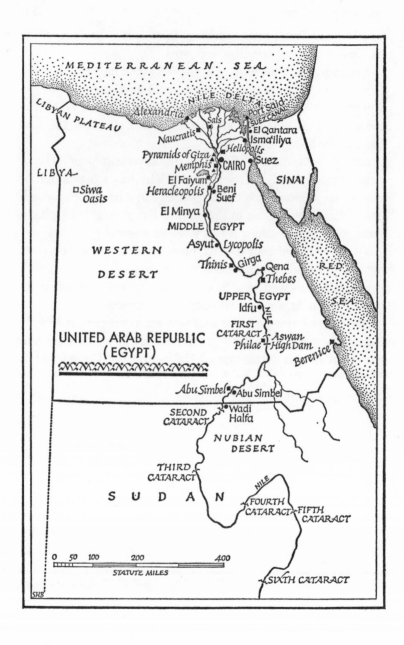

MEDITERRANEAN · SEA

LIBYAN PLATEAU

NILE DELTA

Alexandria
Sais
Naucratis
Port Said
SUEZ CANAL
El Qantara
Isma'iliya

LIBYA

Pyramids of Giza
Memphis
Heliopolis
CAIRO
Suez

□ *Siwa Oasis*

El Faiyum
Heracleopolis
Beni Suef

SINAI

El Minya

MIDDLE   EGYPT

WESTERN

DESERT

Asyut *Lycopolis*

Thinis *Girga*
Qena
Thebes

RED.

UPPER   EGYPT

Idfu

UNITED ARAB REPUBLIC
(EGYPT)

FIRST CATARACT
Philae
Aswan High Dam

SEA

Berenice

Abu Simbel Abu Simbel

SECOND CATARACT
Wadi Halfa

NUBIAN   DESERT

THIRD CATARACT

S U D A N

FOURTH CATARACT
FIFTH CATARACT

0   50   100   200   400
STATUTE MILES

SIXTH CATARACT

SHB

TABLE OF DATES

NOTE: *All dates* B.C. *except where noted otherwise.*

8000	Glaciers begin to recede; Nile Valley to dry out	1790	End of Middle Kingdom
4500	Neolithic villages on shores of Lake Moeris	1720	Hyksos occupy Egypt
3100	Menes unites Egypt; First Dynasty begins	1570	Eighteenth Dynasty begins; Ahmose evicts Hyksos and starts New Kingdom
2800	Egyptian solar calendar adopted	1545	Amenhotep I
2680	Third Dynasty begins; start of Old Kingdom	1525	Thutmose I
2650	Step Pyramid of Zoser completed	1490	Hatshepsut
2614	Fourth Dynasty begins	1469	Thutmose III
2580	Great Pyramid completed; Old Kingdom at peak	1457	Thutmose III defeats Mitanni at Kadesh
2530	Pyramid of Khafre built; Great Sphinx	1397	Amenhotep III; New Kingdom at peak
2510	Pyramid of Menkure built	1371	Ikhnaton
2500	Fifth Dynasty begins	1366	Ikhnaton builds Akhetaton
2430	Sixth Dynasty begins	1353	Death of Ikhnaton
2272	Pepi II	1343	Death of Tutankhamen
2180	End of Old Kingdom	1339	Horemheb restores old religion
2132	Eleventh Dynasty begins	1304	Nineteenth Dynasty begins
2052	Mentuhotep II unites Egypt; start of Middle Kingdom	1303	Seti I
1991	Amenemhat I	1290	Ramses II
1971	Sesostris I	1286	Ramses II draws battle with Hittites at Kadesh
1842	Amenemhat III; building of Labyrinth; Middle Kingdom at peak	1223	Merneptah; Peoples from the Sea; [Exodus?]
		1192	Twentieth Dynasty starts; Ramses III defeats Philis-

tines; end of New Kingdom

1075 Twenty-first Dynasty starts

973 Psusennes II; alliance with Solomon

940 Twenty-second (Libyan) Dynasty. Sheshonk I

929 Sheshonk I invades Judah

730 Twenty-fifth (Nubian) Dynasty starts

701 Senaccherib of Assyria at Egyptian border

671 Esarhaddon of Assyria takes delta

661 Esarhaddon sacks Thebes; Twenty-sixth (Saitic) dynasty starts

640 Greeks found Naucratis in delta

630 Greeks found Cyrene on African coast

610 Necho

608 Necho defeats Josiah of Judah at Megiddo

605 Necho beaten by Nebuchadrezzar of Chaldea at Carchemish

595 Psamtik II

589 Apries

570 Ahmose II. Saitic Egypt at peak

525 Psamtik III. Cambyses of Persia conquers Egypt

486 Egypt revolts after death of Darius I of Persia

464 Egypt revolts after death of Xerxes I of Persia; receives help from Athens

404 Egypt revolts, successfully, after death of Darius II of Persia

378 Thirtieth Dynasty (last native one) founded

360 Agesilaus II of Sparta dies at Cyrene

340 Artaxerxes III of Persia conquers Egypt; end of last native dynasty

332 Alexander the Great conquers Egypt

331 Alexandria founded

323 Death of Alexander the Great; Egypt comes under the rule of his general, Ptolemy

320 Ptolemy captures Jerusalem

306 Ptolemy adopts title of king; founds Ptolemaic Dynasty

285 Ptolemy II; museum, library, and lighthouse built in Alexandria

280 Manetho writes history of Egypt

276 First Syrian War

270 Ptolemy II forms treaty of alliance with Rome

260 Second Syrian War

246 Ptolemy III; Third Syrian War; Egyptian forces enter Babylon; Ptolemaic Egypt at peak

221 Ptolemy IV

220 Cleomenes III of Sparta dies in Alexandria

217 Ptolemy IV defeats Antiochus III of Seleucid Empire at Raphia

205 Ptolemy V

201 Fifth Syrian War. Egypt loses Syria and Judea to Antiochus III

197 Rosetta Stone inscribed

181 Ptolemy VI

171 Sixth Syrian War. Egypt beaten by Antiochus IV of Seleucid Empire

168 Antiochus IV at walls of Alexandria; ordered away by Rome

116 Death of Ptolemy VII. Egypt virtual puppet of Rome

96 Cyrene becomes Roman province

88 Ptolemy VIII sacks Thebes and puts final end to that city

80 Ptolemy XI

75 Cyprus becomes Roman province

51 Ptolemy XII and Cleopatra

48 Cleopatra in revolt; Pompey killed in Alexandria; Julius Caesar lands in Alexandria; Cleopatra sole ruler

42 Mark Antony meets Cleopatra in Tarsus

31 Mark Antony and Cleopatra defeated by Octavian at Actium

30 Octavian takes over Egypt; Cleopatra commits suicide; end of Ptolemaic Egypt

25 Gaius Petronius invades Nubia

NOTE: *All dates after this point are* A.D.

115 Jews revolt in Cyrene

130 Roman Emperor Hadrian visits Egypt

216 Roman Emperor Caracalla visits Egypt; ends state support of Museum

270 Zenobia of Palmyra briefly occupies Egypt

285 Anthony founds monasticism in Egyptian desert

295 Diocletian defeats Achilleus; takes Alexandria

328 Athanasius, bishop of Alexandria

391 Emperor Theodosius orders Serapion in Alexandria destroyed

412 Cyril, bishop of Alexandria

415 Death of Hypatia in Alexandria

451 Monophysitism condemned at fourth ecumenical council

619 Chosroes II of Persia takes Egypt

627 Egypt restored to East Roman Empire

642 Arabs take Alexandria

706 Arabic becomes official language of Egypt

831 Last native Egyptian revolt crushed

973 Cairo founded

1099 Crusaders take Jerusalem

1187 Saladin retakes Jerusalem

1248 Louis IX of France invades Egypt

1260 Baybars defeat Mongols; establish Mameluke power in Egypt

1517 Ottoman sultan, Selim the Grim, takes Egypt

1798 Napoleon Bonaparte invades Egypt

1799 Finding of the Rosetta Stone

1811 Mohammed Ali destroys Mameluke power

1869 Suez Canal opened

1875 Great Britain gains control of Canal

1882 Great Britain occupies Egypt

1922 Tomb of Tutankhamen discovered

1937 Egypt joins League of Nations

1942 Great Britain defeats Germans at El Alamein

1948 Israel gains independence; defeats Egypt

1952 Egypt becomes republic

1954 Nasser seizes power

1956 Egypt nationalizes Suez Canal. Anglo-French-Israeli invasion fails

1967 Continuing hostility between Egypt and Israel.

INDEX